Los Angeles 2009

A Selection
of ***Restaurants*** *&* ***Hotels***

Manufacture française des pneumatiques Michelin
Société en commandite par actions au capital de 304 000 000 EUR
Place des Carmes-Déchaux – 63000 Clermont-Ferrand (France)
R.C.S. Clermont-Fd B 855 200 507

Dépot légal Octobre 2008

Made in Canada

Published in 2008

Cover photograph : Getty Images / Glow Images

Please send your comments to:

Michelin Maps & Guides
One Parkway South
Greenville, SC 29615 USA
Michelinguide.com
Michelin.guides@us.michelin.com

Dear reader

We are thrilled to launch the second edition of our Michelin Guide Los Angeles.

Our teams have made every effort to produce a selection that fully reflects the rich diversity of the restaurant and hotel scene in the City of Angels.

The Michelin Guide provides a comprehensive selection and rating, in all categories of comfort and prices. As part of our meticulous and highly confidential evaluation process, Michelin's American inspectors conducted anonymous visits to restaurants and hotels in Los Angeles. Our inspectors are the eyes and ears of the customers, and thus their anonymity is key to ensure that they receive the same treatment as any other guest. The decision to award a star is a collective one, based on the consensus of all inspectors who have visited a particular establishment.

Our company's two founders, Édouard and André Michelin, published the first Michelin Guide in 1900, to provide motorists with practical information about where they could service and repair their cars, and find quality accommodations and a good meal. The star-rating system for outstanding restaurants was introduced in 1926. The same system is used for our American selections.

We sincerely hope that the Michelin Guide Los Angeles 2009 will become your favorite guide to the city's restaurants and hotels.

The Michelin Guide

"This volume was created at the turn of the century and will last at least as long".

This foreword to the very first edition of the MICHELIN Guide, written in 1900, has become famous over the years and the Guide has lived up to the prediction. It is read across the world and the key to its popularity is the consistency in its commitment to its readers, which is based on the following promises.

→ Anonymous Inspections

Our inspectors make anonymous visits to hotels and restaurants to gauge the quality offered to the ordinary customer. They pay their own bill and make no indication of their presence. These visits are supplemented by comprehensive monitoring of information—our readers' comments are one valuable source, and are always taken into consideration.

→ Independence

Our choice of establishments is a completely independent one, made for the benefit of our readers alone. Decisions are discussed by the inspectors and the editor, with the most important decided at the global level. Inclusion in the guide is always free of charge.

→ The Selection

The Guide offers a selection of the best hotels and restaurants in each category of comfort and price. Inclusion in the guides is a commendable award in itself, and defines the establishment among the "best of the best."

How the MICHELIN Guide Works

→ Annual Updates

All practical information, the classifications, and awards, are revised and updated every year to ensure the most reliable information possible.

→ Consistency & Classifications

The criteria for the classifications are the same in all countries covered by the Michelin Guides. Our system is used worldwide and is easy to apply when choosing a restaurant or hotel.

→ The Classifications

We classify our establishments using XXXXX-X and ⌂⌂⌂⌂⌂-⌂ to indicate the level of comfort. The ✿✿✿-✿ specifically designates an award for cuisine, unique from the classification. For hotels and restaurants, a symbol in red suggests a particularly charming spot with unique décor or ambiance.

→ Our Aim

As part of Michelin's ongoing commitment to improving travel and mobility, we do everything possible to make vacations and eating out a pleasure.

Contents

How to use this guide

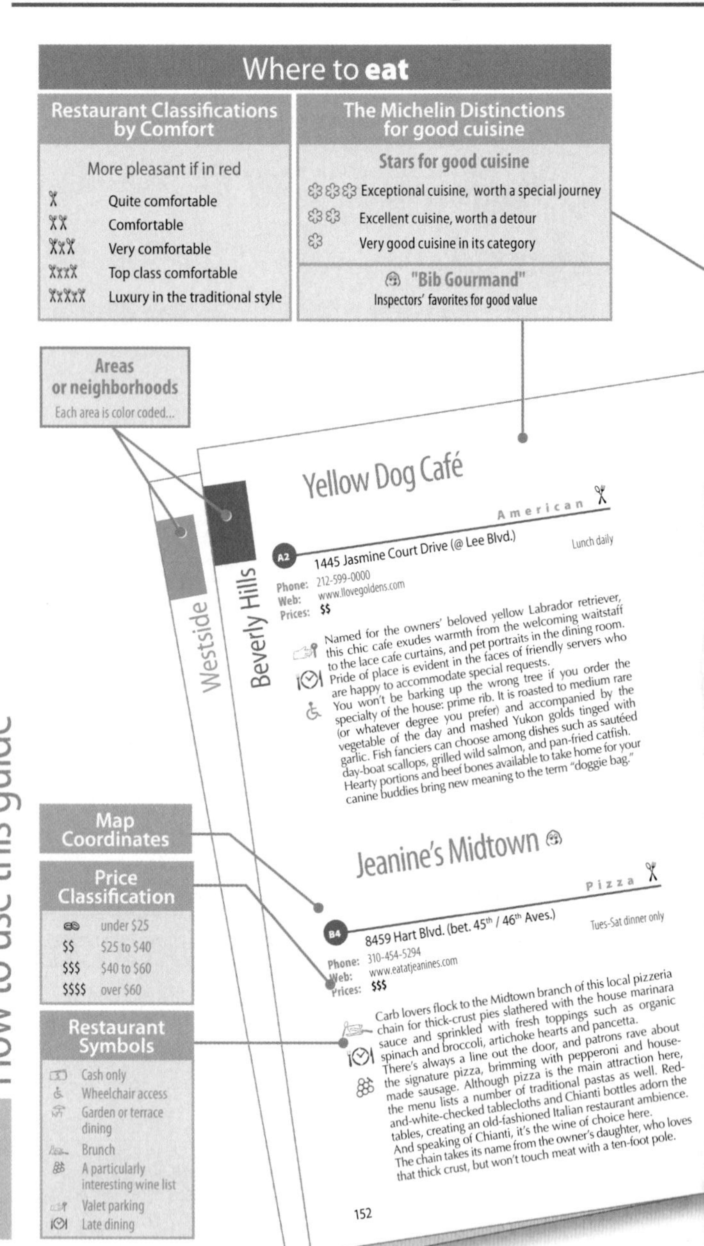

Where to **stay**

Average Prices

Prices do not include applicable taxes

$	under $150
$$	$150 to $250
$$$	$250 to $350
$$$$	over $350

Map Coordinates

Hotel Symbols

149 rooms	No of rooms and suites
♿	Wheelchair access
	Exercise room
	Spa
	Swimming pool
	Equipped conference room
	Pet Friendly

Hotel Classifications by Comfort

More pleasant if in red

- Quite comfortable
- Comfortable
- Very comfortable
- Top class comfortable
- Luxury in the traditional style

The Fan Inn

D1

135 Shanghai Road, Oakland

Phone: 650-345-1440 or 888-222-2424
Fax: 650-397-2408
Web: www.superfaninnoakland.com
Prices: $$

45 Rooms
5 Suites

Housed in an Art Deco-era building, the venerable Fan Inn recently underwent a complete facelift. The hotel now fits in with the new generation of sleekly understated hotels offering a Zen-inspired aesthetic, despite its 1930s origins.

soothing neutral palette runs throughout the property, nctuated with exotic woods, bamboo, and fine fabrics. the lobby, the sultry lounge makes a relaxing place for a l-mixed cocktail or a glass of wine.

linens and down pillows cater to your comfort, while reen TVs, DVD players with iPod docking stations, vireless Internet access satisfy the need for modern ies. For business travelers, nightstands convert to tables and credenzas morph into flip-out desks. printer, fax or scanner? It's just a phone call away. quest, the hotel will even provide office supplies.

half of the accommodations here are suites, where factor ratchets up with marble baths, spacious s, and fully equipped kitchens. Although the inn e a restaurant, the nearby blocks hold nearly ou could want in terms of food, from soup haute cuisine.

Eastside

419

ya's Palace

Italian

uther Place (at 30th Street)
-5309
nyasfabulouspalace.com

Dinner daily

Greater Downtown

Home cooked Italian never tasted so good than at this unpretentious little place. The simple décor claims no big-name designers, and while the Murano glass light fixtures are chic and the velveteen-covered chairs are comfortable, this isn't a restaurant where millions of dollars were spent on the interior.

Instead, food is the focus here. The restaurant's name may not be Italian, but it nonetheless serves some of the best pasta in the city, made fresh in-house. Dishes follow the seasons, thus ravioli may be stuffed with fresh ricotta and herbs in summer, and pumpkin in fall. Most everything is liberally dusted with Parmigiano Reggiano, a favorite ingredient of the chef.

For dessert, you'll have to deliberate between the likes of creamy tiramisu, ricotta cheesecake, and homemade gelato. One thing's for sure: you'll never miss your *nonna's* cooking when you eat at Sonya's.

Appetizers
- Crostini alla Toscana
- Antipasti della Casa
- Funghi con Polenta

Entrées
- Lasagna Bolognese
- Gnocchi alla Sorrentina
- Grilled Lamb Chops "Scotta Dita"

Desserts
- Panna Cotta
- Tiramisú
- Bombolini

153

How to use this guide

A brief history of Los Angeles

The four million people who live inside L.A.'s 469 square miles speak more than 90 languages in a mosaic of communities, comprising one of the nation's most multicultural city—a literal and figurative melting pot that boasts a nearly year-round growing season, as well as some 15,000 restaurants.

PROVINCIAL NO MORE

Our Lady the Queen of the Angels was founded in 1781 by 11 families who answered the call of Felipe de Neve (the Spanish governor of then Alta California) for *pobladores* (settlers), for a new town in Southern California. Food was a priority here from the beginning. The settlement's 44 pioneers were charged with feeding the garrison guarding the pueblo. Grains and game were staples until land-grant ranchers began to produce beef for local tables.

Mexico's independence from Spain in 1821 opened the province to non-Spanish immigrants. In the 1830s, French Angelenos planted the pueblo's first orange grove and California's first vineyards. Ceded to the U.S. in 1848, California soon swarmed with Gold Rush fortune-seekers who brought seeds from afar, sprouting the region's diverse agriculture. In the 1850s, as hunters supplied restaurants with bear meat, émigrés from Italy's high regions were winning tastes away from mining-camp fare in favor of the Northern Italian recipes that still pepper area menus. The Chinese were recruited to build the western leg of the Transcontinental Railroad, and later established

©Mark Gibson

California's fishing industry—selling catches along the Los Angeles shore. In 1885, the city's first Japanese-owned venture, a restaurant, marked the birth of Little Tokyo.

INNOVATION LEADS TO FUSION

Local oil booms in the 1890s and the early 20th century arrival of film companies, created a free-spending elite associated with nightclubbing and fancy dining, who were barely constrained by Prohibition or the Depression that followed. A 1905 *Los Angeles Times* cookbook hints of things to come: a "California Salad" calling for walnuts and the "purest olive oil." Still, through the Eisenhower years, the city remained, as one newspaperman observed, "a red meat, red sauce, heavy cream and butter town."

That changed in the 1960s, as jet planes delivered fresh foods from around the globe and local farmers' markets proliferated. Waves of immigrants from Latin America, Asia, Iran, Africa, and the former Soviet Bloc established vibrant cultural communities, each a constituency for homeland cuisines. The professional stigma associated with their inevitable Americanization began to fade after a chef at one of L.A.'s first sushi bars, unable to find fresh *toro*, substituted creamy avocado for the fatty tuna belly. The California roll's immediate popularity opened the door to cross-culinary combinations. The result is a unique, ever-evolving local cuisine; the best of it fresh, organic, locally produced, and seasonal.

Note that valet parking is available at most restaurants in LA.

Where to **eat**

©Comstock / Jupiter Images

Alphabetical list of restaurants

Restaurants by cuisine type

American

Argentinian

Asian

Bakery

Brazilian

Bulgarian

Californian

Chinese

Contemporary

Ethiopian

European

French

Fusion

Gastropub

Greek

Indian

International

Italian

Japanese

Korean

Latin American

Lebanese

Mediterranean

Mexican

Moroccan

Persian

Seafood

Spanish

Steakhouse

Thai

Vegan

Vietnamese

Cuisine type by area

Bib Gourmand

This symbol indicates our inspectors' favorites for good value. For $40 or less, you can enjoy two courses and a glass of wine or a dessert (not including tax or gratuity).

Starred restaurants

Within the selection we offer you, some restaurants deserve to be highlighted for their particularly good cuisine. When giving one, two or three Michelin stars, there are a number of things that we judge, including the quality of the ingredients, the technical skill and flair that goes into their preparation, the blend and clarity of flavors, and the balance of the menu. Just as important is the ability to produce excellent cooking time and again. We make as many visits as we need, so that our readers can be sure of quality and consistency.

A two- or three-star restaurant has to offer something very special in its cuisine; a real element of creativity, originality or "personality" that sets it apart from the rest. Three stars – our highest award – are given to the very best restaurants, where the whole dining experience is superb.

Cuisine in any style, modern or traditional, may be eligible for a star. Because we apply the same independent standards everywhere, the awards have become benchmarks of reliability and excellence in more than 20 European countries, particularly in France, where we have awarded stars for almost 80 years, and where the expression "Now that's real three-star quality!" has entered into the language.

The awarding of a star is based solely on the quality of the cuisine.

Exceptional cuisine, worth a special journey.

One always eats here extremely well, sometimes superbly. Distinctive dishes are precisely executed, using superlative ingredients.

Excellent cuisine, worth a detour.

Skillfully and carefully crafted dishes of outsanding quality.

Mélisse	XXX	158
Providence	XXX	120
Spago	XXX	50
Urasawa	XX	54

A very good restaurant in its category.

A place offering cuisine prepared to a consistently high standard.

Asanebo	X	175
Bastide	XXX	89
CUT	XXX	39
Dining Room at the Langham (The)	XXXX	135
Gordon Ramsay at the London	XXX	102
Hatfield's	XX	103
La Botte	XX	155
Mori Sushi	X	206
Ortolan	XXX	117
Osteria Mozza	XXX	118
Patina	XXX	73
Sona	XXXX	123
Sushi Zo	X	213
Trattoria Tre Venezie	XX	140
Valentino	XX	167
Water Grill	XXX	76

Where to eat for less than $25

LOUIS ROEDERER
CHAMPAGNE

Where to have brunch

Where to have a late dinner

Beverly Hills

Bel-Air

Between West Hollywood and West Los Angeles, roughly bounded on the south by Whitworth Drive, this palmy city of 36,000 inclines north along curving streets, crossing Sunset Boulevard into the Santa Monica Mountains where its grandest homes rise behind tall hedges and gates.

Nine-tenths of Beverly Hills' 5.7 square miles are residential, so the city's stellar shopping and dining cluster around **Rodeo Drive** in the pedestrian-friendly **Golden Triangle** bound by Santa Monica Boulevard, Wilshire Boulevard, and Rexford Drive. Though most residents are professional and business people, the city remains the perceived capital of A-list extravagance, displayed by a conspicuous minority addicted to pampering, cosmetic surgery, and the costliest of everything.

FROM SWALE TO SWANK

The confluence of streams from Franklin, Coldwater, and Benedict canyons led the native Gabrielino-Tongva people to name this area *The Gathering of the Waters*. In 1838 a land grant to Maria Rita Valdez Villa, the Afro-Latina widow of a Spanish soldier, bestowed the parcel called *El Rodeo de las Aguas*. Employing a corps of *vaqueros* out of her adobe near Sunset Boulevard and Alpine Drive, she raised cattle and horses until 1854, selling her 4,449-acre rancho—more than a square mile larger than present-day Beverly Hills—for $4,000.

The late 1800s brought a run of failed oil and building schemes, the last a North African-themed subdivision called Morocco. In 1907 developers filed papers for "Beverly Hills" (the name reflects a partner's fondness for Beverly Farms, Massachusetts), its big lots and high prices targeting the wealthy. In 1912 the **Beverly Hills Hotel** became the community's social center. Among filmdom's first millionaires were Mary Pickford and husband Douglas Fairbanks, whose 1919 move into their Summit Drive estate, Pickfair, triggered an influx of screen stars.

Less than a mile up Beverly Boulevard from Sunset, Coldwater Canyon Park offers serenity amid the buzz, as do the terraced gardens of the Doheny oil clan's 1928 Greystone estate that overlooks the city. On Sunday mornings, just east of City Hall on Civic Center Drive, the **Beverly Hills Farmers' Market** recalls this area's cultivation by 19th-century vegetable peddlers.

BEL-AIR

Laid out in 1923 behind imposing white gates north of Sunset, this woodsy enclave of Los Angeles climbs the ridges above Beverly Hills. The area is a bastion of privacy, most of its posh residences hidden by greenery. Even its unofficial clubhouse, the Hotel Bel-Air, is easy to miss as you drive by.

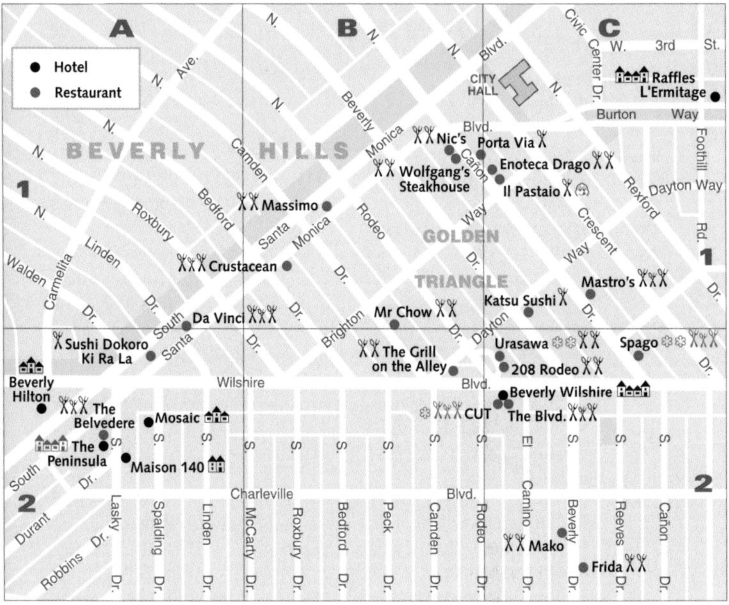

Hotel
Restaurant

A B C
1 2

BEVERLY HILLS
GOLDEN TRIANGLE
CITY HALL

Raffles L'Ermitage
Nic's
Porta Via
Wolfgang's Steakhouse
Enoteca Drago
Il Pastaio
Massimo
Crustacean
Mastro's
Katsu Sushi
Da Vinci
Mr Chow
Sushi Dokoro Ki Ra La
The Grill on the Alley
Urasawa
Spago
208 Rodeo
Beverly Hilton
Beverly Wilshire
The Belvedere
Mosaic
CUT
The Blvd.
The Peninsula
Maison 140
Mako
Frida

W. 3rd St.
Burton Way
Dayton Way
Wilshire Blvd.
Charleville Blvd.
Civic Center Dr.
Foothill Rd.
N. Santa Monica Blvd.
South Santa Monica Blvd.
Brighton Way
Dayton Way
Rexford Dr.
Crescent Dr.
N. Cañon Dr.
N. Beverly Dr.
N. Rodeo Dr.
N. Camden Dr.
N. Bedford Dr.
N. Roxbury Dr.
N. Linden Dr.
N. Carmelita Ave.
N. Walden Dr.
South Santa Monica Blvd.
Durant Dr.
Robbins Dr.
S. Lasky Dr.
S. Spalding Dr.
S. Linden Dr.
S. McCarty Dr.
S. Roxbury Dr.
S. Bedford Dr.
S. Peck Dr.
S. Camden Dr.
S. Rodeo Dr.
El Camino Dr.
S. Beverly Dr.
S. Reeves Dr.
S. Cañon Dr.

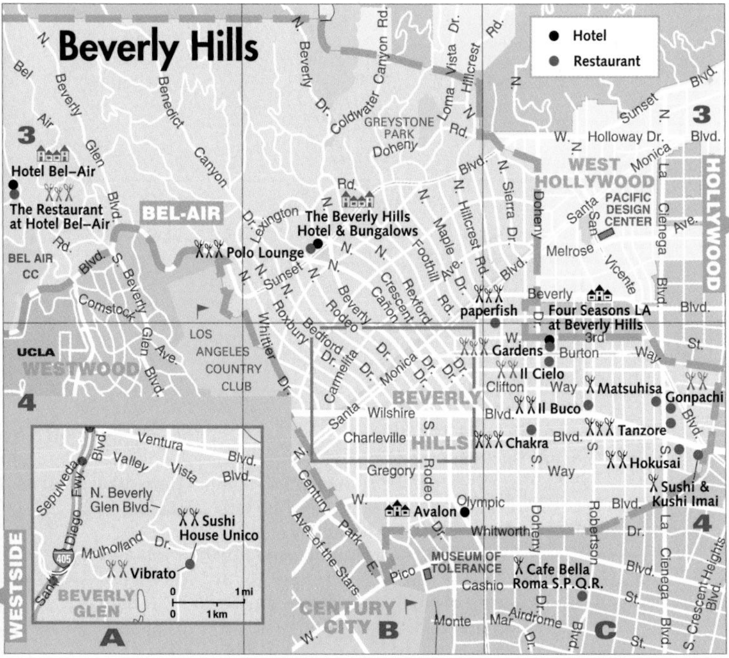

Beverly Hills

Hotel
Restaurant

3 4
A B C

BEL-AIR
WEST HOLLYWOOD
HOLLYWOOD
PACIFIC DESIGN CENTER
GREYSTONE PARK
LOS ANGELES COUNTRY CLUB
BEL AIR CC
UCLA
WESTWOOD
BEVERLY HILLS
CENTURY CITY
WESTSIDE
MUSEUM OF TOLERANCE

Hotel Bel-Air
The Restaurant at Hotel Bel-Air
The Beverly Hills Hotel & Bungalows
Polo Lounge
paperfish
Four Seasons LA at Beverly Hills
Gardens
Il Cielo
Matsuhisa
Gonpachi
Il Buco
Tanzore
Chakra
Hokusai
Sushi & Kushi Imai
Avalon
Cafe Bella Roma S.P.Q.R.

Sunset Blvd.
Holloway Dr.
Santa Monica Blvd.
Melrose Ave.
San Vicente Blvd.
Beverly Blvd.
W. 3rd St.
Burton Way
Clifton Way
Wilshire Blvd.
Charleville Blvd.
Gregory Way
W. Olympic Blvd.
Whitworth Dr.
Pico Blvd.
Cashio
Monte Mar
Airdrome St.
N. Bel Air Rd.
N. Beverly Glen Blvd.
Benedict Canyon Dr.
Lexington Rd.
N. Beverly Dr.
Coldwater Canyon Dr.
Loma Vista Dr.
N. Hillcrest Rd.
Doheny Rd.
N. Sierra Dr.
Doheny Dr.
La Cienega Blvd.
N. Maple Dr.
Foothill Rd.
N. Crescent Dr.
N. Cañon Dr.
Rexford Dr.
N. Rodeo Dr.
N. Roxbury Dr.
N. Sunset Blvd.
Whittier Dr.
S. Beverly Glen Blvd.
Comstock Ave.
N. Bedford Dr.
Carmelita Dr.
Santa Monica Blvd.
Rodeo Dr.
Robertson Blvd.
S. Crescent Heights Blvd.
N. Century Park E.
Ave. of the Stars

Ventura Blvd.
Valley Vista Blvd.
Sepulveda Blvd.
San Diego Fwy.
405
N. Beverly Glen Blvd.
Mulholland Dr.
Sushi House Unico
Vibrato
BEVERLY GLEN
0 1 mi
0 1 km

The Belvedere

A2 — **Contemporary** XXX

9882 South Santa Monica Blvd. (at Wilshire Blvd.)

Phone: 310-788-2306 — Lunch & dinner daily
Web: www.beverlyhills.peninsula.com
Prices: **$$$$**

This restaurant perfectly complements its palatial Beverly Hills hotel home, offering a classic European experience amid formal old-world opulence. Off a marbled hallway, the dining room's pale peach and green tones are reprised in French period décor. Here, the city's elegant senior elite celebrate special occasions, where the casual dress of Los Angeles' younger crowds seems out of place—so come dressed to impress!

Black-suited servers are professional and attentive, presenting ambitious dishes like Hawaiian Blue Prawns with Okinawa sweet potato, hon-shimeji mushrooms, and *beurre noisette*; or a generous striped bass pan, simply seasoned with salt and pepper atop a bed of sautéed mushrooms, shaved zucchini, and a velvety carrot purée. Desserts are as splendid as the setting.

The Blvd

C2 — **American** XXX

9500 Wilshire Blvd. (at Rodeo Dr.)

Phone: 310-275-5200 — Lunch & dinner daily
Web: www.fourseasons.com/beverlywilshire
Prices: **$$$$**

In the Beverly Wilshire hotel *(see hotel listing)* facing Wilshire at Rodeo Drive, this grand room enjoys one of the city's top locations, a reason the sidewalk tables are so highly coveted. High ceilings, panelled walls, graceful armchairs, and finely set wood tables strike a refined tone for hotel guests and locals, including the occasional famous face.

Prepared with skill and superb ingredients, globally influenced cuisine trumps star-gazing. An Ahi tuna sampler presents seared slices of fish atop a julienne of green papaya, as well as a stack of diced avocado crowned with Ahi tartare. The all-day schedule allows the prime sirloin Blvd Burger, with foie gras mousse and sautéed wild mushrooms, to fit right in. Dress to impress—it matters here.

Cafe Bella Roma S.P.Q.R.

Italian 

1513 S. Robertson Blvd. (bet. Cashio & Horner Sts.)

Phone: 310-277-7662 — Tue – Sun lunch & dinner
Web: www.bellaromaspqr.com
Prices: $$

As homey and authentic a neighborhood Italian cafe as *La Città degli Angeli* can offer, what distinguishes this newcomer is homemade pastas, pizzas, *antipasti, salumi,* and more ambitious main courses—all at prices lower than other fine Italian places hereabouts. In front is a small fenced patio with potted foliage and a trickling fountain. Inside, the tiny dining room's cheery yellow walls, vintage posters, displays of Italian crockery, and cozy wood tables create an air of casual panache.

From the first taste of fresh *ciabatta* bread spread with a thick, flavourful black olive tapanade, or a steaming bowl of tender *gnocchi all'arrabiata* in a tomato sauce infused with garlic, basil, and chile, you know you are enjoying the singular luxury of artisanal cooking.

Chakra

Indian 

151 S. Doheny Dr. (at Charleville Blvd.)

Phone: 310-246-3999 — Lunch & dinner daily
Web: www.chakracuisine.com
Prices: $$

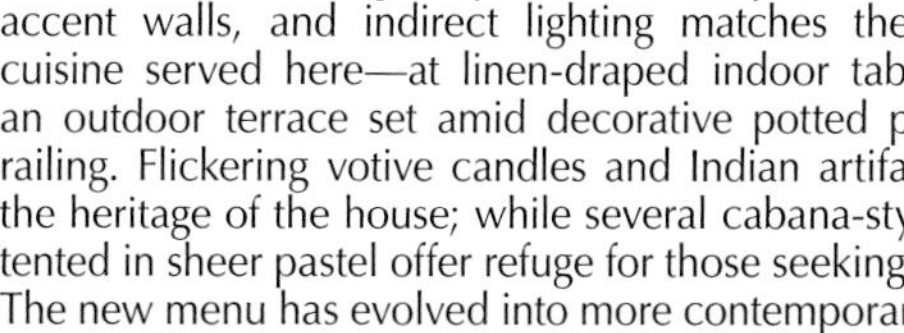

The sleek urban design of polished wood plank floors, stone accent walls, and indirect lighting matches the updated cuisine served here—at linen-draped indoor tables or on an outdoor terrace set amid decorative potted plants and railing. Flickering votive candles and Indian artifacts evoke the heritage of the house; while several cabana-style booths tented in sheer pastel offer refuge for those seeking privacy.

The new menu has evolved into more contemporary cuisine, serving dishes like *papadam* with a quartet of savory chutneys; small whole calamari oven-roasted in intensely flavored red chili-infused oil with minced garlic and scallions; or creamy poached shrimp flavored with red curry paste and leaves of Kaffir lime, served with buttery pancakes.

Crustacean

Asian XXX

B1

9646 South Santa Monica Blvd. (at Bedford Dr.)

Phone: 310-205-8990 — Mon – Fri lunch & dinner
Web: www.anfamily.com — Sat – Sun dinner only
Prices: $$$

Industry players, whose lust for privilege is second only to breathing, buzz over this Euro-Vietnamese extravaganza, sister to Crustacean in San Francisco. Designed by Elizabeth An (a daughter of the family that owns the restaurant), the interior recalls the family's French Colonial estate in Hanoi. A glass walkway spans a koi-stocked "river" that runs from the entrance through the bar area into the paneled, two-story dining room.

Crustacean takes Vietnamese-inspired cuisine to new heights. Just ask the elite Beverly Hills set who mob this place. They're hooked by the exclusivity of dishes—like the whole roasted Dungeness crab, made with An's garlic sauce and secret spices—cooked in the hidden kitchen, where only family members are allowed.

Da Vinci

Italian XXX

A1-2

9737 South Santa Monica Blvd. (at Linden Dr.)

Phone: 310-273-0960 — Mon – Fri lunch & dinner
Web: www.davincibeverlyhills.com — Sat – Sun dinner only
Prices: $$$

His standing order on arrival was two Cutty Sarks, and Dean Martin claimed them often, slipping into his reserved booth in this ornately mirrored place he proclaimed his favorite. Tuxedoed servers may finish dishes tableside, but their easy, friendly manner bans stiffness from the hushed and intimate room, which, besides crooners, attracts an old-school Beverly Hills crowd as well.

The menu presents Italian classics, starting with generous appetizers like prosciutto-wrapped grilled asparagus. A signature dish, *Pollo Da Vinci*, combines thinly pounded chicken breast with rounds of fennel-seed-scented Italian sausage, strips of roasted bell pepper and sliced roasted white mushrooms. For dessert, try the tiramisú; it's one of the best in town.

CUT ✿

Steakhouse XXX

9500 Wilshire Blvd. (at Rodeo Dr.)

Phone: 310-276-8500 Mon – Sat dinner only
Web: www.wolfgangpuck.com
Prices: **$$$$**

Timothy Griffith/Four Seasons

You know what they say in Hollywood: the bigger the marquee, the faster they come. Such is the case with CUT, a sleek, sexy steakhouse tucked into the opulent Beverly Wilshire hotel that boasts a gorgeous Richard Meier interior and a designer menu courtesy of the great Wolfgang Puck. Not surprisingly, then, the beautiful and the wealthy descend on this trendy Beverly Hills restaurant nightly. And though the line of paparazzi hovering near the door can be intimidating, don't be daunted—just don your finest, flip the valet your keys, and get ready to throw down some red meat.

Warm up with a rich, fragrant Austrian oxtail bouillon, simmering with bone marrow dumplings and fresh sprigs of chervil and chive blossoms. For dinner, try the slow-cooked Kobe beef short ribs, tender with Indian spices, served over a pool of creamy cauliflower purée.

Appetizers

- Prime Sirloin Steak Tartare, Herb Aïoli
- Bone Marrow Flan, Mushroom Marmalade, Parsley Salad
- Maryland Blue Crab and Louisiana Shrimp "Louis" Cocktail

Entrées

- Slow-cooked, Indian-spiced Short Ribs
- Grilled U.S.D.A Prime Beef, Nebraska Corn Fed, Dry Aged 35 Days
- Roasted Maine Lobster, Truffle Sabayon

Desserts

- Baby Banana Cream Pie Brûlée, Dark Chocolate Sorbet
- Valrhona Chocolate Soufflé, Milk Chocolate Hazelnut Glacé
- Wild Berry Crumble, Vanilla Ice Cream

Enoteca Drago

C1

Italian XX

410 N. Cañon Dr. (at Brighton Way)

Phone: 310-786-8236 Lunch & dinner daily
Web: www.celestinodrago.com
Prices: $$

Sidewalk tables here are coveted for neighborhood people watching. The lofty wood-floored dining room is abuzz midday with chic shoppers and power players whose vehicles gleam expensively at the valet stand.

A power lunch here might cast a refreshing *panzanella* salad of tomato and crunchy cucumber, briny black olives, raw red onion, ciabatta, and mozzarella with a wonderfully moist halibut steak—crusty from its buttery pan sauté, served atop chunky tomato sauce accented with black olives and green capers. Desserts are seasonal—so see writers in autumn celebrating script sales over crêpes spiced with cinnamon, cloves, nutmeg, and ginger, filled with a pumpkin purée, garnished with tangy crème fraîche, and crunchy toasted walnut halves.

Frida

C2

Mexican XX

236 S. Beverly Dr. (bet. Charleville Blvd. & Gregory Way)

Phone: 310-278-7666 Mon – Sat lunch & dinner
Web: www.fridarestaurant.com Sun dinner only
Prices: $$

Everyone knows which Frida we mean, so it's no surprise the interior is artistically cluttered and colorful, sophisticated and rustic by turns. Stone tile floors, bright walls, a big canvas of rural life, wrought-iron fixtures, and woven reed chairs create a perfect setting for gourmet food that honors Mexican tradition.

You see it in generous dishes that stay true to different regions of Mexico, starting with a large basket of fresh tortilla chips served with a trio of salsas, and perhaps a taste of the day's fresh ceviche. Like the restaurant's namesake, artist Frida Kahlo, the main courses are seductively complicated. Avocado-tomatillo sauce adds depth to a grilled filet mignon *patron*, spiced up with a side of poblano chile mashed potatoes. Brava!

Gardens

Contemporary XXX

C4

300 S. Doheny Dr. (at Burton Way)

Phone: 310-273-2222 Lunch & dinner daily
Web: www.fourseasons.com
Prices: **$$$$**

Surrounded by palms and lush foliage, Gardens' dining room nestles off the lobby of the Four Seasons Beverly Hills *(see hotel listing)*, where it creates a sense of seclusion and luxury befitting its swanky hotel home. The location naturally draws a suit crowd.

Each course unfolds with flavors that are at once intricate and balanced. Good ingredients and artful presentation are evident in dishes such as a fillet of roasted black cod marinated in citrus-sesame dressing, served atop a cylinder of green basmati rice and wilted chard. For the finale, the pastry chef may whip up a flourless chocolate cake with vanilla-bean ice cream.

Well-versed servers proffer an efficiency that marries well with the dining room's 18th-century French style and the casual elegance of the adjoining terrace.

Gonpachi

Japanese XX

C4

134 N. La Cienega Blvd. (bet. Clifton Way & Wilshire Blvd.)

Phone: 310-659-8887 Dinner daily
Web: www.globaldiningca.com
Prices: **$$$**

An authentic experience within a two-story traditional structure fashioned by *miyadaiku* carpenters using native woods and roof tiles, this restaurant is decorated with Japanese artifacts to emulate a vintage estate house. Every detail, from sliding shoji doors to private tatami rooms (where shoes are left behind), adds to the tranquil atmosphere.

A good sake and *shochu* selection complements the extensive traditional menu of *sumiyaki*, sushi, sashimi, and soba. *Shiro miso*, a large hot bowl of white miso soup, is deliciously simple with bonito flakes, scallions, and cubes of soft tofu. Two small pieces of perfectly roasted black cod (*gindara yuan yaki*) glazed with sweet-salty-nutty miso, are served with Japanese eggplant, snow peas, and a ginger shoot.

The Grill on the Alley

American XX

B2

9560 Dayton Way (at Wilshire Blvd.)

Phone: 310-276-0615 — Mon – Sat lunch & dinner
Web: www.thegrill.com — Sun dinner only
Prices: $$$

The interior evokes the confident era when Ike was president, cars with pistons the size of paint cans burned 25-cent-per-gallon gasoline, and day's end meant a martini (mixed here in many varieties) or a scotch. It's all present and accounted for: comfy booths, ceiling molding, a big mirror reflecting an affluent patronage, and a staff focused on service, not the next audition.

Appetizers are a traditional glossary: shrimp cocktail, oysters on the half shell, with sashimi perhaps thrown in for local color. Sides and salads are many and nostalgically familiar—from a big Caesar to a bowl of creamed spinach. The flag flies over steaks and chops—that's what you salute here, aged prime Angus Midwestern corn-fed beef, succulent pork and veal.

Hokusai

Japanese XX

C4

8400 Wilshire Blvd. (at Gale Dr.)

Phone: 323-782-9718 — Mon – Fri lunch & dinner
Web: www.hokusairestaurant.com — Sat dinner only
Prices: $$$

Named for Japanese artist, Katsushika Hokusai, this restaurant similarly captures nature in the wood, stone, and glass elements that illuminate its décor. Dark wood floors and zebra-striped paneling frame the sleek room, lending an intimate and exclusive feel to the panel-enclosed central table.

The front bar area, which offers solo seating and camaraderie with the semi-open kitchen's staff, fills after work with the Beverly Hills happy-hour set. A local favorite, spicy tuna is mounded here atop two round thin disks of pressed rice that are pan-fried until golden brown. The fresh flavor of the minced raw tuna is elevated with red chili paste, sesame oil, ginger, garlic, and scallions.

Note that valet parking is available at the lot next door.

Il Buco

C4 — Italian XX

107 N. Robertson Blvd. (at Wilshire Blvd.)

Phone: 310-657-1345 — Mon – Fri lunch & dinner
Web: www.giacominodrago.com — Sat – Sun dinner only
Prices: $$

Homey rustic food is served in this old-country trattoria, featuring authentic details and vintage touches like white paper-draped tables—each with a bottle of olive oil—as well as a street-side dining patio.

Owner Giacomino Drago also bills this as a pizzeria, *paninoteca*, and wine bar. A Margherita pizza, big enough to be a *secondi*, trumps competitors with a thin crispy crust, savory tomato sauce, and oozing layer of melted mozzarella sprinkled with basil. *Polpettoni di carne*, seared herb and garlic-flavored meatballs, arrive in a bubbling pool of mozzarella-covered tomato sauce with notes of garlic, red chile, and basil. Even the espresso-soaked tiramisú sponge cake, layered with mascarpone cream and bitter chocolate, is pure rustic goodness.

Il Cielo

C4 — Italian 

9018 Burton Way (at Doheny Dr.)

Phone: 310-276-9990 — Mon – Sat lunch & dinner
Web: www.ilcielo.com
Prices: $$$

The lovely flowered, shrubbery-sheltered, shaded dining patio, and rustic dining areas inside "The Sky" impart a secret-garden feel outdoors and a romantic country-cottage ambience indoors, all enhanced by friendly, attentive service.

Lunch and dinner share refined versions of traditional Italian favorites using fresh seasonal ingredients. At lunch, you could make a meal out of the substantial antipasti; and main courses day and night are sumptuously pastoral as well as generous. Their ingredients harmonize in a lovely symphony of flavors—as in ravioli filled with subtly fragrant porcini mushrooms, coated with melted sage butter, and topped with roasted butternut squash. For dessert, tiramisú follows a signature recipe from Italy.

Il Pastaio

Italian

C1

400 N. Cañon Dr. (at Brighton Way)

Phone: 310-205-5444 Lunch & dinner daily
Web: www.giacominodrago.com
Prices: $$

Here, at some of Beverly Hills' most coveted lunchtime patio tables, the sidewalk parade competes against a consistently splendid Italian menu of skillfully prepared pastas, with delicious appetizers and desserts as bookends. The earth-tone dining room offers close, linen-topped tables, with counter seating favored by solo diners.

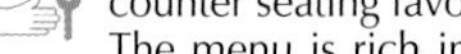

The menu is rich in little marvels like *timballo di zucchine*, a creamy soufflé of zucchini purée enriched by cream and whipped egg whites, inverted onto a dish of roasted yellow bell pepper sauce swirled with a truffle-infused fondue. Among the pastas, bite-sized pieces of *spugnette* are served al dente with a spinach purée, sautéed fresh peas, haricot verts, lima beans, and diced onion, accented with a bit of salty pecorino.

Katsu Sushi

Japanese 

C1

260 N. Beverly Dr. (bet. Dayton Way & Wilshire Blvd.)

Phone: 310-858-0535 Mon – Sat lunch & dinner
Web: www.katsusushibar.com
Prices: $$$

Deep in the heart of L.A.'s legendary zip code, famed chef, Katsu Michite, opens a sleek new sushi joint—minimally dressed in a clean Japanese palette of blond wood, neutral furniture, and bright white walls, in order to allow his impeccably fresh sushi to take center stage.

Nothing is overly complicated, but the unmarked perfection of the fish is astounding—like bright, simple cuts of velvety smooth yellowtail and tuna sashimi; or light, crunchy prawns in tempura batter. Even that old standby, miso soup, gets an upgrade with tender kelp and sweet *kabocha*.

Like his successful Tama Sushi—the Studio City restaurant he named after his wife—Michite's new place is intent on keeping its prices low; it's very possible to get out of here for about $40.

Mako

C2 — Asian XX

225 S. Beverly Dr. (at Charleville Blvd.)

Phone: 310-288-8338 — Wed – Fri lunch & dinner
Web: www.makorestaurant.com — Mon – Tue & Sat dinner only
Prices: $$

Set in a part of Beverly Hills that is removed from the tourist crush, this pleasant stretch of Beverly Drive brims with boutiques, cafes, and restaurants. It is no surprise that these large and small plates of flavorful Asian fare draw local business folks who favor Mako at lunch, while well-to-do residents show up at dinnertime.

Designed by Executive Chef and co-owner Makoto "Mako" Tanaka, the menu lists Japanese-inspired dishes from sushi and sashimi to Wagyu beef meatballs. Save room for desserts, which are as good as the savory courses and include the likes of a tangy yuzu meringue tart with mango sorbet, ending meals on a refreshing note.

For a view of the action, stake out a stool at the counter fronting the gleaming exhibition kitchen.

Massimo

B1 — Italian XX

9513 South Santa Monica Blvd. (at Rodeo Dr.)

Phone: 310-273-7588 — Lunch & dinner daily
Web: www.massimobh.com
Prices: $$$

Fashionistas who lunch take time-outs here, careening off Rodeo Drive with shopping bags and plopping onto chairs in the small, inviting, palm-shaded patio. Watching them is part of the fun, along with sampling copious dishes using local ingredients that impart contemporary California traits to Old World recipes.

The grimly svelte might go no further than the antipasti; mini-entrées in spirit, they encompass eggplant baked with mozzarella and tomato sauce, and beef carpaccio with enough arugula and shaved parmesan to qualify. High culinary craft produces gems like zesty pappardelle sautéed with fresh herb-and-garlic-spiced homemade chicken sausage, the pasta coated with basil pesto. Pay particular attention to the expertly prepared desserts.

Mastro's

Steakhouse XXX

C1

246 N. Cañon Dr. (bet. Clifton & Dayton Ways)

Phone: 310-888-8782 Dinner daily
Web: www.mastrosteakhouse.com
Prices: $$$$

Traditional, with an attentive staff serving large portions of well-prepared classics, this is a favorite among the local chic, who range from neighbors and business people to A-list celebrities and their circles. The small downstairs bar and the formal, dimly lighted dining room's carved paneled ceilings, closely spaced white-linen-covered tables, and black leather banquettes evoke Europe. Upstairs, the bar and casual dining area are more lively.

The bill of fare honors the steakhouse canon. Crab cakes? Of course, atop greens with a creamy lemon sauce. A Porterhouse? Natch, a big one served solo on the plate. Generous sides, cherished Yankee fare, include cheesy potatoes au gratin and sautéed sliced mushrooms and bell peppers. Hail, meat!

Matsuhisa

Japanese X

C4

129 N. La Cienega Blvd. (bet. Clifton Way & Wilshire Blvd.)

Phone: 310-659-9639 Mon – Fri lunch & dinner
Web: www.nobumatsuhisa.com Sat – Sun dinner only
Prices: $$$$

It's hard to imagine it's been 22 years since this Beverly Hills mainstay threw open its doors to critical success in 1987. Things haven't slowed down a bit; given the power crowd that packs this place night and day, one would think it's the newest hot spot.

Expect a casual environment along La Cienega Boulevard's restaurant row, with an informal vibe and a giant dose of character.

On the omakase front, you'll find a quality parade of creative dishes—if not the variety that put this famed chef on the map, then certainly very good sushi, like fresh, beet-red slices of rare tuna, perfectly seared and paired with a delicate onion sauce; or a wickedly fresh collection of sea bream, prawn, red snapper, and toro sashimi, laid over warm bullets of rice.

Mr Chow

B1 **Chinese** XX

344 N. Camden Dr. (bet. Brighton Way & Wilshire Blvd.)

Phone: 310-278-9911 — Mon – Fri lunch & dinner
Web: www.mrchow.com — Sat – Sun dinner only
Prices: **$$$$**

Epitome of a hip-for-the-moment L.A. dining hot spot, Mr Chow caters to an A-list of celebrities. Expect the entrance to be lined with paparazzi on a perpetual star search. So, if you're dining late and you have The Look, prepare to be blinded by a hail of camera flashes by a fleet-fingered cadre of photographers who shoot first and ask questions later.

Expensive Chinese cuisine rambles from lettuce wraps filled with chicken and veggies to spicy-sweet chili prawns. To accommodate the fickle tastes of the glitterati, Mr Chow's tasting menu differs per table. And while you may not find stars on your plate, you'll find plenty in the chic black and white dining room.

If you've been waiting for a place to wear those designer duds, this is it.

Nic's

B1 **International** XX

453 N. Cañon Dr. (at South Santa Monica Blvd.)

Phone: 310-550-5707 — Mon – Sat dinner only
Web: www.nicsbeverlyhills.com
Prices: **$$$**

A self-proclaimed shrine to vodka and the martini, Nic's splashy Fifties décor evokes notions of Rat Pack coolness. That can lead to occasional displays of self-reverential behavior by the terminally trendy in the white faux-leather banquettes, but the overall friendliness of the place compensates for any posturing engendered in wannabes by all those Silver Bullets.

The kitchen, however, is earnest and eclectic, with a Mediterranean bent. Nic's knack with modern cuisine comes to the fore in steamed Parisian gnocchi in a tasty creamy wine sauce with earthy morels, followed by seared *pommery*-crusted free-range chicken over a flavorful ratatouille-style bed of multicolored Asian slaw. Wines by the glass keep pace with the well-prepared dishes.

paperfish

Seafood XXX

345 N. Maple Dr. (bet. Alden Dr. & 3rd St.)

Phone: 310-858-6030 — Mon – Fri lunch & dinner
Web: www.patinagroup.com — Sat dinner only
Prices: **$$$**

Another coup by Joachim Spichal's Patina Restaurant Group is found at paperfish, with all the polish expected. Positioned on leafy Maple Drive, amid homes and offices, the design signature is sleek Retro Modernism; a minimalist décor with repeating contrasts of red and white. Spacious tables host a buzzy lunch crowd and come night, the airy space breathes a sophisticated cool.

The forte here is quality seafood in contemporary preparations—raw, chilled, and warm—as well as *en papillote*, hence the restaurant's name. So a fillet of red snapper plated tableside has been cooked in the aromatic embrace of ginger, scallion, and cilantro. Oyster-sauce covered stalks of stir-fried asparagus and jasmine rice give further Thai influence to this elegant dish.

Polo Lounge

Californian 

9641 Sunset Blvd. (bet. Beverly & Cresent Drs.)

Phone: 310-887-2777 — Lunch & dinner daily
Web: www.thebeverlyhillshotel.com
Prices: **$$$$**

In 1941 this restaurant was renamed to honor polo players such as Will Rogers, Darryl Zanuck, and Spencer Tracy, who often came here after matches. The Polo Lounge, a metaphor for the food-fueled deal-making at the core of the entertainment trade, shares the Beverly Hills Hotel's *(see hotel listing)* trademark pink and green motif and retro California style—right down to the white wrought-iron tables and chairs on the tree-shaded brick patio.

The menu reflects California's embrace of many cuisines: an Ahi tuna tartare topped with mango and firm *tobiko* caviar, and dripped with citrus-infused chili oil; grilled swordfish topped with a creamy garlic aïoli and a slice of smoky Italian bacon. Desserts are deliciously fancy, like most everything here.

Porta Via

Californian 

B-C1

424 N. Cañon Dr. (at South Santa Monica Blvd.)

Phone: 310-274-6534 — Mon – Sat lunch & dinner
Web: N/A — Sun lunch only
Prices: $$

Despite its location at a restaurant-rich Beverly Hills crossroad, Porta Via succeeds in being a convivial neighborhood bistro. Here, the percentage of patrons sporting Dolce & Gabbana sunglasses seems a bit lower than in other eateries in the Golden Triangle bounded by Wilshire and Santa Monica boulevards and Cañon Drive.

Locals come here for breakfast, lunch, and dinner. In the morning, scones and pastries go down well with a cup of espresso—as heady and strong as any you'd find in Milan. At dinnertime, the cornucopia of lunch salads and sandwiches gives way to simply prepared entrées.

Seating is limited to about a dozen tables inside and a few more out on the sidewalk terrace, where you can take in the tony street scene.

The Restaurant at Hotel Bel-Air

French

A3

701 Stone Canyon Rd. (off Sunset Blvd.)

Phone: 310-472-5234 — Lunch & dinner daily
Web: www.hotelbelair.com
Prices: $$$$

Nestled in a lush garden at the Hotel Bel-Air (*see hotel listing*), this restaurant is reached via a curving lane off Sunset Boulevard. Classically formal, the dining room sets a Mediterranean tone with its butter cream and terra-cotta hues, Venetian chandelier, and hand-painted walls—an ambience where jackets are recommended at dinner. French doors open onto a bougainvillea-covered terrace whose banquettes are the turf of Hollywood deal makers.

All this would be window dressing, were it not for the California-inspired French cuisine. As a starter, dishes to share include caviar tastings and samplings of Ahi tuna or foie gras. Refinement rings in a Mediterranean *daurade*, served in a fish *fumet* fragrant with fresh herbs and *pistou* Provençal.

Spago ✿✿

C2 — Californian XXX

176 N. Cañon Dr. (at Wilshire Blvd.)

Phone: 310-385-0880 — Mon – Sat lunch & dinner
Web: www.wolfgangpuck.com — Sun dinner only
Prices: $$$$

Wolfgang Puck's legendary Beverly Hills flagship, Spago, has evolved into a venerable institution in its second decade—a go-to place for the well-heeled to break bread, or a notch-in-the-belt for out-of-towners looking to indulge. You can try to nail down a reservation on the see-and-be-seen courtyard underneath the trees illuminated by garlands, but A-listers tend to rule this area. The good news is that with a grand dining room laid out underneath a striking pyramid-shaped skylight, Plan B doesn't look so bad.

Barring a smidgeon of Puck's Austrian influence, Spago's award-winning cuisine epitomizes Californian cooking—with a healthy obsession for fresh, seasonal ingredients. A tender squab is grilled to perfection and served over a tangle of pancetta, bacon, mushrooms, and brussels sprouts; and a warm toffee cake arrives oozing with crème fraîche and tangerine ice cream.

Appetizers

- Chino Farms Beet Salad, Goat Cheese, Hazelnuts and Shallot-Citrus Vinaigrette
- White Asparagus with Yuzu-Miso Vinaigrette, Upland Cress, Favas, and Baby Beets

Entrées

- Steamed Black Bass "Hong Kong" Style with Ginger, Garlic, Chili, and Bok Choy
- Pan-roasted Liberty Farms Duck Breast with Morels, Ramps, and Sweet Pea Flan

Desserts

- "Kaiserchmarren" Crème Fraîche Soufflé Pancake with Sautéed Chino Ranch Strawberries
- 12 Layers of Flourless Chocolate Cake with Mocha Praline Cream

Sushi Dokoro Ki Ra La

A2 **Japanese**

9777 South Santa Monica Blvd. (at Wilshire Blvd.)

Phone: 310-275-9003 Mon – Fri lunch & dinner
Web: www.sushikirala.com Sat – Sun dinner only
Prices: $$

Floor-to-ceiling windows brighten the gray-concrete interior, whose spare walls and furnishings impart calm to this small, fashionable yet low-key fishbowl of a sushi house, located on a quiet block.
An excellent and generous lunch with salad, soup, edamame, and tea costs about $20. There are hot dishes, or gourmet omakase lunch and dinner menus for those who relish the adventure of bowing to the competent chef's choices.
Leafy greens are fresh and subtly seasoned with touches like a miso-based vinaigrette. Slightly warm sushi rice tops slices of firm, mild fish, some garnished with sliced scallions, minced pickled daikon, or grated ginger. A cut roll of diced yellowtail mixes the fish with crunchy *tobiko* and aïoli seasoned with red chili and onion.

Sushi House Unico

A4 **Japanese**

2932 1/2 Beverly Glen Circle (at Beverly Glen Blvd.)

Phone: 310-474-2740 Mon – Fri lunch & dinner
Web: www.shusushi.com Sat – Sun dinner only
Prices: $$$

Another bold venture by Chef Giacomino Drago (of Il Pastaio), "Shu" (as it's known) fuses Japanese and Latin flavors in a brown-hued modern space in the Beverly Glen shopping center. A haven for well-heeled Bel-Air ladies who lunch, the dining space incorporates a contemporary Japanese sensibility with lots of natural elements (stone, wood, bamboo) and bright red accents.
There is fusion here. Ahi tuna in jalapeño and ginger sauce with Japanese risotto certainly qualifies, as do the signature "Shu" tacos—creamy ripe avocado, ground raw tuna, shredded crab meat, and a fresh prawn tucked inside crispy fried wonton-like wrappers. Most dishes, including first-quality sushi, hover closer to Japanese technique and taste.
Both valet and self-parking apply.

Sushi & Kushi Imai

Japanese

C4

8300 Wilshire Blvd. (at San Vicente Blvd.)

Phone: 323-655-2253 Mon – Fri lunch & dinner
Web: www.sushiandkushiimai.com Sat – Sun dinner only
Prices:

This inexpensive spot serving sushi and *kushi* (grilled skewers like whitefish dripping with lemon, teriyaki-marinated chicken, or green *shisito* peppers) is well above the ranks of the average Beverly Hills sushi-ya. In addition to short-order lunch combinations popular among the local business set, a more extensive dinner menu is also offered.

The wedge-shaped restaurant is decorated in shades of gray and brown wood trim, with a center sushi bar flanked by simple wood tables. Its name honors Takeo Imai, who helped introduce the city to Tokyo-style nigiri sushi, known for small portions of seafood on seasoned rice. The house embellishes tradition: the minced raw tuna roll is spiced with chili paste, sesame oil, and diced scallion. Imai-sensei would approve.

Tanzore

Indian

C4

50 N. La Cienega Blvd. (bet. Clifton Way & Wilshire Blvd.)

Phone: 310-652-3894 Tue – Sun lunch & dinner
Web: www.tanzore.com
Prices: $$$

Subtlety guides the skillful preparations here, with an attention to detail that creates an Indian cuisine as sophisticated as its clientele. Flavors are refined rather than aggressive; spices are thoughtful, with results that are fresh, earthy, and fragrant.

Thus, a Punjabi chicken curry is milder than its usual presentation—cumin seeds and green coriander stewed into a thick glaze infusing the fork-tender meat with a pleasing herbal zip to the flavors of the curry, chicken, and stewed onions.

The reserve of this new restaurant is matched by an understated contemporary décor of soft lighting, rich fabrics, marble accents, dark red polished concrete floors, and dark wood panels, with a pleasantly illuminated wine cellar dividing the dining area from the bar.

208 Rodeo

C2 — Californian XX

208 Via Rodeo (at Wilshire Blvd.)

Phone: 310-275-2428 — Lunch & dinner daily
Web: www.208rodeo.com
Prices: $$$

Boasting one of the best dining terraces in town, 208 Rodeo affords prime people-watching from its perpetually packed patio. You may have to line up for an outdoor table, but this is worth the wait to be among the casual-chic patrons and survey the wealthy or wannabes shopping on Via Rodeo—although sitting in the bold, black-and-white dining room is certainly no hardship.

In either venue, lunch on the likes of crispy, golden-brown Maryland crab cakes served atop a refreshing salad of shaved cucumbers, red peppers, and crunchy green apples. Well-marbled meat, smoked-paprika aïoli, and a caramelized-onion brioche bun raise the American Kobe burger a cut above.

From the underground valet parking lot, an elevator whisks you directly to Via Rodeo.

Vibrato

A4 — American XX

2930 Beverly Glen Circle (at Beverly Glen Blvd.)

Phone: 310-474-9400 — Tue – Sun dinner only
Web: www.vibratogrilljazz.com
Prices: $$$$

With its tables and banquettes arranged to afford clear views of a stage where first-rate jazz musicians perform nightly, some might ask if as much attention is paid to the food. The answer is yes. Up in the Bel-Air hills, Vibrato's swanky interior mixes elements of a posh recording studio and an eclectic art gallery.

Part supper club, part steakhouse, it ventures skillfully into seafood, chicken, and even lamb dishes. A filet mignon is grilled to order and paired with a creamy sauce and some onion here, some blue cheese there. You see the balance in the sides: herbed shoestring French fries versus grilled buttery broccolini topped with toasted almonds and grated Parmigiano Reggiano. The wine list includes some unsung yet exceptional labels.

Urasawa ✿✿

Japanese

218 N. Rodeo Dr. (at Wilshire Blvd.)

Phone: 310-247-8939

Dinner daily

Web: N/A

Prices: **$$$$**

Ken Sugiyama

There is no street sign marking the way to sushi nirvana, so pay close attention. Make your way to the Rodeo Collection's second floor, where you'll find a series of signs directing you to a small, sleek interior. Inside, you'll find a polished wood sushi bar with ten seats. This is Urasawa—and in a town known for good sushi, many would argue that this is the best.

Unassuming interiors aside, be forewarned that Chef Hiroyuki Urasawa's omakase dinner will lighten your wallet considerably. But for the few hours you are here, you'll be treated like royalty—the doting staff never leaves your side, and the multi-course dinner might include a silky sesame seed tofu dumpling, topped by gold flakes; scrumptious sea urchin and shrimp *maki*, humming with olive paste; bright slices of sashimi, presented in carved ice; or a soft piece of barely-seared wagyu beef from Hokkaido, Japan.

Appetizers

- Uni Nikogori: Terrine of Sea Urchin, White Shrimp, Shiso, Mountain Potato and Gelatin from Fish
- Junsai "Shot" with Myoga, Shiso, Negi and Yuzu Zest

Entrées

- Chef's Sashimi Selection on Carved Ice with Pickles and Edible Garnishes
- Kinuta Maki of Snapper, Shrimp, Shiso, Takuan and Myoga with Pickled Daikon, Nori and Ponzu

Desserts

- Seasame Seed Ice Cream
- Grapefruit "Jello" with Goji Berries

Wolfgang's Steakhouse

B1 Steakhouse XX

445 N. Cañon Dr. (bet. Brighton Way
& Santa Monica Blvd.)

Phone: 310-385-0640 Lunch & dinner daily
Web: www.wolfgangssteakhouse.com
Prices: **$$$$**

One of several new steakhouses to debut on the L.A. restaurant scene this year, Wolfgang's stands out from the others as a true New York-style concept. No surprise, since the originals reside in Manhattan.

Don't confuse your Wolfgangs. This one is Wolfgang Zwiener, who cut his teeth for some 40 years as a headwaiter at the mother of all steakhouses—Peter Luger's in Brooklyn. Zwiener's West Coast satellite accommodates sports fans with flat-screen TVs over the bar; others favor the dining room with its vaulted ceiling trimmed in decorative tile.

On the menu are all the usual suspects—from crab cakes to a massive Porterhouse for two or more. Pecan pie comes à la New York mode with a dollop of *schlag*. Mammoth portions mean that doggie bags are de rigueur.

Feast for under $25 at all restaurants with ☺.

Beverly Hills

Eastside

Owing to its diverse ethnic heritage, the Eastside is characterized by one of the most vibrant cultural landscapes in LA County. Leaning slightly northeast of the city, west of San Bernadino Valley, south of the San Gabriel Mountains and north of the Puente Hills, the area covers cities in the **San Gabriel Valley** (north of the mostly Hispanic enclave commonly known as *East L.A.*) These include **Alhambra, Arcadia, San Gabriel**, and **Monterey Park**.

THE MISSION

For nearly 7,000 years, the Native American ***Tongva*** tribe—whose name means "people of the earth"—populated much of what is now modern day Los Angeles. When Spanish missionaries settled the area, they assigned their indigenous inhabitants the name *Gabrielino*, as it was customary to rename local tribes after nearby missions. **The Mission San Gabriel Arcángel** was established in 1771 under the auspices of Franciscan father Junipero Serro. Natives either fled or were forced to relocate; those who stayed eventually lived and worked on the property. (Although Catholics contend that missionaries and natives worked together in relative harmony, the *Tongva-Gabrielino* of today maintain that their people were enslaved to build the mission.) Ultimately, the natives perished due to Old World diseases or maltreatment by occupying Spanish soldiers. Some 6,000 *Gabrielino* are buried at the grounds of their namesake mission; the cemetery remains to this day.

The fourth in a string of twenty-one, the San Gabriel Arcángel flourished and became known as the "Pride of the Missions," providing provisions to other settlements throughout California. Today, it stands as a historical landmark in the City of San Gabriel.

DEMOGRAPHIC SHIFTS

With a combined population of roughly two million, San Gabriel Valley now has one of the largest enclaves of Asian-Americans in the United States. Weathy Chinese professionals (mostly from Taiwan) streamed into Monterey Park in the 1970s, soon expanding into the more affluent Arcadia. In the late 1980s and 90s, white residents performed a mass exodus from the area, while Cantonese and Vietnamese immigrants established large communities in San Gabriel, Monterey Park, and Alhambra. Today, Chinese-owned banks,

boutiqes, supermarkets, and restaurants line the streets, transforming what were once almost entirely Caucasian neighborhoods.

In celebration of the Chinese New Year, San Gabriel and Alhambra co-host the annual **Lunar and New Year Parade and Festival.** Colorful floats, lively marching bands, and acrobatic dance troupes take a 1.5 mile march from San Gabriel to Alhambra, drawing nearly 30,000 spectators. The popular event is even broadcast on radio stations in China.

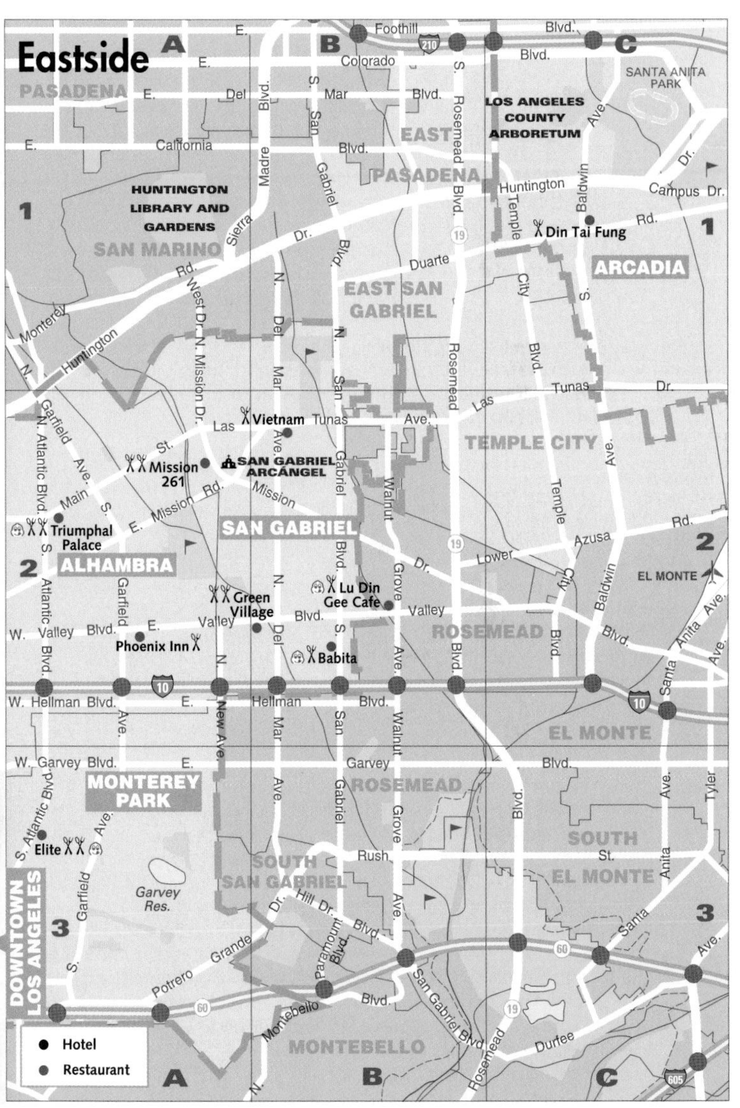

Babita

Mexican

B2

1823 S. San Gabriel Blvd. (at Norwood Pl.), San Gabriel

Phone: 626-288-7265 — Tue – Fri lunch & dinner
Web: N/A — Sat – Sun dinner only
Prices: $$

Fans of this family-run establishment believe its ten tables, squeezed into an unassuming cottage in downtown San Gabriel's Chinese district, serve the area's finest traditional, regional fare.
The menu may feature the velvety smooth banana soup (*sopa nueva*) richly flavored with sweetly caramelized bananas. *Panuchos yucatecos*, a rustic open-faced tostada, is heaped with earthy black beans and flavorful strips of seasoned chicken. Pan-sautéed chicken, laid atop chayote gratin, is smothered in a thick, smoky sauce, topped with prawns. Daily specials are popular, often served with sauces rich with tropical fruit purées, spices, and ground nuts.
Everything here is homemade, with an eye on authenticity rather than concessions to American tastes.

Din Tai Fung

Chinese

C1

1108 S. Baldwin Ave. (at Rosemead Blvd.), Arcadia

Phone: 626-574-7068 — Lunch & dinner daily
Web: www.dintaifungusa.com
Prices: ©

Part of a dumpling house chain born in Taiwan, success on the mainland and in Japan led to this U.S. strip-mall location. Here, the signature décor showcases immaculately clean, glass-enclosed kitchens where teams make fluffy buns and juicy dumplings with trademark efficiency: waiters wear wireless microphones; orders speed to the kitchen by computer.
The menu is partial to steamed-dough delicacies like *siu mai* dumplings holding ground pork and shredded crab in a fragrant pork broth, served with a dish of julienned ginger. The same white dough is steamed to produce favorites like the sesame bun, plump with a sweet paste of ground black sesame and sugar.
Generous servings make this location well suited to large groups sharing family-style meals.

Elite

Chinese XX

A3

700 S. Atlantic Blvd. (at El Portal Pl.), Monterey Park

Phone: 626-282-9998 Lunch & dinner daily
Web: N/A
Prices: $$

Elite is known among residents of this vast Asian community for generous servings of well-prepared and full-flavored dim sum, noodle dishes, congee, and many other specialty foods. Add good prices and an elegant gilded interior of reds, greens, and yellows, to understand why it is usually thronged with enthusiasts.

Fragrant steamed dumplings of rice dough filled with meat, fish, or poultry are tasty, filling, and infused with flavor, served simply with a soy-sesame oil dipping sauce. *Chow fun* noodles are stir-fried with thin beef slices accented by white onion and scallions, and capture the rich flavor of the brown oyster sauce.

Try a traditional dim sum pastry, like the perfectly smooth Macau egg custard, for dessert.

Green Village

Chinese XX

B2

250 W. Valley Blvd. (at Abbot Ave.), San Gabriel

Phone: 626-576-2228 Lunch & dinner daily
Web: N/A
Prices: ☺

To be precise, this is a Shanghainese restaurant, the most elegant and comfortable in town, with a sleekly sober décor. On the second floor of a strip mall, its dishes are fresh, well-prepared, and flavorful.

There is a large Asian population hereabouts, and the patronage reflects that, with many coming here to savor dishes difficult to realize at home—like *Ning Bo* seaweed-flavored yellow fish or pig kidney in hot chili sauce.

Regional flavors shine through in the Shanghainese noodle soup, the soft wheat noodles served in an aromatic broth of pickles, cabbage, pork, and tofu; as well as spicy salt pork wrapped in a mild spice crumb and served with steamed rice. An extensive tasting menu showcases the best of the skilled kitchen's refinements.

Lu Din Gee Cafe

B2 — Chinese

1039 E. Valley Blvd. (bet. Delta Ave. & Walnut Grove Ave.), San Gabriel

Phone: 626-288-0588 — Lunch & dinner daily
Web: www.pearlcatering.com
Prices: $$

Given its unassuming location in an urban strip mall, it might be surprising to hear that this friendly, pleasantly-decorated homage to Northern Chinese cuisine is the premiere Peking duck restaurant in the Los Angeles area. The reason, however, is simple: top quality ingredients prepared with extraordinary skill. To ensure a table for the signature dish, you are advised to reserve in advance, ideally a day or more.

The roasted duck is moist inside its marvelously crispy skin, arriving with shredded scallion, cucumber, hoisin sauce, and delicately thin, warm pancakes for wrapping these ingredients. Among other rare offerings—here are stir-fried salads of bean sprouts and duck meat; or braised pan-fried tofu, based on a classic regional recipe.

Mission 261

A2 — Chinese

261 S. Mission Dr. (at Broadway), San Gabriel

Phone: 626-588-1666 — Lunch & dinner daily
Web: www.mission261.com
Prices:

An elegant dim sum palace in a vintage Spanish Colonial building decorated with contemporary paintings, fresh flowers, and comfortable round tables, its dining areas include a courtyard of umbrella-shaded tables.

Here, ingredients are of the highest quality in preparing dim sum plates to order—realize that their presentation by the attentive staff may take a bit longer.

The dinner menu offers a choice of Cantonese specialties plus assorted dim sum favorites well-seasoned with vinegar, chili, and mustard sauces. The classic steamed shrimp and pork dumpling, *siu mai,* is soft and savory. An especially flavorful pairing of flavor and texture, *sui mui* is composed of steamed sticky rice wrapped in a tofu skin, the rice spiced with bits of Chinese sausage and green onion.

Phoenix Inn

Chinese

208 E. Valley Blvd. (at Monterey St.), Alhambra

Phone: 626-399-1238 Lunch & dinner daily
Web: www.phoenixfoodboutique.com
Prices: ⊜

This menu features meals of traditional soups, seafood, noodles, and meats. While such hearty food satisfies, what shines here are the pastries, custards, and specialty drinks like tapioca shakes. The ambiance may not be thrilling here—most unique and exciting, however, is the adjoining pastry shop serving both the public and the restaurant.

There is a homey aspect to the cooking, as in fragrant Chinese chicken soup with winter melon and ginseng; or thin slices of tender flank steak stir-fried in black pepper sauce with crunchy white onion and bell pepper.

Remember to stay focused on desserts and to indulge in mango-coconut rice dough balls; nutty black sesame-almond custard; or pastries of green tea rice dough swirled with sticky red bean paste.

Triumphal Palace 

Chinese

500 W. Main St. (at Fifth St.), Alhambra

Phone: 626-308-3222 Lunch & dinner daily
Web: N/A
Prices: $$

Credit this dim sum spot's popularity to its spacious, elegant, contemporary interior, and huge servings of high-quality food. Their particularly traditional dumplings, congee, and rice noodle dishes are not often seen on Americanized menus.

Here, the tender pork and shrimp *siu mai* dumplings are well infused with the flavors of garlic and ginger. Rich Shanghai juicy buns hold seasoned ground pork in a fragrant soup broth, served with red vinegar and chili paste. A *chow fun* masterpiece, enough for a family, lies on wide, thick pillows of folded, slightly sweet rice dough noodles, steamed and then stir-fried with pork short ribs in salty-smoky black bean sauce, and garnished with chopped scallions, sliced white onions, and bell peppers.

Vietnam

B2 Vietnamese X

340 W. Las Tunas Dr. (bet. San Marino Ave.
& Santa Anita St.), San Gabriel

Phone: 626-281-5577 Fri – Wed lunch & dinner
Web: N/A
Prices: ⇔

A relative newcomer to the Eastside, Vietnam has clearly and quickly emerged as a leader in the area for generous portions of tasty, authentic Vietnamese dishes at very inexpensive prices.

Just off of the sidewalk, along busy Las Tunas Drive, enter into the small, homey, and cheery yellow bungalow. Two simple and immaculate dining rooms are dressed in rose-tiled floors, and dark-stained wood furnishings. Each tabletop is set with a variety of chili paste pots and canisters for paper napkins, flatware, and chopsticks. Floral arrangements and potted palms complete the minimal, clean décor.

The menu offers traditional, hearty dishes that stand out for using superbly fresh, robust, and flavorful combinations of ingredients in their preparation.

Do not confuse X with ✿ ! X defines comfort, while ✿ are awarded for the best cuisine. Stars are awarded across all categories of comfort.

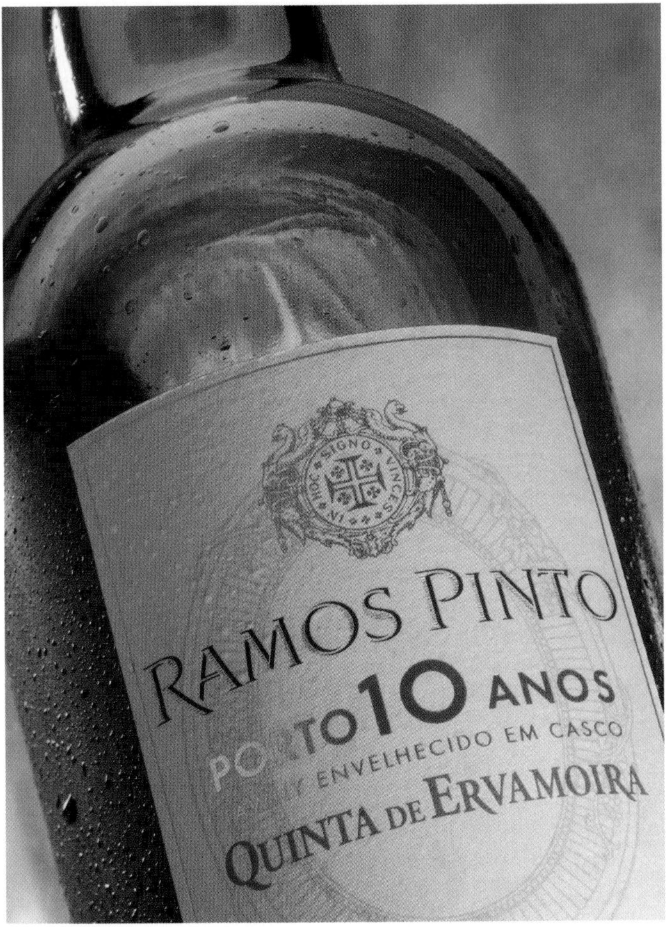
IN HOC SIGNO VINCES
RAMOS PINTO
PORTO 10 ANOS
ENVELHECIDO EM CASCO
QUINTA DE ERVAMOIRA

Greater Downtown

Chinatown - Koreatown

Within the eight square miles bounded by Chinatown, the Los Angeles River, the University of Southern California (USC), and Western Avenue, Downtown LA is a reviving inner city enjoying the return of nightlife. Until the 1980s, Downtown dining meant a vintage steakhouse or a cafeteria. The nation's first cafeteria opened here in the late 1800s, adopting the Spanish term for coffeehouse. Today LA's Downtown claims some of the city's finest restaurants and cultural venues, including the **Music Center**, the **Walt Disney Concert Hall**, and the **Museum of Contemporary Art**. A 1981 ordinance legalizing artists/squatters in vacant warehouse space on the east side created the **Arts District**, a community of studio lofts and galleries.

AN URBAN RENAISSANCE

Where settlers staked out the farming village that became Los Angeles in 1781, the 44-acre **El Pueblo** historical monument now preserves its oldest building, Avila Adobe, in the Olvera Street marketplace. Nearby **Little Tokyo**, center of LA's Japanese community, retains many original 19th-century buildings—not to mention some good sushi.

Southern California's first oil well was drilled northeast of Downtown in 1892. By 1897 there were 500 wells in the area overseen by a mercantile elite, who rode the Angels Flight funicular railway to Victorian manses crowning Bunker Hill. Spring Street, the self-proclaimed Wall Street of the West in the 20th century, boasts a rare unbroken string of pre-1931 buildings. The **Broadway Theater District** holds a dozen pre-World War II movie houses; the refurbished Orpheum is still active.

Grand Central Market at 317 Broadway has sold fresh fruits, vegetables, meats, poultry, and fish since 1917. Hub of the West's apparel trade, the **Fashion District** (bounded by I-10 and Main, 7th and San Pedro streets) caters to bargain hunters and wholesale buyers. The vast **Flower Mart** centers around 8th Street, while the 3,000 dealers in the **Jewelry District** (most along Olive and Broadway between 5th and 8th streets) offer competitive prices.

ASIAN INFLUENCE

Although LA's Chinese population is now concentrated east of the city in San Gabriel Valley, Chinatown still holds significance. A fixture in LA since the mid-19th-century, the Downtown district was founded in the 1930s by those displaced when Union Station was built. Today it brims with dim sum parlors, food markets, Taoist temples, and curio shops. An influx of South Koreans in the 1960s transformed the languishing Wilshire Center district, though today Latinos and African Americans still outnumber Asians here. Restaurants in **Koreatown** dish up authentic fare, while its bars and clubs now attract hipsters.

Yellow Cab Co

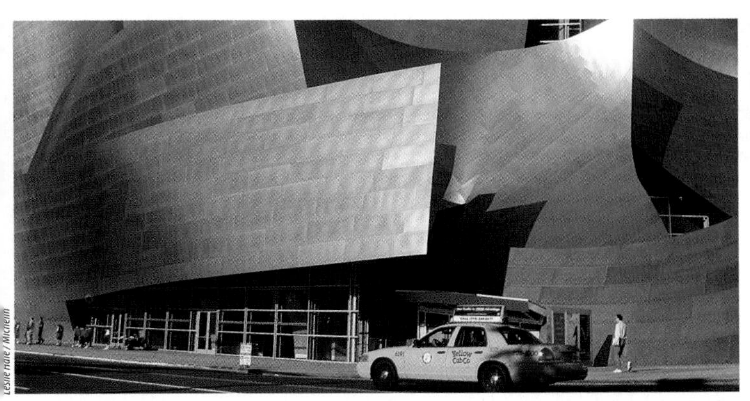

Leslie Hale / Michelin

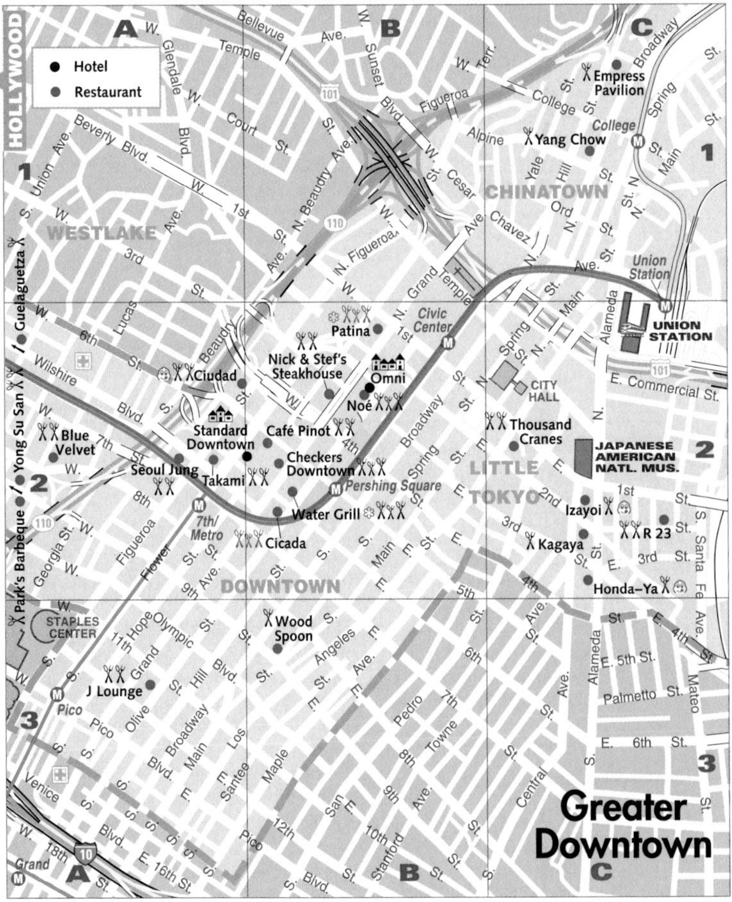
Greater Downtown
Hotel
Restaurant
HOLLYWOOD
A
B
C
1
2
3
WESTLAKE
CHINATOWN
LITTLE TOKYO
DOWNTOWN
Civic Center
UNION STATION
Union Station
CITY HALL
JAPANESE AMERICAN NATL. MUS.
STAPLES CENTER
Pershing Square
7th/Metro
College
Pico
Grand
Empress Pavilion
Yang Chow
Patina
Nick & Stef's Steakhouse
Omni
Noé
Ciudad
Standard Downtown
Café Pinot
Checkers Downtown
Takami
Seoul Jung
Blue Velvet
Water Grill
Cicada
Thousand Cranes
Izayoi
R 23
Kagaya
Honda-Ya
Wood Spoon
J Lounge
Guelaguetza
Yong Su San
Park's Barbeque
W. Bellevue Ave.
W. Temple St.
W. Sunset Blvd.
Figueroa
W. Glendale Blvd.
W. Court St.
Beverly Blvd.
W. 1st St.
N. Beaudry Ave.
N. Figueroa
Grand
Temple
Alpine
W. Cesar Chavez Ave.
W. College St.
Yale
Hill
Ord
N. Spring St.
N. Main St.
Broadway
Alameda
E. Commercial St.
W. 3rd St.
W. 6th St.
Wilshire Blvd.
W. 7th St.
W. 8th St.
Georgia St.
S. Figueroa St.
Flower
W. 9th
Ave.
Lucas
S. Union Ave.
S. Hope
W. 11th
Olympic
Grand
Olive
S. Hill
Broadway
Main
Los Angeles
Spring
E. 1st St.
E. 2nd
E. 3rd St.
E. 4th
5th
6th
7th
8th
9th
10th
12th
E. 16th St.
W. 18th St.
Venice Blvd.
Pico Blvd.
San Pedro
Santee
Maple
Stanford
Towne Ave.
Central
Alameda
E. 5th St.
Palmetto St.
E. 6th St.
S. Santa Fe Ave.
Mateo
101
110
10

Blue Velvet

A2 Contemporary XX

750 S. Garland Ave. (at 7th St.)

Phone: 213-239-0061 Mon – Fri lunch & dinner
Web: www.bluevelvetrestaurant.com Sat dinner only
Prices: $$

Come evening, this former Holiday Inn becomes a hot spot, with tall windows framing the city's bar-graph skyline, smart eco-friendly minimalist interior, and a skilled kitchen that stays open late. Weather permitting, one can also choose to dine on the poolside terrace,

Lunches are simple, featuring the likes of salads and gourmet burgers. Toward sundown the menu expands with an international spin, as colorful organic ingredients and carefully presented dishes are pleasantly served to the young, upscale crowd.

Typical of the innovative cuisine, a pair of eel fillets in a wine sauce is presented over a coconut rice quenelle, with kumquat confit adding a bittersweet touch. Desserts are sophisticated and fun. A parking lot is available.

Cafe Pinot

B2 Contemporary XX

700 W. 5th St. (at Flower St.)

Phone: 213-239-6500 Mon – Fri lunch & dinner
Web: www.patinagroup.com Sat – Sun dinner only
Prices: $$$

You couldn't ask for a more ideal location Downtown, overlooking Maguire Gardens' terraces and fountains, unveiled in the 1920s as the grand entrance to the Los Angeles Central Library. The twin dining rooms' ceiling-high windows frame skyscrapers, but the best seats are on the outdoor patio—a rose-edged oasis by day, a romantic lair by night.

Fish-market specials may feature *Loup de Mer*, lemon verbena tomato water, charred spinach, and macerated heirloom tomatoes; while filet mignon, rotisserie chicken, and Colorado lamb are regular entrées. The wine list is well chosen, as are the cheeses (Petit Basque, anyone?)—an alternative to tantalizing desserts.

If you don't take advantage of the cafe's valet parking, there's two-hour validated parking in the library, off Flower Street.

Checkers Downtown

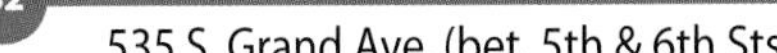

B2 **Californian**

535 S. Grand Ave. (bet. 5th & 6th Sts.)

Phone: 213-624-0000 Lunch & dinner daily
Web: www.checkershotel.com
Prices: $$$

Tucked inside the boutique Hilton Checkers Hotel, this Financial District hideaway sports a clubby ambience equally suited to serious business or earnest romancing. Credit the interior's warm colors, fine fabrics, comfy seating, English china, and soft jazz. A heated patio offers sheltered open-air dining.

One of the best options Downtown for lunch, dinner, or Sunday brunch—Checkers serves refined Californian cuisine with Asian, Italian, and French accents. Dessert brings perennial favorites like crème brûlée and bread pudding. And at lunchtime the friendly waitstaff respects diners' time limits with snap-to-it efficiency.

A pre-theater dinner package includes complimentary town-car service to nearby venues, including Disney Hall.

Cicada

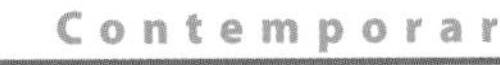

B2 **Contemporary**

617 S. Olive St. (bet. 6th & 7th Sts.)

Phone: 213-488-9488 Tue – Sun dinner only
Web: www.cicadarestaurant.com
Prices: $$$$

This opulent room, in the 1928 Oviatt Building inspired by the 1925 Paris Exposition, is as elegant a restaurant setting as exists in Los Angeles. Enter through a dazzling lobby embellished with over 30 tons of René Lalique designed glass; original art deco fixtures are offset by contemporary touches, adding wonder to this posh interior.

Nostalgic background music accompanies plates of marinated artichokes split lengthwise and grilled until smoky-tender. The cuisine often departs from the Italian canon, which explains a moist cut of mahi mahi dusted in blackening spices, roasted until just cooked through, served over earthy, chewy lentils mixed, wilted Swiss chard, atop a velvety pool of lobster butter. Honor this jewel by dressing up.

Ciudad

Latin American 

445 S. Figueroa St. (at 5th St.)

Phone: 213-486-5171 — Mon – Fri lunch & dinner
Web: www.ciudad-la.com — Sat – Sun dinner only
Prices: $$

Mary Sue Miliker and Susan Feniger (of Santa Monica's Border Grill) serve both authentic and innovative dishes from Cuba, Central and South America, Portugal, and Spain. The vibrant bar, elegant dining area featuring eye-popping murals, and a welcoming patio with sunny parasols and olive trees, evoke the stylish modernity of mid-20th century Latin America.

From Spanish paellas to Cuban pressed sandwiches, Argentine empanadas, and Bolivian tamales—it is all here. Newer offerings may include an olive oil-poached salmon served with braised orange, fennel, and *tacu tacu* (Peruvian pan-fried "dirty" rice made with mashed lentils). The wine list features the best of Spain, Argentina, and Chile.

Validated valet and self-parking are available.

Empress Pavilion

Chinese 

C1

988 N. Hill St. (at Bernard St.)

Phone: 213-617-9898 — Lunch & dinner daily
Web: www.empresspavilion.com
Prices:

An encyclopedic choice of dim sum and Mandarin Szechwan specialties draws a largely Asian crowd to this Chinatown emporium, whose popularity with locals can mean a long wait for a table. Adjoining the picturesque Bamboo Plaza, the big banquet-style dining room is noisy but table service is quick, with cart-pushing waitresses offering an endless stream of courses such as pork buns, beef meatballs, dried-shrimp rice noodles, and sticky rice wrapped in a lotus leaf.

The regular menu lists dozens of traditional favorites like fried noodle and rice dishes; stir-fried beef with ginger and onion; as well as shark-fin soup and Peking duck. Sharing courses, family style, is the best way to sample the enticing variety of dishes.

Guelaguetza

Mexican 

3337 1/2 W. 8th St. (bet. Ardmore Ave. & Irolo St.)

Phone: 213-427-0601 — Mon – Fri lunch & dinner
Web: www.guelaguetzarestaurante.com — Sat – Sun dinner only
Prices:

Only in LA would you be likely to find authentic homemade Oaxacan food in the middle of Koreatown—a testament to the melting pot of cultures that blends together in the City of Angels. Located on a dingy block, Guelaguetza takes its moniker from a Zapotec word meaning "shared offering," a reference to the restaurant's generous spirit.

Many of the intriguing dishes will surprise, since the menu does not bow to American palates. Thus a large platter of *nopal Zapoteco* holds a tender grilled cactus leaf heaped with thinly sliced skirt steak, slices of white onion, green bell pepper, and wedges of roasted tomato. Moles are exceptional here, starting with the thick red mole enhanced with smoked chile and hints of chocolate that accompanies the chips.

Honda-Ya

Japanese 

333 S. Alameda St. (bet. 3rd & 4th Sts.)

Phone: 213-625-1184 — Dinner daily
Web: N/A
Prices:

A true *izakaya,* or pub favoring fried and *robata*-grilled small plates, this newcomer on the third floor of the Little Tokyo shopping center attracts a mainly Japanese-American business lunch and evening crowd, seeking native beer, sake, *shochu,* and the nightly list of specials. At the evening hour, families fill raised tatami rooms.

Unusual surprises include broiled Japanese sweet potatoes, nearly melting with their sticky-sweet natural sugars; shrimp dumplings with a soy-rice wine vinegar dipping sauce spiked with spicy mustard; and thin pounded strips of skewered, grilled steak whose smokiness makes embellishment unnecessary.

The conviviality is enhanced by dark wood tables and benches, with a U-shaped bar embracing the glass-enclosed *robata.*

Izayoi

C2 — Japanese

132 S. Central Ave. (bet. 1st & 2nd Sts.)

Phone: 213-613-9554
Web: N/A
Prices: $$

Mon – Fri lunch & dinner
Sat dinner only

Reward yourself with flavorful, simply-prepared sushi, sashimi, and hot dishes—all prepared with quality ingredients in an open kitchen behind a wood sushi bar. This will seem all the more appealing after locating this jewel amid fairly nondescript storefronts—in an area short on parking.

Six chefs deftly prepare traditional treasures like *konnyaku*, a chewy, gelatinous cake, tossed in red chili paste and sesame oil. Watch them slice halibut for sashimi, place it atop a *shiso* leaf, shredded daikon, with a dab of fresh wasabi. Let yourself down gently from these exotic tastes and textures with a creamy mound of homemade custard-like tofu, served cool with a warm, sweet, nutty sauce of toasted black sesame seeds. Reservations are recommended.

J Lounge

A3 — Californian

1119 S. Olive St. (bet. 11th & 12th Sts.)

Phone: 213-746-7746
Web: www.jloungela.com
Prices: $$

Mon – Fri lunch & dinner
Sat dinner only
Sun lunch only

The frisson of big ideas is palpable in many L.A. debuts, from films to restaurants like the 25,000-square-foot J Lounge. With live entertainment, a humidor, and a wonderful patio for outdoor dining, J-Lounge attracts young film and media types who fancy that whatever they wear is fashionable and wherever they land is hip. But this place delivers more than attitude. Its postmodern décor suits the wide-ranging menu, which melds American favorites with California panache.

With its signature cocktails and menu of pizzas, charcuterie, and burgers, the sexy lounge is the place to schmooze, smooch, or party until the wee hours of the night. Events are celebrated on the huge outdoor patio, which includes private cabanas for that intimate tête-à-tête.

Kagaya

Japanese

418 E. 2nd St. (at Central Ave.)

Phone: 213-617-1016 — Tue – Sun dinner only
Web: N/A
Prices: $$$

With counter seating for ten and tables for maybe twice that, this wildly popular Little Tokyo spot elevates *shabu shabu* to an art. Reservations are a must, but once in, a meal at Kagaya progresses smoothly. Diners first choose a protein from prime beef, mixed seafood, and varied grades of Wagyu beef (note that prices can escalate well over $100 when Wagyu is involved). Then a series of appetizers arrives, followed by the *shabu shabu* ingredients, which diners cook in a metal bowl of steaming broth placed over the table's central hot plate.
During this process, chefs circulate through the room to skim the froth that forms on top of the liquid. When finished cooking, chefs return to season the remaining broth and add rice or udon noodles.

Nick & Stef's Steakhouse

Steakhouse

330 S. Hope St. (bet. 3rd & 4th Sts.)

Phone: 213-680-0330 — Mon – Sat lunch & dinner
Web: www.patinagroup.com — Sun dinner only
Prices: $$$

A classic steakhouse, Nick & Stef's dishes up unabashedly hearty food in a pair of modern woodsy-warm rooms and on an open-air terrace. From ribeyes to veal cheeks, this place worships prime dry-aged beef, but organic chicken, wild salmon, lamb chops, and even free-range buffalo co-star. Daily specials tout seafood and pasta.
A classic Caesar prepared tableside tops the salad list, which includes salt-roasted baby beets tossed with walnuts and goat cheese, as well as a seared-tuna Niçoise. Pumpkin and butternut-squash hash; broccoli rabe; and braised beans with prosciutto raise the bar on steakhouse sides.
The restaurant offers two-hour validated parking in the building and a complimentary shuttle to the Music Center and the Staples Center.

Noé

B2 Contemporary XXX

251 S. Olive St. (at 2nd St.)

Phone: 213-356-4100 — Dinner daily
Web: www.noerestaurant.com
Prices: $$$

Noé heralds its food as "progressive American cuisine," melding a strong Japanese influence with a French sensibility. "Progressive" implies change, and the menu does, constantly, along ingenious but disciplined lines. Miso stuffed eggplant salad with mizuna and citrus vinaigrette, and Arctic char with artichoke *barigoule*, onion glace, and caviar will give you the picture.

Its location, in the Omni Hotel *(see hotel listing)* next to the Walt Disney Concert Hall and the Museum of Contemporary Art, makes Noé a natural for a pre-theater nosh. But with stylish service, more than 100 foreign wines, a well-stocked humidor, and a "cigar-friendly" outdoor patio, this is a place to linger, rathen than rush through en route to a performance.

Park's Barbeque

A2 Korean 

955 S. Vermont Ave. (at San Marino St.)

Phone: 213-380-1717 — Lunch & dinner daily
Web: N/A
Prices: ⓑ

Park's location in an undistinguished Koreatown mall makes it easy to overlook this authentic restaurant. Inside, however, is a large, clean, well-ventilated space of black-granite tables equipped with charcoal grills. Young servers are knowledgeable and friendly.

Start with the *pan chan* appetizers, a variety of little dishes such as tofu and vegetables seasoned with cabbage condiment and garlic. You can grill Kobe beef, marinated pork belly, and other meats to your taste. A spicy beef stew with seasonal vegetables comes with sticky rice. Chef's specials may offer hearty portions of items like a seafood pancake, beef leg tendons, and pickled raw Dungeness crab in soy sauce.

There's a very small fee for valet parking at lunch and dinner.

Patina

Contemporary

141 S. Grand Ave. (at 2nd St.)

Phone: 213-972-3331 — Tue – Fri lunch & dinner
Web: www.patinagroup.com — Sat – Sun dinner only
Prices: $$$$

Patina Restaurant Group

A playful, endlessly creative menu sets the stage for an exquisite meal at Patina, tucked inside downtown L.A.'s landmark Walt Disney Concert Hall. Dinner might begin with an elegant starter of bright white asparagus stalks, perfectly blanched, and topped with a crispy, shredded potato-enclosed poached egg, laced with a silky tarragon mayonnaise. Next, set your sights on a criminally fresh California squab, expertly seared to golden perfection and set alongside a crunchy mix of organic *risi bisi* (an Italian dish of rice and peas) and bright spring leeks.

The man to thank for the seasonally-inspired menu is Chef/founder Joachim Splichal, but the well-trained kitchen keeps the motor running in this Frank Gehry designed building. The elegant room's interior is a handsome sight, with an almost regal brigade of perfectly-spaced white-cloth tables lining the floor.

Appetizers

- Caviar with Traditional Accompaniments
- White Asparagus, Crispy Poached Market Egg, Tarragon Mayonnaise
- Maine Lobster Tail, Melting Pig's Trotters, Hon Shimeji Mushrooms

Entrées

- Squab, "Risi Bisi", Leeks, Brandy Reduction
- Lamb Saddle, Fava, Potato, Almond Romesco Soil
- Salmon, Baby Artichoke, Carrot-Ginger Air

Desserts

- French Toast, Poached Apricot-Cardamom Crumble
- Chocolate Tuile, Macadamia Nut
- Vanilla Panna Cotta and Citrus Salad with a Madeleine

R 23

Japanese XX

C2

923 E. 2nd St. (bet. Alameda St. & Santa Fe Ave.)

Phone: 213-687-7178 — Mon – Fri lunch & dinner
Web: www.r23.com — Sat dinner only
Prices: $$$

This "Japanese restaurant+gallery" has won a decade of praise for artfully presenting a broad array of sushi on lovely ceramic platters. Fresh sushi and sashimi form the kitchen's focus, while daily chef's specials pay homage to tradition with fried Sawa crab; ribeye steak with ponzu; and sautéed maitake mushrooms with chili pepper.

In the large dining room, the décor is chic with its soaring ceilings, large canvases of contemporary art, and Frank Gehry's comfy cardboard chairs. The convivial sushi bar adds an extra seating option. The exterior is gritty urban; one enters via a narrow alley in an erstwhile warehouse district now filled with artists' studios. Valet parking (signs are clearly indicated) or taxi service is the best way to go here.

Seoul Jung

Korean XX

A2

930 Wilshire Blvd. (at Figueroa St.)

Phone: 213-688-7880 — Mon – Fri lunch & dinner
Web: www.wilshiregrand.com — Sat – Sun dinner only
Prices: $$$

Smoothly serving traditional dishes deftly cooked and beautifully presented by native chefs in a comfortable, contemporary setting, this authentic experience is truly above typical hotel dining. It consistently draws a loyal crowd who linger over settings of imported Korean porcelain in booths and alcoves tucked into four dining rooms.

Renowned tabletop barbecue specialties include sliced marinated pork in a spicy beef broth, topped with shredded beef, scallions, and vermicelli. A tasting menu offers a cook's tour of the finest Korean cuisine, with classics from lightly seasoned seafood scallion pancakes topped with calamari, baby shrimp, and bell pepper; to Kobe short ribs cooked with onion and served with dipping sauce.

Takami

Japanese XX

811 Wilshire Blvd. (at Lebanon St.)

Phone: 213-236-9600 — Mon – Fri lunch & dinner
Web: www.takimisushi.com — Sat – Sun dinner only
Prices: $$

Executive Chef Kenny Yamada, celebrated for his creative sushi, unveiled this modern minimalist restaurant atop a 21-story office tower. The view is stunning and grand—especially from tables on the outdoor terrace at night.

Quality ingredients and innovative presentations prevail, along with a friendly air at the sushi bar, where chefs are happy to suggest their preferred picks of the day, such as rolls of mixed crab, avocado, and cucumber in a soy and seaweed wrap. A choice of meats, vegetables, poultry, or fish, gently grilled over the *robata*, and attractively-priced *bento* box lunches round out the menu.

More hip and ambient during evenings, dancing is featured in the clubby lounge area, fueled by a solid sake list and creative cocktails.

Thousand Cranes

Japanese XX

120 S. Los Angeles St. (bet. 1st & 2nd Sts.)

Phone: 213-253-9255 — Sun – Fri lunch & dinner
Web: www.newotani.com — Sat dinner only
Prices: $$

Asymmetry, simplicity, austerity, naturalness, calmness, spirituality, subtlety: the seven principles of Zen define this serene restaurant. Located on the garden level (third floor) of the New Otani Hotel in Little Tokyo, Thousand Cranes peers out on a manicured Japanese garden. The garden's waterfall burbles soothingly in the background as you mindfully savor each bite.

Intriguing combinations of sushi, sashimi, soba, and tempura are offered at lunch; while evening rolls out a more expansive and pricey menu including chef's special sushi assortments, as well as a nine-course *kaiseki* dinner based on the freshest seasonal products.

A favorite haunt of local Japanese business people, the sushi and tempura bars are open at dinnertime only.

Water Grill

Seafood

B2

544 S. Grand Ave. (bet. 5th & 6th Sts.)

Phone: 213-891-0900
Web: www.watergrill.com
Prices: **$$$$**

Mon – Fri lunch & dinner
Sat – Sun dinner only

Critically acclaimed Chef David LeFevre, helms the ship at the beloved Water Grill, and downtown L.A. is lucky for it. Duck into this airy, elegant brasserie, located just a block off Pershing Square, and you'll discover a handsome room with wood panelling, curving banquettes, and an ever tempting raw bar stuffed with succulent oysters and plump shellfish.

Fresh is the name of the game here, so the menu changes accordingly—but dinner might begin with a crispy croquette, stuffed with succulent blue and Dungeness crab meat, and served over a creamy yogurt and cucumber sauce humming with *harissa*. A collection of New Zealand John Dory fillets might follow, crisped to golden perfection and dusted with paprika.

Save room for a lip-smacking finale like the Meyer lemon and cinnamon doughnuts, served with a lavender crème brûlée, and a coffee and chocolate pâtisserie.

Appetizers

- Santa Barbara Spot Prawn with Charred Octopus, Lemon Curd, Smoked Paprika Oil
- Blue Crab Cake, Harissa, Couscous, Yogurt-Lime-Cucumber Sauce

Entrées

- Wild Swordfish, Tomato-Date Chutney, Cumin-scented Zucchini Purée, Chick Pea Panisse
- Wild Tasmanian King Salmon, Soba Noodles and Gingered Katsuodashi Broth

Desserts

- Chocolate and Peanut Butter Coulant with Cracker Johns, Vanilla Marshmallows, Banana
- Blueberry and Mascarpone Cake with Candied Corn, Crème Fraîche Ice Cream

Wood Spoon

B3 — Brazilian

107 W. 9th St. (at Main St.)

Phone: 213-629-1765 — Tue – Sat lunch & dinner
Web: N/A — Mon lunch only
Prices: $$

This small, friendly, and unpretentious new eatery near the Fashion and Jewelry Districts has quickly won a local following. Basic and comfortable, it combines bright colors in a simple, clean, Art Deco style with a short, affordable menu of petite, tasty dishes.

Among the favorites are *feijoada,* a bean stew served (on Saturdays) with rice and salted pork, or pork burger with roasted cabbage and onion. A good selection of small plates may include *cohinha,* beignets filled with shredded chicken or shrimp with spicy mayonnaise; as well as skewer-grilled pork sausage with black beans, excellent roasted plantain, and spicy salsa.

The caffeine-loaded *Guarama,* a Brazilian staple, goes down smoothly with a dessert of flan or *Brigadeiro*—simple chocolate candy.

Yang Chow

Chinese

819 N. Broadway (bet. Alpine & College Sts.)

Phone: 213-625-0811 — Lunch & dinner daily
Web: www.yangchow.com
Prices: $$

Look at Yang Chow's pink façade and its basic décor, and you might conclude that this is a run-of-the-mill Chinatown restaurant. But look again: the line of regulars waiting to order savory Mandarin and Szechwan dishes at this family-run restaurant will tell you a different story.

Traditional fare—wonton soup, noodles, and made-to-order spring rolls, as well as seafood, beef, pork, and poultry in all their Asian incarnations—fills the menu; and specialties encompass spicy dishes such as Szechwan chicken, slippery shrimp, and Kung Pao fresh conch. Lunch combos and family dinners provide the most bang for the buck.

Visit Yang Chow's two other locations: in Canoga Park *(6443 Topanga Canyon Blvd.),* and in Pasadena *(3777 E. Colorado Blvd.).*

Yong Su San

Korean XX

A2

950 S. Vermont Ave. (at Olympic Blvd.)

Phone: 213-388-3042 Lunch & dinner daily
Web: N/A
Prices: **$$**

The Korean consular crowd who regularly dines here, quietly fussed over by traditionally costumed hostesses, may prize Yong Su San for its many small private rooms that offer discreet diplomacy. More likely it is the refined and traditional cuisine they favor—especially the set menus for two or more.

What is familiar to Koreans seems exotic to most everyone else, like a clear mungbean-jelly appetizer mixed with mushroom and seaweed; a cold buckwheat-noodle soup; steamed pork with pan-fried green beans; or barbecued sliced short ribs over a bed of onions. You may order à la carte, but know that the chef's tastings are interesting, balanced, and abundant. Rolling out up to 20 courses, these set menus dish up a memorable feast fit for an emperor.

The ✿ award is the crème de la crème. This is awarded to restaurants which are really special for their cuisine.

Hollywood

Midtown - West Hollywood

Is any American institution more durable than Hollywood, still a tourist magnet despite the loss of most of its film and TV studios? A 2002 bid failed to incorporate set boundaries claiming about 170,000 residents in a roughly four-mile square between the cities of Beverly Hills, West Hollywood and Burbank, and Melrose Avenue on the south. Since that annexes Los Feliz, Griffith Park, and the iconic Hollywood Sign, all claimed by other constituencies, Hollywood's boundaries are far from settled.

THE TOWN THAT MOVIES BUILT

Subdivided in the 1880s by Prohibitionist Horace Wilcox and named by his wife after a friend's country home, Hollywood was an independent city until water shortages compelled its annexation to Los Angeles in 1910. The following year the first movie studio opened on **Sunset Boulevard** at Gower Street, where CBS' former Columbia Square studio now stands. Paramount Pictures began in 1913 in a rented horse barn near Sunset and Vine, moving to its current location a mile south in 1926. Between the world wars the industry boomed, showcasing its product in **Hollywood Boulevard** movie palaces like Grauman's Chinese Theatre, El Capitan, and the Egyptian, now home to the American Cinematheque.

By the 1960s, rising land prices were driving production away as urban blight spread. A grassroots redevelopment movement began in the 1990s. Proof of its progress is the renovated Hollywood Bowl and the return of the Academy Awards, first bestowed at the Hollywood Roosevelt Hotel, now permanently ensconced in the new **Kodak Theatre**. Confidence in the future of rapidly gentrifying Hollywood has encouraged entrepreneurial chefs and restaurateurs to set up shop in chic new spaces throughout the area.

WEST HOLLYWOOD

Beyond the LA city limits and the reach of its vice squads, the neighborhood adjoining Beverly Hills enabled Hollywood's smart set to defy Prohibition and convention in **Sunset Strip** casinos and speakeasies like the Mocambo, the Café Trocadero, and Ciro's (now the Comedy Store), whose Sunday night "tea dances" allowed men to dance together in defiance of city law. Posh residence hotels like the Chateau Marmont attracted an upscale demimonde. Nightlife soared again during the 1960s, when clubs like Whiskey a Go Go and the Troubadour introduced many music legends.

Today the Strip (between Crescent Heights Boulevard and Doheny Drive) boasts rock clubs, restaurants and boutiques that attract an A-list clientele. Credit the sizeable gay community (about 40 percent of the 37,000 residents), which led the 1984 movement to incorporate the city of West Hollywood, now known for its progressive policies and civic pride.

The highest concentration of notable restaurants in the area can be found on 3rd Street, Beverly Boulevard, and Melrose Avenue.

© Mark Gibson

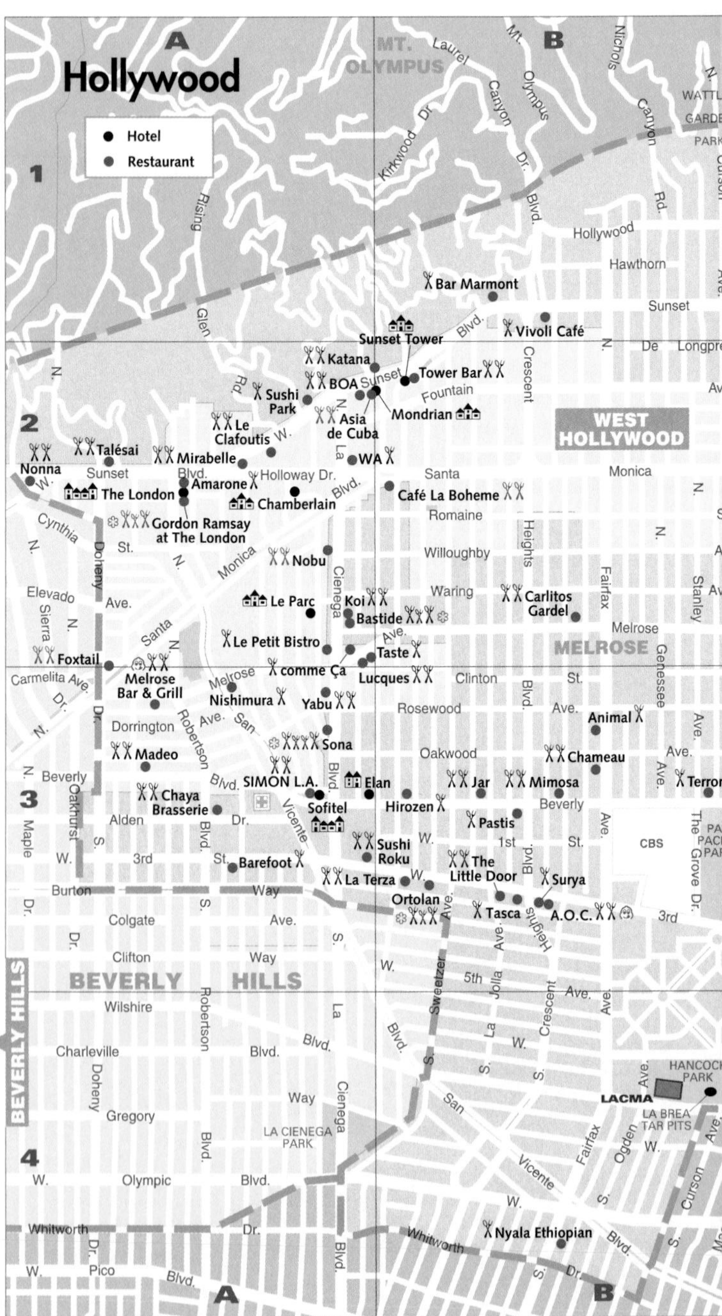

Hollywood
Hotel
Restaurant
A
B
1
2
3
4
MT. OLYMPUS
WEST HOLLYWOOD
MELROSE
BEVERLY HILLS
Bar Marmont
Vivoli Café
Sunset Tower
Katana
BOA
Tower Bar
Sushi Park
Mondrian
Asia de Cuba
Le Clafoutis
Talésai
Nonna
Mirabelle
WA
Amarone
The London
Chamberlain
Café La Boheme
Gordon Ramsay at The London
Nobu
Carlitos Gardel
Le Parc
Koi
Bastide
Le Petit Bistro
Taste
Foxtail
comme Ça
Lucques
Melrose Bar & Grill
Nishimura
Yabu
Animal
Sona
Chameau
Madeo
SIMON L.A.
Elan
Jar
Mimosa
Terroni
Chaya Brasserie
Sofitel
Hirozen
Pastis
Sushi Roku
Barefoot
The Little Door
La Terza
Surya
Ortolan
Tasca
A.O.C.
CBS
PAN PACIFIC PARK
HANCOCK PARK
LACMA
LA BREA TAR PITS
LA CIENEGA PARK
Nyala Ethiopian
WATTLE GARDEN PARK
Hollywood
Hawthorn
Sunset
De Longpre
Fountain
Santa Monica
Romaine
Willoughby
Waring
Melrose
Clinton
Rosewood
Oakwood
Beverly
1st
3rd
Burton Way
Colgate Ave.
Clifton Way
5th
Wilshire
Charleville Blvd.
Gregory Way
Olympic Blvd.
Whitworth Dr.
Pico Blvd.
Holloway Dr.
Cynthia St.
Elevado Ave.
Carmelita Ave.
Dorrington Ave.
Alden Dr.
Doheny Dr.
Robertson Blvd.
La Cienega Blvd.
San Vicente Blvd.
Sweetzer Ave.
La Jolla Ave.
Crescent Heights Blvd.
Fairfax Ave.
Genessee Ave.
Stanley Ave.
Curson Ave.
The Grove Dr.
Ogden
Laurel Canyon Blvd.
Mt. Olympus Dr.
Kirkwood Dr.
Nichols Canyon Rd.
Rising Glen Rd.
Sierra
Oakhurst
Maple Dr.

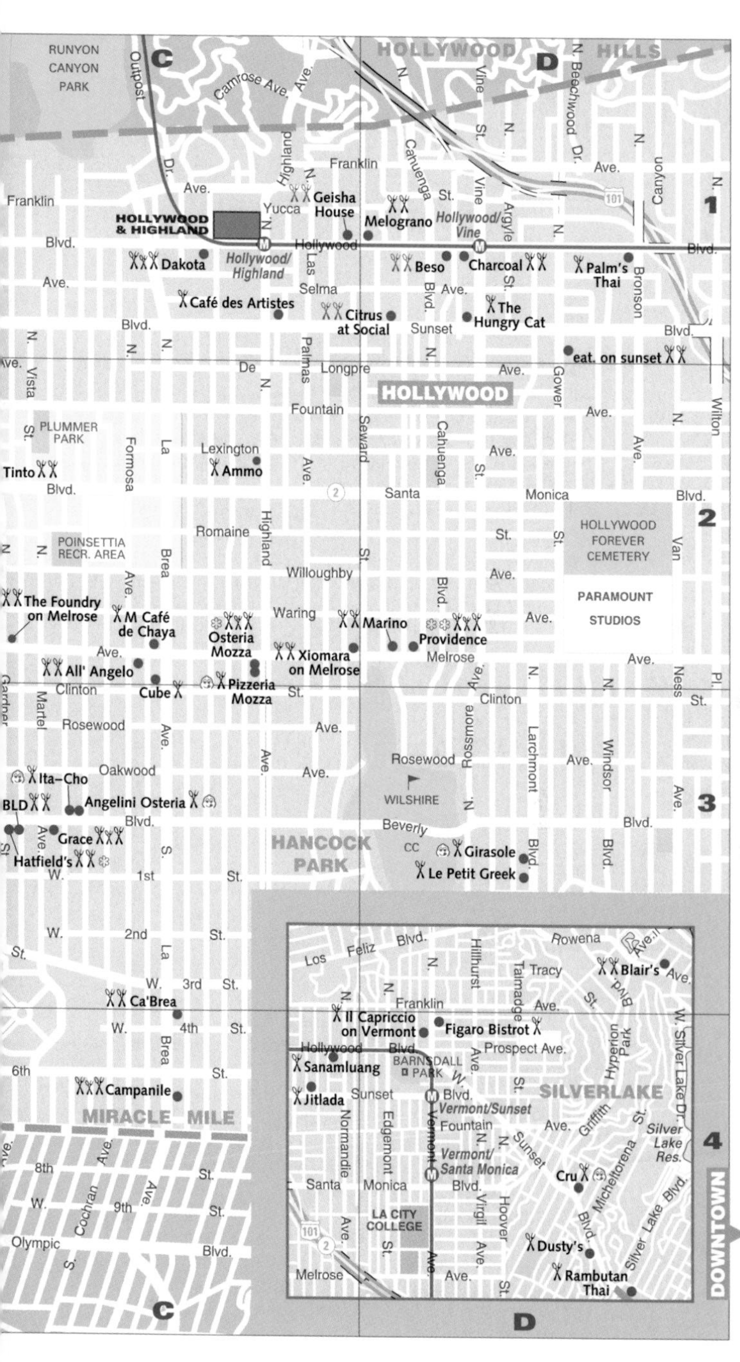

HOLLYWOOD
HOLLYWOOD HILLS
HOLLYWOOD & HIGHLAND
Geisha House
Melograno
Dakota
Café des Artistes
Citrus at Social
Beso
Charcoal
The Hungry Cat
Palm's Thai
eat. on sunset
Ammo
Tinto
The Foundry on Melrose
M Café de Chaya
Osteria Mozza
Xiomara on Melrose
Marino
Providence
All' Angelo
Cube
Pizzeria Mozza
Ita-Cho
Angelini Osteria
BLD
Grace
Hatfield's
Girasole
Le Petit Greek
Ca'Brea
Campanile
MIRACLE MILE
HANCOCK PARK
WILSHIRE CC
HOLLYWOOD FOREVER CEMETERY
PARAMOUNT STUDIOS
RUNYON CANYON PARK
PLUMMER PARK
POINSETTIA RECR. AREA
Blair's
Il Capriccio on Vermont
Figaro Bistrot
Sanamluang
Jitlada
SILVERLAKE
BARNSDALL PARK
LA CITY COLLEGE
Silver Lake Res.
Cru
Dusty's
Rambutan Thai
Hollywood/Highland
Hollywood/Vine
Vermont/Sunset
Vermont/Santa Monica
DOWNTOWN

All' Angelo

Italian XX

7166 Melrose Ave. (bet. Detroit St. & La Brea Ave.)

Phone: 323-933-9540
Web: www.allangelo.com
Prices: **$$$**

Mon – Thu & Sat dinner only
Fri lunch & dinner

Authentic, with reliably good food, impeccable table settings, and a wine list sampling the finest from Piedmont to Sicily, this youngster features straightforward dishes without superfluous sophistication. Seasonal menus feature what is freshest.
There is no scene here. Within tawny walls softly lighted by hand-blown Murano glass sconces and candles, a domestic warmth pervades. So, a braised radicchio lasagna with porcini mushrooms and melted mozzarella seems appropriate. Dishes display deft accents like a porcini mushroom sauce and sautéed rapini and add rustic flavor to a baked Alaskan black cod. Wrap it up grandly with, say, a flourless chocolate tart served with cocoa-hazelnut *gianduja*, or the simple grace notes of a caffè espresso e biscotti.

Amarone

A2

8868 W. Sunset Blvd. (at San Vicente Blvd.)

Phone: 310-652-2233
Web: www.amarone-la.com
Prices: **$$**

Mon – Sat dinner only

Small, casual, and friendly, Amarone's authentic cuisine is unique on this stretch of Sunset Strip, better known for the nightclub scene at the nearby Viper Room. The tiny ground-floor dining room has but 20 seats but an upstairs mezzanine holds 20 more, with comfy banquette seating creating a cozy intimate air.
The food is classic Italian, with superb pasta, fine meats, and organic ingredients cooked to showcase natural flavors. Expect rustic recipes like homemade fresh pappardelle with prosciutto, cherry tomatoes, and pecorino; or veal saltimbocca, the meat pounded thin, topped with sage and a slice of prosciutto, sautéed in butter, then marsala.
The wine list is exclusively Italian, competently chosen, and reasonably priced.

Ammo

Californian

1155 N. Highland Ave. (bet. Lexington Ave. & Santa Monica Blvd.)

Phone: 323-871-2666 — Lunch & dinner daily
Web: www.ammocafe.com
Prices: $$

Film industry denizens favor this cafe for its cool vibe, its background of indie rock, and its well-executed Californian fare. Self-taught Chef Amy Sweeney opened Ammo as a catering business in 1996, and expanded it into a full-service restaurant four years later. Recently, the place has enjoyed a new surge of popularity, owing to its new Executive Chef, Julia Wolfson, whose culinary pedigree includes a position in the kitchen at Le Bernardin in New York.

The menu is all about fresh organic ingredients gathered at the farmers' market. A playful, creative touch raises the house-made pappardelle with dandelion greens, sweet onion, and pancetta way above a common pasta. Likewise, a honey *gastrique* elevates the much-ordered pan-roasted Sonoma duck breast.

Angelini Osteria

Italian

7313 Beverly Blvd. (at Poinsettia Pl.)

Phone: 323-297-0070 — Tue – Fri lunch & dinner
Web: www.angeliniosteria.com — Sat – Sun dinner only
Prices: $$$

Here is an authentic trattoria whose native-born Chef/ owner and knowledgeable waitstaff serve traditional dishes with a friendly flair. Menus range from pizza and pasta to ambitious meat and fish recipes, perfectly executed without presumptuous presentation.

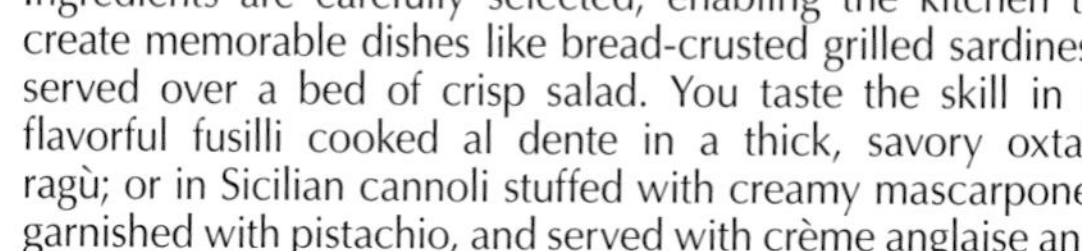

Ingredients are carefully selected, enabling the kitchen to create memorable dishes like bread-crusted grilled sardines, served over a bed of crisp salad. You taste the skill in a flavorful fusilli cooked al dente in a thick, savory oxtail ragù; or in Sicilian cannoli stuffed with creamy mascarpone, garnished with pistachio, and served with crème anglaise and vanilla ice cream.

The simple, comfortable interior sets a casual mood, enhanced at the pizza counter and on the sidewalk terrace.

Animal

Mediterranean

B3

435 N. Fairfax Ave. (bet. Oakwood & Rosewood Aves.)

Phone: 323-782-9225 Dinner daily
Web: www.animalrestaurant.com
Prices: $$

Food Dudes, Jon Shook and Vinny Dotolo, are on the prowl again—this time with their own restaurant, a hip new Hollywood hotspot near CBS Studios. Surrounded by vintage furniture and clothing shops, Animal exudes a bohemian spirit in its artsy minimalist décor: an unmarked door, naked light bulbs, and a wooden bench running along one wall.

The kitchen's inner beast emerges in its Cal-Med cooking, with an obvious fondness for pork. A fried pork chop with slow-cooked greens and slab bacon will give you the idea; while the likes of fresh monkfish cooked with Rancho Gordo scarlet beans, favas, and artichokes also relies on locally raised products.

A good selection of reasonably priced wine by the glass, carafe, or bottle, will keep you running with the pack.

A.O.C.

Mediterranean

B3

8022 W. 3rd St. (bet. Crescent Heights Blvd. & Edinburgh Ave.)

Phone: 323-653-6359 Dinner daily
Web: www.aocwinebar.com
Prices: $$

It stands for *Appellation d'Origine Contrôlée*, the certification granted to French regions for labeling wines and other agricultural products. And so, the bottles racked in this convivial gem are a design element amid the main room's warm yellow walls and leather-toned wood and fabrics. A.O.C. expanded their range of tapas, to include anything prepared fresh with flair. It is luscious stuff presented simply. A salad of smoked trout, persimmon, endive, and blue cheese-accented crème fraîche contrasts perfectly; while a rabbit ragoût with dijon mustard, chestnuts, and tarragon is an exercise in balance.

For twosomes, the best seating is at the wine bar, or the charcuterie and cheese counter—where knowledgeable staff will slice and cut as you chat.

Asia de Cuba

A-B2 — Fusion XX

8440 Sunset Blvd. (bet. La Cienega Blvd. & Olive Dr.)

Phone: 323-848-6000 — Lunch & dinner daily
Web: www.chinagrillmanagement.com
Prices: $$$

In the fancifully decorated Mondrian Hotel, this chic hot spot serves boldly flavorful combinations of Asian and Northern African-Caribbean ingredients. Panoramic city views from the outside dining patio, a see-and-be-seen young and fabulous crowd buzzing in the white-on-white dining room, and the poolside Skybar add glamour. Cordially attentive servers keep the hip vibe friendly.

The kitchen is innovative. As an appetizer, large sea scallops, simply sautéed and nicely browned, are served atop a generous dollop of caramelized plantain purée and smartly garnished with tropical fruit accents. Sliced roast duck with a thick hoisin glaze is surrounded by a salad of microgreens and shredded semi-ripe papaya. An A-list scene with food in a supporting role.

Barefoot

A3 — Californian

8722 W. 3rd St. (at Robertson Blvd.)

Phone: 310-276-6223 — Lunch & dinner daily
Web: www.barefootrestaurant.com
Prices: $$

The front wood and wrought-iron patio and its vine-covered façade, with flower pots and window boxes, are among L.A.'s loveliest. The food is solid and simple with salads popular at lunchtime, when the fashionable drawn by the nearby Robertson Boulevard boutiques, mix with medics in scrubs from the adjoining Cedars-Sinai Medical Center.

Here, Californian means things like a tower of finely diced raw Ahi tuna tartare, flavored with minced ginger and garlic, served atop simple radish greens—the whole shebang drizzled with green wasabi aïoli. A filet of fresh grilled salmon is simply seasoned with salt and pepper and served over fresh field greens. Californians are cosmopolitan, hence a robust cappuccino comes in a mug nearly the width of a soup bowl.

Bar Marmont

Contemporary

B1

8171 Sunset Blvd. (bet. Havenhurst Dr. & Selma Ave.)

Phone: 323-656-0575 Dinner daily
Web: www.chateaumarmont.com
Prices: $$

Long a hideaway for the glitterati, Chateau Marmont looks down on the Sunset Strip from its hilltop perch. If you can't get a room at the hotel, you can soak up a bit of the rarified atmosphere down the hill at Bar Marmont.

The Bar, facing Sunset Boulevard, greets patrons with a courtyard lounge. Inside, hundreds of butterflies decorate the ceiling over the sunken bar area, and sculpted walls and plush banquettes bespeak glamour in the elevated dining room.

Chef Carolynn Spence offers well-prepared, simple dishes. Entrées like a rustic lamb and feta sandwich, and a steak and portobello salad will give you the idea. The place caters to the fickle Hollywood set, which means that some nights it's standing-room only and other evenings the room is half-empty.

Beso

Latin American

D1

6350 Hollywood Blvd. (at Ivar Ave.)

Phone: 323-467-7991 Mon – Sat dinner only
Web: www.toddenglish.com
Prices: $$$

This newcomer on Hollywood Boulevard has been getting a lot of buzz owing to its celebrity pedigree—notably Chef Todd English and backers such as Eva Longoria among others. Outside, the building may look like a warehouse, but inside well-spaced tables and roomy demilune banquettes pair with stunning raindrop-shaped chandeliers, a back-lit glass wine wall, and glowing candlelight create an ambience worthy of the A-list crowd that frequents the place.

The menu globetrots through Mexico with tortilla soup and crab tacos, and on to Asia with an innovative crudo of yellowtail mixed with creamy coconut milk and tart yuzu juice. Despite these detours, the cuisine returns frequently to Spain for inspiration, as in a tasty saffron-scented seafood paella.

Bastide ✿

Contemporary

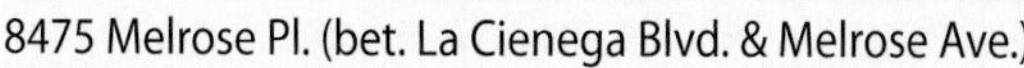
A2

8475 Melrose Pl. (bet. La Cienega Blvd. & Melrose Ave.)

Phone: 323-651-5950
Web: N/A
Prices: $$$$

Tue – Fri lunch & dinner
Sat dinner only

Hector Giraldo

Rising up from the ashes of Hollywood's fiery-hot restaurant scene is a sexy new contender for the patronage of L.A.'s power set. Housed amongst the designer shops that line tree-studded Melrose Avenue, Bastide was designed to impress with a lovely front garden, shaded with olive trees—and a smattering of beautiful, eccentric interior rooms to choose from, including a wild indoor atrium.

Heading the kitchen is Paul Shoemaker (formerly of Providence) who spins two nightly menus in 4- or 7-course options. The offerings change with the season, but might include a perfectly al dente, saffron-dusted risotto, sporting a piece of succulent Alaskan King Crab; two crunchy little squares of moist pork belly coated with coarse salt, served with roasted apricot and a spring onion bulb; or a succulent, marbled ribeye, topped with silky beads of bone marrow and crispy grains of faro.

Appetizers

- Kumomoto Oysters, Apple, Wasabi, Daikon-Yuzu Granité
- Apple-fed Black Pig, Poached Egg, Bacon, Frisée
- Thai Curry-Coconut Soup, Basil Infusion, King Crab

Entrées

- Milk-fed Poularde, Black Truffle, Coq au Vin Sauce
- Hawaiian Moi, Morel Mushrooms and White Asparagus
- Dry-aged Pennsylvania Beef Ribeye, Palate of Accompanying Flavors

Desserts

- Mango-Jasmine Rice Pudding Ravioli, Passion Fruit,Coconut
- Pineapple "Martini", Raspberry Tapioca, Yuzu Granité, Coconut Sorbet
- Chocolate, Peanut Butter and Banana

Blair's

Californian XX

D3

2903 Rowena Ave. (bet. Glendale & Hyperion Blvds.)

Phone: 323-660-1882 — Lunch & dinner daily
Web: www.blairsrestaurant.com
Prices: $$

Though mostly gentrified by creative sorts, the Silverlake area wasn't known for dining until this convivial neighborhood spot auditioned and won raves. One room stands in as a breakfast, lunch, and brunch cafe—mostly salads and burgers, but the former are organic and the latter sirloin—with bare bistro tables and a counter of fresh pastries on display.

The second room plays a more elegant role, serving dinner on white tablecloths amid chocolate-colored walls and soft music. Its more ambitious menu features risotto with roasted butternut squash, applewood bacon, and fontina cheese. Ingredients are fresh, the mood laid-back, and the service efficient.

If you can't find street parking, there's a small lot behind the restaurant.

BLD

American XX

C3

7450 Beverly Blvd. (at N. Vista St.)

Phone: 323-930-9744 — Lunch & dinner daily
Web: www.bldrestaurant.com
Prices: $$

The menu and minimalist décor are simple at this sibling of the ambitious Grace next door, which is open for breakfast, lunch, and dinner, (hence the name). Large windows frame Beverly Boulevard and inside, the ambiance is young, urban, and lively.

The menu features a wide choice of charcuterie from Italy and Spain, as well as local and European cheeses, dried fruits, and excellent bread.

There is simple fare, such as a Spanish dry-cured peppery salami served with dried fruits and a baguette. More exotic items run to things like wild Australian sea bass with roasted *fregola sarda*, wild mushrooms, sautéed pea tendrils, walnuts, and a garnish of garlic, lemon, and chopped fresh parsley. Wines sorted by character are mostly offered by the glass.

BOA

Steakhouse XX

A2

8462 W. Sunset Blvd. (at La Cienega Blvd.)

Phone: 323-650-8383 Lunch & dinner daily
Web: www.boasteak.com
Prices: $$$

BOA is currently located inside the swanky Grafton Hotel on the Sunset Strip, but is scheduled to move to a new location on Sunset within the year. This ultra-modern steakhouse is a far cry from the clubby classic that your grandfather frequented. Happily, BOA reveres doing things right, beginning with polite and careful service, and extending to impeccably prepared salads—applewood-smoked bacon, Maytag blue cheese, and buttermilk ranch dressing in the Cobb, for instance—and a "Turf" menu hewing to tradition with a bone-in Kansas City filet mignon and a 40-day dry-aged New York strip. The burgers are not your grand-dad's either; bet he never had one with Kobe beef and black-truffle shavings.

Ca'Brea

Italian XX

C4

346 S. La Brea Ave. (bet. 3rd & 4th Sts.)

Phone: 323-938-2863 Mon – Fri lunch & dinner
Web: www.cabrearestaurant.com Sat dinner only
Prices: $$

After undergoing significant renovation, Ca'Brea now feels like an authentic Italian trattoria. Its upscale country house décor mixes urbanity and *rustica* with a knowing panache. Friendly, attentive service adds appealing warmth. Given the chef is Antonio Tommasi, founder of much-praised Locanda Veneta, expect consistently well-executed dishes prepared from quality ingredients with respect for tradition.

That means antipasti classics like *carpaccio di manzo e Parmigiano*, thinly sliced raw beef garnished with shaved parmesan, chopped arugula, and mushrooms served with a mustard dressing; and pastas like plump *gnocci di patate* in a rich beef and veal ragù sauce accented with fresh herbs. This kind of cooking begs for a glass of Chianti classico in your hand.

Café des Artistes

French

C1

1534 N. Mc Cadden Pl. (at Sunset Blvd.)

Phone: 323-469-7300 Mon – Fri lunch & dinner
Web: www.cafedesartistes.info Sat – Sun dinner only
Prices: $$

In this bungalow-cum-French bistro, on a street chockablock with studio buildings, sound stages, and post-production houses, the buzzing in the dining room and pretty courtyard comes from a lot of "below-the-line" folks who actually *make* movies—the editors, technicians, and craftspeople whose names account for most of the credit roll.

The décor is a bright mélange of paintings and antiques. *Les créations culinaires* are classic bistro fare, like onion soup gratinée, pâté with cornichons, and grilled spicy merguez sausage. Jean Renoir and François Truffaut would find the "Main Courses Avec Les Frites"—the steamed mussels, the steak tartare prepared tableside, the filet with peppercorns and *sauce flambée Cognac*—as familiar as an old Arriflex.

Café La Bohème

Fusion

B2

8400 Santa Monica Blvd. (at Orlando Ave.)

Phone: 323-848-2360 Dinner daily
Web: www.globaldiningca.com
Prices: $$$

Named for the Puccini opera, La Boheme serves food that sings with high-quality ingredients, both local and seasonal. On any given day, simple pastas include rich and earthy mixtures like roasted mushrooms and brown butter sauce, a chestnut ravioli, and a Maine lobster risotto with corn purée; while main courses run from seared wild salmon to an aged sirloin strip steak. Unusual desserts share Italian touches and full-voiced sweetness.

In keeping with the restaurant's bohemian spirit, the dressy-casual crowd reflects West Hollywood's indie-film community. There are two dinner seatings, and their popularity makes reservations a must. This spacious production closed for a few months to undergo a significant facelift, creating a more relaxed ambiance.

Campanile

Mediterranean XXX

C4

624 S. La Brea Ave. (bet. W. 6th St. & Wilshire Blvd.)

Phone: 323-938-1447 — Mon – Sat lunch & dinner
Web: www.campanilerestaurant.com — Sun lunch only
Prices: $$$$

Charlie Chaplin built this gem, whose tiled fountain and dramatic rooms, two with glass atrium ceilings, have a theatrical flair suited to the show-biz neighborhood. Expect rustic fare and fresh seasonal ingredients at this popular place, whose loyals forgive the occasional lapse. Simple weekly specials add to the menu, offering less expensive choices.

You'll taste Italian and Southern French influences, as in a heaping pile of steaming Bouchot mussels drizzled with a creamy rouille, with a slight garlic and red chile flavor, served with roasted cherry tomatoes, and smoky-charred slices of grilled rustic bread from the next-door bakery.

The wine list is strong in Italian, Californian, and French labels, and the desserts can steal the show.

Carlitos Gardel

Argentinian XX

B2

7963 Melrose Ave. (bet. Crescent Heights Blvd. & Fairfax Ave.)

Phone: 323-655-0891 — Mon – Fri lunch & dinner
Web: www.carlitosgardel.com — Sat – Sun dinner only
Prices: $$

Stars, including Lauren Bacall not long ago, used to speak fondly of dining on Santa Monica's stretch of Montana Avenue the way they do today about Melrose Avenue's run east from Beverly Hills. Stars frequent Carlitos Gardel too, their chummy photos with the owner decorating the masculine, old-fashioned dining room.

Named for Carlos Gardel (ca.1890-1935), the still-revered King of Tango, the restaurant features the *parrillada mixta*, or mixed grill, so popular in Argentina. Here that can mean short ribs, grilled skirt steak, sweetbreads, chorizo, and black sausage finished at your table on a small grill. All else on the menu revolves around meat, about which—to borrow the title of one of Gardel's films, *La Casa es Seria*—the house is serious.

Chameau

Moroccan XX

B3

339 N. Fairfax Ave. (bet. Beverly Blvd. & Oakwood Ave.)

Phone: 323-951-0039 Tue – Sat dinner only
Web: www.chameaurestaurant.com
Prices: $$

This French-Moroccan restaurant forsakes the North African Casbah motif for a contemporary French-Arab look of vivid blue and red surfaces, modern furnishings, and dramatic accent lighting. That it is discreetly tucked into the Fairfax district, known for its Orthodox Jewish community, is very L.A.—a city whose schools recognize more than 90 languages.

The menu is seasonal, but favorites like duck *bastilla,* grilled merguez sausage with chickpea purée, and grilled skewered beef and lamb shank grace the selection year-round. Market-fresh daily fish specials are prepared Mediterranean-style. Traditional couscous courses run the gamut: vegetable, lamb, beef, sausage, game hen, fish. The wine list includes Moroccan, Spanish, and Californian labels.

Charcoal

Steakhouse XX

D1

6372 W. Sunset Blvd. (bet. Ivar Ave. & Vine St.)

Phone: 323-465-8500 Lunch & dinner daily
Web: www.charcoalhollywood.com
Prices: $$

The American comfort food served here suits the callow buzz in the ArcLight Cinema complex. The objective is not to push the culinary envelope, but to please. The décor is Hollywood glam, with high booths hinting there's Somebody in them. Elk horn chandeliers and wood panels suggest a clubby hipness. This is where fledgling sophisticates might order their first martini or canned malt liquor. The menu takes no chances, what with jumbo shrimp, sugary baked beans, homemade coleslaw, oysters, Caesar salad, skewered Kobe beef, mesquite-grilled burgers, ribs, salmon, and a filet mignon served with crispy French fries and no-nonsense ketchup. And then there's the giant funnel cake topped with fruit purées, vanilla ice cream, and chocolate sauce.

Chaya Brasserie

Fusion XX

A3

8741 Alden Dr. (bet. Georges Burns Rd. & Robertson Blvd.)

Phone: 310-859-8833 Lunch & dinner daily
Web: www.thechaya.com
Prices: $$$

In feudal Japan, a *chaya* was a roadhouse where travelers found rest, a meal, and a pot of tea. For more than 20 years in this high-end shopping district, loyals have filled the bar, the stylish dining room, the interior bamboo garden, and the flowered patio into the late-night hours. The draw? Top-notch fusion fare in a space filled with flowing fabrics and Asian objets d'art—and live jazz on Sundays.

The menu changes, but defers to fans of special sushi rolls like the Banzai—spiced soft-shell crab with sprouted radish seeds and cucumber—while offering seductive pasta, fish, and meat entrées (lobster ravioli; miso-marinated sea bass; hot and cold paella with chicken and saffron). This brasserie is as locally secure as the one in Paris called Lipp.

Citrus at Social

Contemporary XX

D1

6525 W. Sunset Blvd. (at Hudson Ave.)

Phone: 323-462-5222 Tue – Sat dinner only
Web: www.citrusatsocial.com
Prices: $$$$

The name is now Citrus at Social, the décor is no longer Moroccan, and the new menu is Franco-Californian inspired. The main dining room is more airy, with rich fabrics in hues of gray, green and, well, citrus. The power diners still gather at week's end, and A-list events book the upstairs private dining room and lounge.

The cooking remains sharp, using ingredients of excellent quality. The classic Lyonnaise salad is smartly updated with an original presentation, with the egg perfectly poached and the grilled lardons crisp. The kitchen's ability is evident in dishes like a very fresh halibut filet pan-seared, with an orange-lime lemon grass essence delicately infusing the meat.

Of course the desserts, wines, and spirits are A-list too.

comme Ça

A2 French

8479 Melrose Ave. (at La Cienega Blvd.)

Phone: 323-782-1104 — Lunch & dinner daily
Web: www.commecarestaurant.com
Prices: **$$**

Celebrity Chef/owner David Meyers is the inspiration behind this upscale brasserie on Melrose. The characteristic contemporary look and old-style devotion to quality food including an appetizing cheese bar merely adds to its charm. No zinc bar or posters, but rather a décor of black, white, and brown set off by antique mirrors.

From breakfast to late supper, the menu hews to classics: *plateau de fruits de mer, specialites du jour, tarte flambée,* coq au vin, and of course steak frites. The bar is skilled, and there's a wine list to match. Any of these, say a frisée salad of warm bacon and vinaigrette with a perfectly poached egg, or a venison, or rabbit terrine with mustard *a l'ancienne* will transport you to the arrondissement dearest to your heart.

Cru 

D4 Vegan

1521 Griffith Park Blvd. (bet. Edgecliffe Dr. & Sunset Blvd.)

Phone: 323-667-1551 — Sun – Mon & Wed – Thu dinner only
Web: www.crusilverlake.com — Fri – Sat lunch & dinner
Prices: **$$**

The wonder here is the marriage between raw organic vegan cuisine and flavor; and the innovation that flows from adhering to both vegan and raw food standards.

You taste the proof when you sip the smooth purée of a spicy curried squash soup flavored with curry and a purée of onion and garlic. It is semi-heated but not cooked to preserve the natural raw flavor of the squash, and garnished with fresh herbs, a bit of herb-cashew nut cream, and a drizzle of fragrant olive oil. Dress rutabaga noodles in ground sunflower seed sauce flavored with ginger and garlic; top them with red bell pepper, red cabbage, shiitake mushrooms, coconut meat, and cucumber garnished with jalapeño, raw cashew nuts, sprigs of cilantro, and lime, and you have a delicious vegan pad Thai.

Cube

Italian

615 N. La Brea Ave. (at Clinton St.)

Phone: 323-939-1148 Mon – Sat lunch & dinner
Web: N/A
Prices: $$

Cube is a neat little place. Half gourmet retail store, half modern-chic restaurant owned by a famed Italian food retailer, it's dining and market all in one. The restaurant was created to showcase ingredients from producers carried by the retail shop, and you'll find classics on the menu with Californian twists.

Dine amid the marketplace from the menu changing every Thursday to feature the cooking of a particular region. Lighter items may include a tangy, creamy *buratta* drizzled with a premium balsamic vinegar over a bed of arugula, and sliced heirloom tomatoes. Heartier dishes might include gnocchi in an intensely flavored veal, pork, and beef ragout topped with Red Cow Parmesan cheese.

There are over 85 cheeses offered from artisan producers.

Dakota

American

7000 Hollywood Blvd. (at Orange Ave.)

Phone: 323-769-8888 Dinner daily
Web: www.dakota-restaurant.com
Prices: $$$

Housed within the Roosevelt Hotel across from Grauman's Chinese Theatre is an enclave of brown suede armchairs, leather-topped tables, and warm-toned wood paneling. With its Spanish Renaissance exterior and supper-club atmosphere inside, the Dakota is a rare find in this touristy part of Hollywood, attracting a mixed crowd of casual diners who favor designer jeans over suits and ties.

Though the restaurant describes itself as a steakhouse, Dakota reaches well beyond typical steakhouse fare with a diverse selection of expertly prepared entrées. A wonderfully composed dish of tender, bacon-wrapped pork shoulder plated with buttery soft polenta and earthy, wilted Swiss chard epitomizes the slow-food style of cooking espoused by this kitchen.

Dusty's

Contemporary X

D4

3200 W. Sunset Blvd. (at Descanso Dr.)

Phone: 323-906-1018 Lunch & dinner daily
Web: www.dustysbistro.com
Prices: $$

Opened by a Québécoise several years ago, this chic little bistro quickly became a Silver Lake hit, a phenomenon encouraged by the generous portions. Locals crowd in for breakfast omelets, crêpes, and French toast. Lunch features organic salad, grilled French sandwiches, and burgers of lamb, turkey, crab, and Black Angus beef. French influences flavor dinner entrées such as duck sautéed in a Merlot sauce, and a goat-cheese-crusted, thyme-infused rack of lamb. Among the hearty sides is *poutine*—Quebec's famed snack—fries covered with mozzarella curds and gravy.
Spare and swanky by turns—a ruler-straight row of tables, a swoopy banquette—the interior reflects the enthusiasm that revitalized this area, home to early motion-picture studios.

eat. on sunset

Contemporary XX

D1

1448 N. Gower Ave. (at Sunset Blvd.)

Phone: 323-461-8800 Tue – Fri lunch & dinner
Web: www.patinagroup.com Sat dinner only
Prices: $$$

This stylish brick house represents the Patina Group's makeover of its former Pinot Hollywood. The restaurant has a restful air, drawing locals with its serious cooking and reasonable prices. On the patio, olive trees and vine-laced walls create a bit of serenity. Couches under the stars and inside add a homey feel to cocktail parties. The dining room is made luminous by an atrium ceiling and warmed by a fireplace when it's cool outside.
American favorites fill the bill in the form of hamburgers, meatloaf, and macaroni and cheese; as well as salads, sandwiches, and salmon (the latter slow-baked to preserve the delicate texture within, served over leeks and garnished with crispy onion rings). The kitchen is open late on Friday and Saturday.

Figaro Bistrot

French

D4

1802 N. Vermont Ave. (bet. Franklin Ave. & Hollywood Blvd.)

Phone: 323-662-1587 — Lunch & dinner daily
Web: N/A
Prices: $$

From the remarkably authentic décor—banquettes, a zinc bar, paneled mirrors, cast iron chandeliers, and tiled floors—you'd expect Parisians frowning at *le Figaro*. But this is bohemian Loz Feliz where from breakfast to dinner you'll more likely see film types intent on the *Hollywood Reporter* or *Variety*.
The kitchen uses mostly organic ingredients in classics like quiche Lorraine with a perfect crust, the egg custard studded with crusted bacon and served with a green salad in vinaigrette. *Poulet roti* comes as a half chicken, au jus, with crispy frites. The bar features Ricard aperitifs, with knowing touches like Lillet and French beer.
The adjacent bakery (same name and owner) supplies pastries, tarts, bread and, *naturellement*, croissants.

The Foundry on Melrose

Contemporary 

C2

7445 Melrose Ave. (at Gardner St.)

Phone: 323-651-0915 — Tue – Sat dinner only
Web: www.thefoundryonmelrose.com — Sun lunch & dinner
Prices: $$$

The Moderne curve of the yellow, black-ribbed bar, the art deco dining room's leather chairs and banquettes, and Pop Art canvases impart warmth inside this pleasant and popular establishment. A fireplace and seductive lighting do the same on the open-air terrace (tented in winter), where a graceful olive tree and the well-organized waitstaff hover over a stylish, mostly entertainment industry crowd.
They come for dishes like a hand-rolled, chervil-seasoned fettuccini appetizer, topped with Parmesan foam, presented on a bed of heirloom tomatoes. Or some enjoy entrées such as Alaskan halibut cooked with a dash of crusty sea salt, served with a leek fondue, red onion, and a soft, light saffron risotto.
There is live music here on some evenings.

Foxtail

Contemporary XX

A2-3

9077 Santa Monica Blvd. (bet. Almont & Doheny Drs.)

Phone: 310-859-8369 — Mon – Sat dinner only
Web: www.sbeent.com
Prices: $$$

You won't have to hunt long to track down this foxy West Hollywood newbie, which splits its space between a serious restaurant downstairs and a posh dance club upstairs. Art Deco and Art Nouveau styles fashion a swanky and seductive spot where deep armchairs cozy up to low octagonal marble tables, and back lighting sets off panels of stained glass.

It's a see-and-be-seen scene in the dining room, yet the kitchen stays focused. An updated take on lobster ravioli, for instance, folds large sheets of pasta over sweet chunks of butter-poached lobster and surrounds all with a velvety tomato-basil sauce. Fresh lavender might infuse a pot de crème for dessert.

Dress to impress if you hope to gain entry to the über-exclusive lounge and club upstairs.

Geisha House

Japanese XX

C1

6633 Hollywood Blvd. (at Cherokee St.)

Phone: 323-460-6300 — Dinner daily
Web: www.geishahousehollywood.com
Prices: $$$

Where else but in Hollywood, where anything can be a movie set, would you find this sexual fantasy of a restaurant? Perfumed with incense and exploding on your senses from the moment you enter, Geisha House envelops you in red. A red tower of stacked fireplaces rises toward the ceiling, lending its flickering glow to the downstairs dining room and the mezzanine above.

While there's much to distract you (even the waitresses are eye-candy), don't ignore the share-able dishes that fill the menu with everything from sushi, hand rolls, and *robata-yaki* to the delicious miso-marinated black cod—a house specialty.

Kimono-clad geishas roam the floor, while the twenty-something crowd sports designer jeans and includes an A-list of Hollywood hotties.

Girasole 

Italian 

D3

225 1/2 N. Larchmont Blvd. (bet. Beverly Blvd. & 3rd St.)

Phone: 323-464-6978 — Wed – Fri lunch & dinner
Web: www.girasolecucina.com — Tue & Sat dinner only
Prices: $$

In Hancock Park's Larchmont Village, a district evoking the red-brick Old Midwest, the Tolot family serves up authentic cuisine with a Venetian flair for seafood. The narrow, high-ceiling room has the intimate chatterbox air of the neighborhood spot it is. There is no bar, but when did you last find a restaurant that doesn't charge for corkage?

Every day features a pasta, soup, and dessert special, mostly Old County fare like eggplant and zucchini marinated in olive oil, garlic, and tomato and softly grilled; or a tomato, spinach, and white fettuccini in a seductive thick mozzarella cream sauce accented with shredded grilled ham.

Sidewalk tables add people-watching to the menu. Don't just drop in; this place is too popular for that.

Grace

American 

C3

7360 Beverly Blvd. (at Fuller Ave.)

Phone: 323-934-4400 — Tue – Sun dinner only
Web: www.gracerestaurant.com
Prices: $$$$

This is a handsome place, with a beautiful exposed wine cellar, minimalist furniture, and earth tones to warm the power scene that gives this Midtown spot its imprimatur.

The menu features both comfort food (burgers on Sunday night) and innovative fare, changing seasonally to feature the freshest ingredients. Dishes are prepared with care, and served in generous portions by a knowledgeable and efficient waitstaff.

In the innovative column you find seared foie gras with a batter-topped, custard-like, baked seasonal fruit clafoutis. Following you might try a wild boar tenderloin garnished with roasted brussels sprouts and herbed Yukon Gold potato spaetzle, accented with a discreet violet mustard sauce.

The desserts are luscious and the wines well-chosen.

Gordon Ramsay at the London ✿

A2 Contemporary XXX

1020 N. San Vicente Blvd. (bet. Cynthia St. & Sunset Blvd.)

Phone: 310-358-7788 Lunch & dinner daily
Web: www.gordonramsay.com
Prices: $$$$

The London West Hollywood

He's totally disagreeable, an unrepentant perfectionist, and prone to four-letter words. We're thinking that London's prized son is going to get along just fine in Hollywood. The famed Gordon Ramsay's newest is tucked into the London West Hollywood, a luxury hotel with a dining room dressed in pale, luminescent wallpaper, white-washed beams, and dripping chandeliers.

As for the groceries, Ramsay's high-end culinary vision is in full effect—look for starters like a soft trio of seared scallops, served over a creamy cauliflower purée; or delicate slices of fresh, scarlet tuna over a sesame biscuit. For dinner, a tender rack of Sonoma lamb arrives juicy to the fork, laced with fresh thyme and shiny pearl onions.

Save room for a milk chocolate sticky pudding, drizzled with caramel and finished with a creamy, roasted banana ice cream infused with black cardamom.

Appetizers

- Smoked Pork Belly, Scottish Langoustine, Celeriac and Apple
- Honey Soy-roasted Quail, Foie Gras, Saffron-Pear Chutney
- Apple-cured Duck Breast, Crispy Tounge, Amaranth

Entrées

- Loin of Rabbit, Black Olives, Tomato-Basil Confit
- Braised Poussin, White Cabbage, Pickled Ginger
- Monkfish with Crispy Chicken Skin, Lemon-Thyme Consommé

Desserts

- Milk Chocolate & Butter-Caramel Fondant
- Pineapple Soufflé, Toasted Coconut and Thai Curry Ice Cream
- Chilled Coconut Tapioca, Passion Fruit, Star Anise Sorbet

Hatfield's ✿

7458 Beverly Blvd. (bet. Gardner & Vista Sts.)

Phone: 323-935-2977 Mon – Sat dinner only
Web: www.hatfieldsrestaurant.com
Prices: **$$$**

Hatfield's

After pocketing their share of critical success in New York and San Francisco, husband-and-wife restaurateurs, Quinn and Karen Hatfield, have laid down their roots in Hollywood's thriving restaurant scene. They're sticklers for keeping things simple—which begins with the restaurant's décor, kept minimal with white walls, concrete floors, and rows of sparingly, but elegantly appointed, tables.

All the more reason for your focus to land on the food, a small, creative Californian menu devoted to the rotating seasonal market. And though it changes frequently, you might find silky crab folded into a wheat crêpe, paired with cool pickled beets and radish; or perfect pink fillets of trout, gently poached in olive oil, and laid over cardoons, potato purée, ruby grapefruit slices, and watercress salad; or for dessert, a Napoleon, dancing with creamy mascarpone and a tangerine sorbet.

Appetizers

- "Croque Madame", Brioche, Hamachi, Prosciutto, Quail Egg
- Roasted Foie Gras, Beluga Lentils, Apple-Rosemary Purée
- Diver Scallops, Braised Celery, Apple Froth

Entrées

- Trout, Herbed Cardoons, Smoked Potato Purée
- Date & Mint-crusted Rack of Lamb, Carrot, Kohlrabi, Fava
- Beef Rib, Spaetzle, Rapini, Mustard-infused Yam Purée

Desserts

- Citrus Napoleon, Almond Cake, Mascarpone
- Sugar and Spice Dusted Beignets, Vanilla-Chai Milkshake Shot
- Chocolate Mousse Tart, Chewy Caramel, Chocolate-Coffee Crumble

Hirozen

B3 Japanese 

8385 Beverly Blvd. (at Orlando Ave.)

Phone: 323-652-0470 — Mon – Fri lunch & dinner
Web: www.hirozen.com — Sat dinner only
Prices: $$

This small, friendly, unpretentious place serves excellent Japanese cuisine at a considerable value. The service here is well-organized, attentive, and truly charming.

Skilled chefs here are serious about their craft and present an impressive assortment of super-fresh sushi; exotica like Spanish mackerel with ponzu sauce and green onion; fresh octopus with salt and lemon; or a king mackerel with miso vinaigrette. The large list of nigiri sushi reflects the best available from the markets.

Though most of the menu is classically Japanese, a few dishes are accented by touches from other cuisines, even Mexican (this being Los Angeles), such as a crab meat chile relleno with salsa; or a salmon tempura roll with avocado and sushi rice in deep fried chile.

The Hungry Cat

D1 Seafood

1535 N. Vine St. (at Sunset Blvd.)

Phone: 323-462-2155 — Lunch & dinner daily
Web: www.thehungrycat.com
Prices: $$

Open late nightly, this is as urban a place as you'll find in Old Hollywood, in the retail-residential complex at Sunset and Vine. Here there is an extensive raw bar with oysters, clams, shrimp, Florida stone crab claws, Maine lobster, Pacific blue prawns, mussels, and caviar. It's all laid out for hungry cats off the district's ever-hipper streets.

The kitchen's creative flair shows in items like fried whitefish tacos with sliced red onions, shredded red cabbage, rich avocado, and sour cream wrapped in corn tortillas. Or something a little more sophisticated might be a filet of Alaskan halibut served with morel mushrooms and a fava bean purée; or even a tempura-fried soft shell "chili crab" accented with cilantro, mint, and peanuts.

Il Capriccio on Vermont

Italian

1757 N. Vermont Ave. (bet. Kingswell & Melbourne Aves.)

Phone: 323-662-5900 — Mon – Fri lunch & dinner
Web: www.ilcapriccioonvermont.com — Sat – Sun dinner only
Prices:

Rustic Italian dishes reign here, made of the freshest ingredients and served in copious portions. The food is traditional, featuring trattoria recipes the owners claim date back to the Renaissance—al dente pasta dishes with strong, aromatic flavors, polenta, and *frutti di mare*. The atmosphere is casual, the prices most affordable, and the staff will welcome you as if you were already a regular.

With its tinted Tuscany-style walls hung with regional paintings, the dining room lies within view of the open kitchen. Large rows of wooden tables, dressed with white linen and brown butcher paper, are most appealing at night under soft lighting. Best place for lunch? On the heated sidewalk patio, where you can feel the neighborhood's bohemian vibe.

Ita-Cho

Japanese

7311 Beverly Blvd. (bet. Fuller Ave. & Poinsettia Pl.)

Phone: 323-938-9009 — Mon – Fri lunch & dinner
Web: www.itachorestaurant.com — Sat dinner only
Prices:

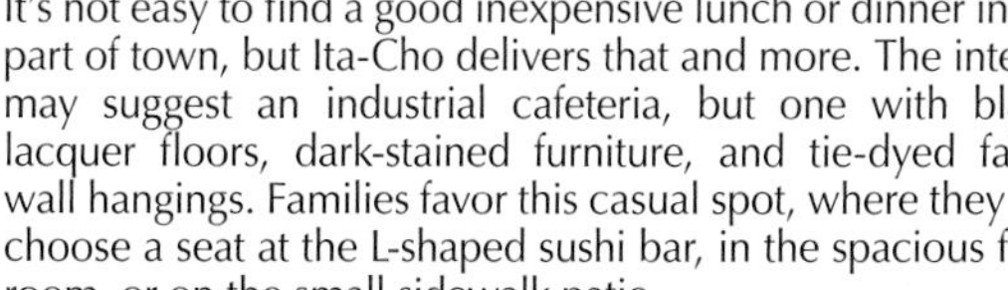

It's not easy to find a good inexpensive lunch or dinner in this part of town, but Ita-Cho delivers that and more. The interior may suggest an industrial cafeteria, but one with black-lacquer floors, dark-stained furniture, and tie-dyed fabric wall hangings. Families favor this casual spot, where they can choose a seat at the L-shaped sushi bar, in the spacious front room, or on the small sidewalk patio.

Simple and well-prepared sushi, sashimi, and à la carte dishes are made with great ingredients, as in light, steamed *shu mai* filled with sweet shrimp and presented with a soy-hot mustard sauce. Dishes, like a terrific steamed white fish infused with floral notes on a bed of wilted chrysanthemum leaves, give you more for your money here.

Jar

B3 — American XX

8225 Beverly Blvd. (at Harper Ave.)

Phone: 323-655-6566 — Mon – Sat dinner only
Web: www.thejar.com — Sun lunch & dinner
Prices: $$$

Chef Susan Tracht's chophouse offers a sophisticated menu of signature classics—her locally famed pot roast, Kansas City steak, and rib eye among the best in town. Perfectly executed by a serious kitchen using the highest quality meats, Tracht calls it "retro" fare "from the American culinary repertoire," right down to "perfect martinis."

Jar's curved wood walls, flying saucer lamps, and banquette evoke the seventies, the last time when you could order a 14-ounce ribeye with a side of crispy garlic and parsley French fries, served with béarnaise and a creamy horseradish sauce without guilt.

The amiably knowledgeable waitstaff, including a sommelier, will alert you to specials like the Monday mozzarella menu, and wines not on the list.

Jitlada

C4 — Thai X

5233 1/2 W. Sunset Blvd. (at Harvard Blvd.)

Phone: 323-667-9809 — Lunch & dinner daily
Web: N/A
Prices: $$

Though this Thai Town veteran has been on the scene for some time, a recent revival can be attributed to the 2007 discovery of a rare, but exciting, side menu: apparently, in addition to Jitlada's traditional Thai offerings, the restaurant was also offering a heat-packing, not-for-the-faint-of-heart, Southern Thai menu. Only problem was the menu was written in Thai. One neat English translation and a few critical reviews later, and Jitlada is firmly back on the foodie map.

But before you go bouncing down to get in line, keep in mind two things. No one comes for the ambience, so don't expect a tree-studded locale or charming interior. And not all of the dishes pack heat, so you'll need to drive it home if you want it spicy. Just don't say we didn't warn you.

Katana

Japanese XX

A-B2

8439 W. Sunset Blvd. (at La Cienega Blvd.)

Phone: 323-650-8585 Dinner daily
Web: www.katanarobata.com
Prices: $$$

The Piazza del Sol building, located on one of the hippest stretches of Sunset Boulevard, is home to Katana. Celebrities and wannabes turn out in droves to this Hollywood hotspot, yet they don't upstage the skewers of meat and vegetables that come from the *robata* grill. Smoky and delicious, items like flaky seabass, miso-marinated cod, and tender asparagus wrapped in bacon are the stars of a meal here. Nigiri, maki, and a host of hot entrées make a great chorus line.

If you're concerned about ambiance, note that the bar facing the *robata* grill can get a bit smoky, so sushi bar seating might make a better option. Or request a table on the lovely outdoor patio. Be sure to make reservations either way, as the buzz at this place has yet to die down.

Koi

Japanese XX

A2

730 N. La Cienega Blvd. (at Melrose Blvd.)

Phone: 310-659-9449 Dinner daily
Web: www.koirestaurant.com
Prices: $$$

Rock and movie stars and the people who orbit them celebrate themselves in this stylish establishment, where black floors, an earth-toned palette with red accents, polished wood, and the flickering light from scores of small white candles honor Asian aesthetic traditions in a contemporary form.

The same attention is given to the preparation of signature dishes like the baked crab hand roll with crispy rice. There's innovation here—California rolls with baked scallops, sautéed shrimp, tuna tartare on crispy wontons, or Kobe beef carpaccio with fried shiitakes and a yuzu citrus sauce. Sake comes "by the bamboo" or the bottle; brands are described by taste.

Pulsing club music, security bouncers, and paparazzi out front foster the private-club vibe.

La Terza

Italian XX

B3

8384 W. 3rd St. (at Orlando Ave.)

Phone: 323-782-8384 Lunch & dinner daily
Web: N/A
Prices: **$$**

At age 23, Gino Angelini was the youngest chef in an upscale hotel restaurant in his native Italy, where he cooked for presidents (Mitterand, Gorbachev) and popes (John Paul II). *La Terza* ("third" in Italian) is owner Angelini's latest L.A. venture, and it's primo in many Angelenos' hearts.

His bright bi-level space has an open wood-burning rotisserie and grill where most of the meats are prepared. Portions are small, strongly flavored, and well-executed from high-quality, and often imported ingredients. Many of the specials trace their heritage to Italy's Piemonte and Emilia-Romagna regions.

Street parking can be challenging to find in this area of West Hollywood, but the valet at the adjoining Orlando Hotel also accommodates La Terza's guests.

Le Clafoutis

Contemporary XX

A2

8630 Sunset Blvd. (at Sunset Plaza Dr.)

Phone: 310-659-5233 Lunch & dinner daily
Web: N/A
Prices: **$$**

The pretty, sunny outdoor patio of this brasserie-cafe-bakery on Sunset Plaza adds people-watching to the cosmopolitan menu of carefully prepared French, American, Californian, and Italian items.

You could order the decadent *croque monsieur,* but first you should consider the daily specials, reflecting the chef's whimsy and the market's best. Signature dishes like Chicken Sunset, a grilled breast topped with a tomato and basil sauce, are reliably satisfying. The freshness and quality of ingredients is evident in a seared Ahi tuna, served in a refined cabernet sauce with mashed potatoes and Niçoise salad. The desserts and pastries made here are *très Français* and excellent.

Come night, enjoy the city lights from the balcony at the back of the dining room.

Le Petit Bistro

French

A2

631 N. La Cienega Blvd. (at Melrose Ave.)

Phone: 310-289-9797 — Mon – Fri lunch & dinner
Web: www.lepetitbistro.us — Sat – Sun dinner only
Prices: $$

Surrounded by hip eateries and a hot nightclub, this old-fashioned Paris-style bistro seems out of time and place, and so offers a refreshing respite. The narrow dining room is usually crowded. The décor is bistro basic, with a burgundy banquette, vintage liquor ads, butcher-paper-covered tables, and waiters dressed in *garçon de café* garb.

Escargots, onion soup gratinée, mussels cooked with white wine and shallots, roasted chicken with herbs de Provence, and grilled ribeye with pommes frites constitute traditionally Gallic fare; while California-style grilled fish and salads cater to those with more health-conscious tastes. Desserts include classic profiteroles and a buttery bread pudding. Portions are honest, tasty, and moderately priced.

Le Petit Greek

Greek 

127 N. Larchmont Blvd. (bet. Beverly Blvd. & 1st St.)

Phone: 323-464-5160 — Lunch & dinner daily
Web: www.lepetitgreek.com
Prices: $$

It's not surprising that the food, décor, and music here are authentic, for the Houndalas family was in the restaurant business in Greece for generations before setting up shop in Larchmont Village in 1988. In a little house, complete with a sidewalk patio, the green and white dining room is decorated with Old Country photos and bottles of wine from around the world—including, of course, a wonderful collection of Greek labels.

The signature baby rack of lamb shares menu space with an abundance of Mediterranean salads, dips, moussaka, kebobs, and pasta dishes. Unpretentious and affordable, with casual yet efficient service and generous portions, Le Petit Greek is a refreshing alternative to L.A.'s often trendy and pricey restaurant scene.

The Little Door

B3 Mediterranean XX

8164 W. 3rd St. (bet. Crescent Heights Blvd. & La Jolla Ave.)

Phone: 323-951-1210 Dinner daily
Web: www.thelittledoor.com
Prices: $$$

What's behind the Little Door? It's worth your while to find out. Once inside, you'll step into a garden patio overflowing with bright flowers, ferns, and lush greenery. By day, sunlight filters in through the open skylight; after dark, the stars twinkle overhead in the night sky. In back you'll discover the open-air winter garden, its sparkling blue and white color scheme conjuring up the Mediterranean.

Hip, moneyed Beverly Hills denizens who frequent this place have no qualms about shelling out big bucks for the wine and food. The menu summons each season with premium ingredients and generous portions of pasta, small plates, and daily specials.

Check out The Little Next Door for breakfast and lunch, or gourmet goodies to go.

Lucques

A2 Mediterranean XX

8474 Melrose Ave. (at La Cienega Blvd.)

Phone: 323-655-6277 Tue – Sat lunch & dinner
Web: www.lucques.com Sun – Mon dinner only
Prices: $$$

Red roof tiles and ivy cloak the brick and wood interior of this old carriage house. The main room's simple décor, crackling fireplace, and covered patio with cushioned wrought-iron chairs, impart a serene, sheltered feel.

Menus change seasonally and focus on local produce. At lunch, the selection is limited but expands come evening.

Overtures include flavorful salads, such as an apricot and cherry salad with seal bay triple crème, and crushed hazelnuts. These set the stage for entrées like a naturally sweet black cod finished with sliced chocolate persimmon, buckwheat crêpes with Gruyère, wild mushrooms, and walnuts; or a pancetta-wrapped stuffed guinea hen. Alluring desserts run to things like buttery crêpes folded over a filling of chopped chestnuts.

Madeo

Italian XX

A3

8897 Beverly Blvd. (bet. Doheny Dr. & Robertson Blvd.)

Phone: 310-859-4903 — Mon – Fri lunch & dinner
Web: N/A — Sat – Sun dinner only
Prices: $$$

This is a friendly establishment whose owners, two Italian-speaking brothers and their sons, and their Tuscan kinfolk are on a first-name basis with many of the A-list regulars. They serve generously-sized, rustic Northern Italian dishes like porcini risotto and veal Milanese, backed by good wines from Naples to Napa. The relaxing, old-fashioned setting where crisp table linens glow, and the crowd around the main room's circular bar, is at ease with the prices.

Menu items are classic, like *buratta caprese*, the tangy, creamy cheese matched with basil leaves and heirloom tomatoes accented with balsamic vinegar, and fruity olive oil. A tender lamb chop cooked medium rare arrives with roasted potatoes and spinach. Very Tuscan, rural, and tasty.

Marino

Italian XX

D2

6001 Melrose Ave. (at Wilcox Ave.)

Phone: 323-466-8812 — Mon – Fri lunch & dinner
Web: N/A — Sat dinner only
Prices: $$$

If you're in the mood for something traditional and romantic, rather than avant-garde, this family-run restaurant is a fine choice. The calm atmosphere, old-fashioned décor (eclectic Italian paintings and antiques), intimate lighting, and polite, efficient service seem to have all been in place here for decades.

Upon entering, patrons are immediately tempted by a glass-fronted armoire displaying antipasti—meats, aged cheeses, marinated olives, and vegetables. If you order the *branzino*, a whole fish cooked en *papillote*, Marino's owner may do the honors himself, deboning the fish at your table before dressing it with olive oil and pepper, then presenting it with a creamy asparagus risotto.

The solid wine list finds strength in Italian vintages.

M Café de Chaya

Californian

C2

7119 Melrose Ave. (at La Brea Ave.)

Phone: 310-525-0588 — Lunch & dinner daily
Web: www.mcafedechaya.com
Prices:

Sequestered in a tiny strip on Melrose at La Brea (around the corner from Pink's Hot Dogs), this cafe is the most casual of the family of restaurants that started with Chaya Brasserie in Beverly Hills.

Quintessentially Californian, made-to-order salads (tuna tataki topped with greens and fresh avocado) share the menu with rice bowls, hot and cold sandwiches, and wraps. Avoiding refined sugars, dairy products, red meat, and poultry, the cafe uses tempeh "bacon" in its California club, and thinly sliced grilled seitan (wheat gluten) in its Carolina-style barbecue.

They do a brisk carry-out business for customers who can't find a seat among the handful of tables inside and out on the sidewalk—where traffic noise can interrupt conversation.

Melograno

Italian

D1

6541 Hollywood Blvd. (at Schrader Blvd.)

Phone: 323-465-6650 — Tue – Thu & Sun dinner only
Web: www.melogranohollywood.com — Fri – Sat lunch & dinner
Prices: $$$

After running some of the best Italian restaurants in Los Angeles, Piedmont-born Alberto Lazarrino opened his own. An ambitious addition to Hollywood Boulevard, the elegantly narrow dining room features leather seats, impeccable white table linens, and a large outdoor patio. It draws a crowd more chic than the district's typical denizens, and the all-Italian wine list is not over-priced.

The name, Italian for pomegranate, hints at touches of the fruit found in most dishes. Precisely cooked, they bear homeland touches such as the grapes and sunflower seeds in an "autumn" salad; the vincotto and pomegranate-shallot dressing in a marinated Cornish hen; and slow-braised short ribs in a densely powerful Barolo wine, served with pan-roasted polenta.

Melrose Bar & Grill

American

8826 Melrose Ave. (at Robertson Blvd.)

Phone: 310-278-3684 — Mon – Fri lunch & dinner
Web: www.melrosebarandgrill.com — Sat dinner only
Prices: $$

This friendly neighborhood bistro serves Yankee dishes and nightly specials chalked on big wall-hung blackboards. Prices are reasonable, ingredients are tops, preparations simple, and the kitchen is open to watch. The atmosphere is relaxed and the staff welcoming.

Wood tables embraced by creamy banquettes under soft lights, a roaring fireplace, sanguine tile floors, and a v-shaped bar (where you can order off the menu) make this a low-tension joint.

Specials include appetizers like tender, roasted mussels in a fragrant tomato broth jacked up with sliced garlic, fennel, and thyme sprigs. Or how about a richly flavorful duck burger, with dried cherry ketchup, gouda, and lettuce? This kitchen is not coy and you'll find the desserts, in studio lingo, are killer.

Mimosa

French 

8009 Beverly Blvd. (bet. Edinburgh & Laurel Aves.)

Phone: 323-655-8895 — Tue – Sat dinner only
Web: www.mimosarestaurant.com
Prices: $$

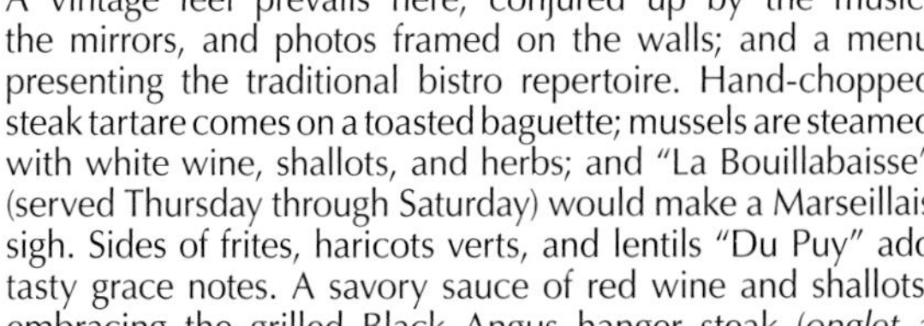

A vintage feel prevails here, conjured up by the music, the mirrors, and photos framed on the walls; and a menu presenting the traditional bistro repertoire. Hand-chopped steak tartare comes on a toasted baguette; mussels are steamed with white wine, shallots, and herbs; and "La Bouillabaisse" (served Thursday through Saturday) would make a Marseillais sigh. Sides of frites, haricots verts, and lentils "Du Puy" add tasty grace notes. A savory sauce of red wine and shallots, embracing the grilled Black Angus hanger steak (*onglet a l'echalotte*) evokes Paris for all the right reasons.

Adding to bistro verisimilitude are desserts like *pot de chocolat* mousse, or pear financier, an almond cake of poached pears served with a walnut caramel sauce.

Mirabelle

Californian

A2

8768 Sunset Blvd. (bet. Horn Ave. & Sherbourne Dr.)

Phone: 310-659-6022 — Lunch & dinner daily
Web: www.mirabellehollywood.com
Prices: **$$**

A serious kitchen open late and a friendly staff offer guests a choice between an intimate dining room of European style (cafe chairs, banquette seating, a wrought iron chandelier above terra-cotta walls) or a clubby boisterous lounge bar.
Here, seafood is prepared with eclectic pan-Latin influences using choice organic ingredients. Sautéed Cajun shrimp, for example, are served with herbed rice and Spanish chorizo in a thick spicy tomato sauce. A filet of brick oven-baked salmon, topped by a cilantro-honey pumpkin seed pesto, is garnished with braised portobello mushrooms in a sweet yellow mole.
A signature chocolate soufflé (requiring 20 minutes of preparation) features a subtly salted caramel ice cream and crème anglaise.

Nishimura

Japanese

A3

8684 Melrose Ave. (at San Vicente Blvd.)

Phone: 310-659-4770 — Mon – Fri lunch & dinner
Web: N/A — Sat dinner only
Prices: **$$$**

It's easy to miss this modest ivy-covered bungalow, across the street from the Pacific Design Center. Once you spot the number on the façade, you'll note there's no entrance on the street side. To find the door, discreetly hidden behind a high wood fence, you'll have to walk through a little courtyard garden.
Once inside the bright little dining room—with its sushi bar and smattering of tables—you'll be treated to a selection of sushi and sashimi, along with thin-sliced hamachi (with Serrano chili, dai-dai sauce, and cilantro), and seared dishes (konpachi with ginger, grated garlic, and yuzu pepper sauce). Depending on what's in season, specials add local seafood such as grilled Santa Barbara shrimp.
Expect gracious service and high prices.

Nobu

Japanese XX

A2

903 N. La Cienega Blvd. (bet. Melrose Ave. & Santa Monica Blvd.)

Phone: 310-657-5711 Dinner daily
Web: www.noburestaurants.com
Prices: **$$$$**

Yet another hit from Nobuyuki Matsuhisa, the newest Nobu presents the chef's unique flavorful cuisine. Virtuoso signature dishes include live scallop *tiradito*, with thin slices fanned out and drizzled with lemon juice. Or look for red snapper sashimi, accented with olive oil and sea salt, accompanied by a nutty mound of dried, powdered red miso and shaved garlic chips. Fish is delicately steamed to preserve its moisture, and innovatively garnished. The omakase always presents the chef's pick of the day's best.

The simply chic richly-hued rooms with dark wood floors contain sleek wood furnishings, a blond wood sushi bar, screened walls back-lit in red, and cocoon-like modernist light fixtures.

Nonna

Italian XX

9255 Sunset Blvd. (at N. Sierra Dr.)

Phone: 310-270-4455 Mon – Fri lunch & dinner
Web: N/A Sat dinner only
Prices: **$$**

Nonna is Italian for grandmother, but besides respect for tradition, this spacious Sunset Strip ingénue is *molto moderno*. The restrained elegance of gleaming wood floors, paneled walls, and minimalist furnishings is offset by the exuberant energy from the large display kitchen.

Dishes are carefully made from superior ingredients and presented simply in generous portions. The menu showcases excellent products in plates of tangy, imported *buratta*, or prosciutto and melon. A bowl of orecchiette topped with ground sausage and aged pecorino is nothing fancy but made with care. Lighter Californian fare like thin-crust pizza and seared ahi tuna can also be found.

A glassed-in wine cellar has a strong collection of reds from Tuscany and Piedmont.

Nyala Ethiopian

Ethiopian

B4

1076 S. Fairfax Ave. (bet. Olympic Blvd. & Witworth Dr.)

Phone: 323-936-5918 Lunch & dinner daily
Web: www.nyala-la.com
Prices:

This family-owned enterprise is said to be the best in L.A.'s Little Ethiopia. Behind a modest storefront façade, a small dining room decorated with African artifacts attracts a boisterous bunch for combination platters of chicken, lamb, or beef; as well as seafood and vegetarian dishes. The cuisine is authentic, flavorful, and reasonably priced.

Pleasantly sour pancake-like bread known as *injera,* ubiquitous in Ethiopia, is a staple here too. The spongy crêpes of teff flour serve as both platter and utensil; tear off a piece and pinch your fingers to pick up portions, or use the bread to soak up the various aromatic sauces. In addition to Ethiopian wine, you can quench your thirst with strong coffee, hot spiced tea, or African beer.

Palm's Thai

Thai 

D1

5900 Hollywood Blvd. (at Bronson Ave.)

Phone: 323-462-5073 Lunch & dinner daily
Web: www.palmsthai.com
Prices: 

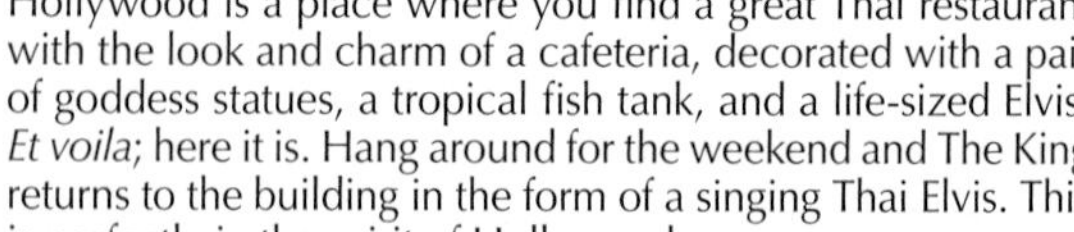

Hollywood is a place where you find a great Thai restaurant with the look and charm of a cafeteria, decorated with a pair of goddess statues, a tropical fish tank, and a life-sized Elvis. *Et voila*; here it is. Hang around for the weekend and The King returns to the building in the form of a singing Thai Elvis. This is perfectly in the spirit of Hollywood.

It's the food and low prices that draw the crowd, however, not Elvis, from the sophisticated spicy soups, the large choice of curries accented with bamboo shoots and coconut milk, and the piquant salads—sometimes grilled beef infused with lime and cilantro. It's all Top 40 hits, all the time.

To top it all off, there's wine, beer, a sidewalk patio, and parking in the back.

Ortolan ✿

French 

8338 W. 3rd St. (bet. Orlando & Sweetzer Aves.)

Phone: 323-653-3300 Tue – Sat dinner only
Web: www.ortolanrestaurant.com
Prices: **$$$$**

It's now illegal to hunt the small European songbird for which Ortolan is named, though their meat was once prized for gourmands in the know. Today's foodies will sign a breath of relief knowing that the restaurant, however, is still very much fair game.

Step back into a time when luxurious surroundings were the mark of fine dining with this ethereally beautiful dining room, cloaked in cream drapes, vanilla leather banquettes, and dripping chandeliers. Behind it, you'll uncover a dark, sultry bar with a striking garden wall.

Chef Christophe Émé keeps his French menu interesting by spinning his creative wheels whenever he can. A simple starter of three fresh langoustines arrives on a stone slate—the crustaceans fried in a tissue-thin pastry and served over a streak of chickpea purée. Paired with two shooters of minestrone soup, capped with basil foam—the result is sensational.

Appetizers

- Seared Calamari with Oxtail and Spaghetti, and Porcini, Scallion, Beef Jus Reduction
- Vegetables in Five Ways: Consommé, Coulis, Carpaccio, Emulsion and Parfait

Entrées

- Roasted Lobster with Morels, Fiddlehead, Watercress Sauce and Fava Bean
- Roast Rack of Lamb with Crispy Mozzarella, Ricotta Gnocchi, Tomato Confit and Baby Artichoke

Desserts

- Chocolate Tart, Raspberry,and Vanilla Ice Cream
- Panna Cotta with Pear "Caviar"
- Baba au Rhum with Mascarpone-Chestnut Sorbet, Clementine

Osteria Mozza ✿

6602 Melrose Ave. (at Highland Ave.)

Phone: 323-297-0100 — Dinner daily
Web: www.mozza-la.com
Prices: **$$$**

Don't tell Pizzeria Mozza, but her little sister has stolen the spotlight. Mario Batali and Nancy Silverton's second Hollywood venture is not as relaxed as their pizzeria, but that could be in part to the mix of chowhounds and scenesters that flood this joint nightly. Who can blame them, with Osteria's urban good looks and killer mozzarella bar, where even Silverton has been known to throw together an antipasti plate or two?

The dishes made with *burrata*—a type of fresh Italian cheese with an oozing cream middle—are a specialty, but those looking for Batali's trademark rustic Italian fare will find plenty to rave about elsewhere.

The menu runs deep, with homemade pastas like the orecchiette, chock-a-block with fiery sausage and silky Swiss chard; or heartier fare like the perfectly roasted quail, wrapped in crispy pancetta and finished with a sage and honey reduction.

Appetizers

- Mussels with Passato di Pomodoro, Chilies & Herbs
- Braised Artichokes, Pine nuts, Currants & Mint Pesto
- Sheep's Milk Ricotta with Hazelnuts, Garlic & Lemon Zest

Entrées

- Radicchio-wrapped and Grilled Whole Orata, with Olio Nuovo
- Duck "al Mattone", Pear Mostarda, Brussels Sprouts
- Garganelli with Ragú alla Bolognese

Desserts

- Bombolini, Huckleberry Compote & Vanilla Gelato
- Moscato di Trani Gelato, Apricot Tart & Hazelnut Nougatine
- Bitter Chocolate, Warm Chocolate Cake & Bourbon Gelato

Pastis

8114 Beverly Blvd. (at Crescent Heights Blvd.)

Phone: 323-655-8822 Dinner daily
Web: www.lapastis.com
Prices: **$$$**

LA's Pastis (no relation to the boisterous bistro in Manhattan's Meatpacking District) welcomes guests into a tiny, candlelit interior, where bare farm tables, framed mirrors and vintage photos of the French countryside are juxtaposed with the sounds of club music—a distinctly LA twist.

Charcuterie, pâté, and *coq au vin* bespeak the traditional, while bouillabaisse, mussels *marinière*, and a lovely lavender crème brulée add Provençal accents. On Wednesdays, buy a bottle of wine and get a complimentary bottle to take home. (Alas, you can't drink it here.)

For a splurge, indulge in the five-course pairing menu. In this feast, the chef matches up imported wines with dishes like lobster bisque, roasted monkfish and walnut-crust strawberry tart.

Pizzeria Mozza

641 N. Highland Ave. (at Melrose Ave.)

Phone: 323-297-0101 Lunch & dinner daily
Web: www.mozza-la.com
Prices: **$$**

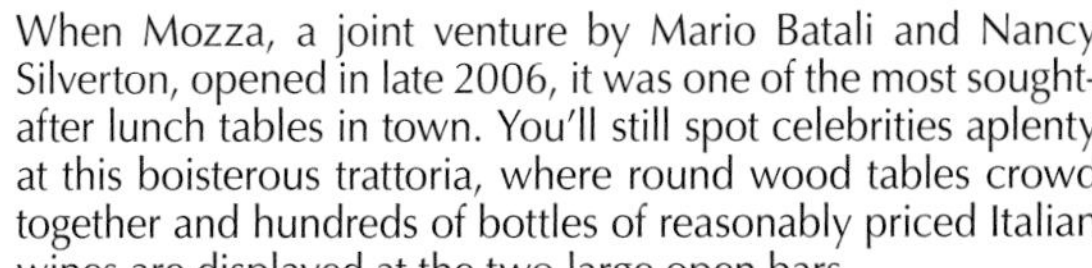

When Mozza, a joint venture by Mario Batali and Nancy Silverton, opened in late 2006, it was one of the most sought-after lunch tables in town. You'll still spot celebrities aplenty at this boisterous trattoria, where round wood tables crowd together and hundreds of bottles of reasonably priced Italian wines are displayed at the two large open bars.

Every day brings a new special. The antipasti are house originals with surprises like green asparagus in a grain-mustard sauce with almonds and caponata, and roasted corn with green-garlic butter. Pizzas have thin crusts, and toppings run from prosciutto, tomato, and mozzarella to littleneck clams. Osteria Mozza, with an entrance off Melrose around the corner, tends to offer more ambitious items.

Providence ✿✿

Seafood 

D2

5955 Melrose Ave. (at Cole Ave.)

Phone: 323-460-4170 — Sat – Thu dinner only
Web: www.providencela.com — Fri lunch & dinner
Prices: **$$$$**

If you were speeding along this unpretentious stretch of Melrose Avenue, past the gas stations and garages, it would be very easy to rush past the discreet little sign that marks the entrance to Providence. But that would—as its many loyalists would tell you—be a shame, for inside this little two-story building resides a lovely restaurant pushing out some of the most inventive seafood in Los Angeles.

For that, we have the visionary chef, Michael Cimarusti, to thank—who headed the kitchen at Water Grill before taking the leap to open Providence in 2005. No one is regretting the move—not when dinner kicks off with a mix of field greens sporting sweet, tender claws of Dungeness and plump pastry pockets of shredded crab and aïoli, set over contrasting streaks of nutty black sesame and red streaks of piquillo pepper coulis. And believe it or not, it just keeps getting better.

Appetizers

- Scallop-Lobster Raviolo, Champagne-Ginger Reduction, Compote of Tomato
- Yellowfin Tuna, Blood Orange, Green Onion, Jalapeño-infused Olive Oil
- Foie Gras a la Plancha

Entrées

- Nancy's Down-East Scallops, Asparagus, Almond Infusion, Sherry
- Wild Salmon, Purée of Parsnips, with Wasabi Peas and Butter
- Tenderloin of Veal, Salsify, Jus de Veau

Desserts

- Chocolate Ganache, Sesame-Soy Milk Ice Cream
- Miso-glazed Pineapple, Yuzu Curd, Praline, Sorbet
- Vanilla Cream, Tangerine, Rose, Pistachio

Rambutan Thai

Thai

D4

2835 Sunset Blvd. (at Silver Lake Blvd.)

Phone: 213-273-8424 — Lunch & dinner daily
Web: www.rambutanthai.com
Prices: $$

As Silverlake's hipness upticks, places like this reflect the district's steady gentrification. Rambutan is another strip mall tenant reflecting the dearth of space in L.A. The compact interior is smartly done with one mirrored green tea wall, and a second bright orange wall framing a huge golden Buddha. Come night it takes on a clubby character more suited to a youngish crowd and a DJ on weekends spices things up.

The extensive, nicely-priced menu is flavorful, and dishes colorful, if perhaps under-spiced. The Thai trademarks are here: pad Thai, satays and such, along with aromatic salads, meat spicy-cooked in a wok, seafood, and noodles galore. There's innovation too, like char-broiled marinated ribeye thinly sliced and cooked with hot pepper sauce.

Sanamluang

Thai 

5176 Hollywood Blvd. (at Kingsley Dr.)

Phone: 323-660-8006 — Lunch & dinner daily
Web: N/A
Prices:

Sanamluang's awning—gracing a small, dingy strip mall in East Hollywood's Thai Town—boasts "The Best Noodles in Town." And despite the less-than-charming locale, they could very well be right. The traditional Thai noodle soups (often called boat noodle soups), might arrive with an indifferent nod from the wait staff, but are flat-out irresistible. Take the beef noodle soup, stuffed with bold chunks of beef and offal in a beef-blood broth humming with bold, exotic spices, and sprinkled with crunchy pork skin. Even the non-noodle dishes are worth the trip, like a spicy lime and chili salad, topped with tender slices of beef marinated in garlic and lime, then grilled to smoky perfection.

Should a noodle craving hit you late, Sanamluang is open until 3:00 A.M.

SIMON L.A.

A3 Contemporary XX

8555 Beverly Blvd. (at La Cienega Blvd.)

Phone: 310-278-5444 Lunch & dinner daily
Web: www.sofitella.com
Prices: $$$

Chef Kerry Simon's crowd-pleaser in the hip Sofitel suggests a high-end coffee shop with its curved booths, open kitchen, and devotion to boldly flavored American comfort food—but a coffee shop for Beautiful People who want *his* Black Angus burger, Tuscan fries, and his truffle macaroni and cheese.

At lunchtime, local business folks favor the 30-minute lunch specials that feature a full meal plus dessert for under $25. If you're still recovering from the previous night's revelry, you'll no doubt appreciate the Breakfast at Lunch portion of the midday menu.

With decorative wood screens partitioning the dining room, there are plenty of intimate spaces in which to hide. On sunny days, the outdoor patio—complete with water fountains—is dreamy.

Surya

B3 Indian 

8048 W. 3rd St. (bet. Crescent Heights Blvd. & Laurel Ave.)

Phone: 323-653-5151 Tue – Fri lunch & dinner
Web: www.surya-india.com Sat – Mon dinner only
Prices: $$

Named after the Hindu Sun God, this contemporary restaurant sits on one of the most pleasant blocks of Third Street. Red walls hung with photos of Indian landmarks are offset by the black ceiling and blond wood floors.

Crisp samosas (pastry shells with savory fillings) make a good place to start. They come with a pair of aromatic mint and tamarind dipping sauces. Tandoori (chicken, lamb, turkey, prawns) dishes, curries, and vegetarian choices are served with freshly baked naan and saffron-infused basmati rice.

Chef/owner Sheel Joshi is half English, which may explain desserts like bread pudding with marmalade, and saffron rice pudding. To drink, there's a Euro-American wine list, or *lassi,* a non-alcoholic yogurt drink served sweet or salted.

Sona ✿

Contemporary XXXX

A3

401 N. La Cienega Blvd. (bet. Beverly Blvd. & Melrose Ave.)

Phone: 310-659-7708 Tue – Sat dinner only
Web: www.sonarestaurant.com
Prices: **$$$$**

FoodArt Group

On the corner of La Cienega Boulevard and Westmount Drive sits a cute little white house with an itty-bitty sign—and a big old reputation for cutting-edge, high-end dining. As night falls, stylish couples descend on the place, flipping the valet their keys, and making their way into the sleek eatery, with its stark gray walls, bright linens, and polished stone. It's a dramatically minimalist background, but the message is simple—all eyes on the plate, thank you very much. It's hardly a problem with Chef/owner David Myers at the wheel, pushing out inventive six and nine course dégustation menus that change with the season.

Dinner might begin with a sashimi presentation of thick, scarlet tuna, ever-so-gently seared and accompanied by a peekytoe crab in ponzu sauce, garnished with fresh wasabi and nori sheets; and continue on to a row of perfectly cooked, salt-dusted lamb chops, paired with a grainy, mustard-based spaetzle.

After dinner, save room to hit Myer's newly expanded bakery, Boule Los Angeles, located across the street.

Appetizers

- Crispy Sweetbread, Tofu, Poached Quail Egg
- Hamachi, Truffle Vinaigrette, Celery Root Purée
- Tuna, Smoked Eggplant, Apple-Ginger Vinaigrette

Entrées

- Salmon Confit, Oyster-Dashi Sauce, Pig's Feet
- Duck, Cilantro-Yogurt Sauce, "Forbidden Rice"
- Rack of Lamb, Herbed-Burrata Ravioli, Tomato Confit

Desserts

- Mango Mousse, Coconut Pearls, Lime "Pop Rocks", Turmeric Ice Cream
- Honey-spiced Tangerine, Peppercorn Vinaigrette, Fennel Ice Cream

Sushi Park

Japanese

A2

8539 Sunset Blvd. (at Alta Loma Rd.)

Phone: 310-652-0523 — Mon – Fri lunch & dinner
Web: www.sushiparkonsunset.com — Sat dinner only
Prices: $$$

Signs on the door and wall clearly indicate the policies here: No California Rolls, No Spicy Tuna, No Teriyaki, and No Tempura. However, these warnings have zero impact on the size of the lunch crowd in this tiny space (only ten seats at the sushi bar and a handful of tables). Sushi purists, aficionados, even celebrities know this gem (in plain sight on the second floor at Sunset Plaza) offers traditional sushi prepared with the best ingredients. Chose from the à la carte or omakase, the latter ranging from $40 - $100 per person.

The low-key, no frills dining room has minimal décor with tile floors, wood furniture, and a flat-screen TV. Ceramic dishes and sake bottles line shelves behind the sushi bar—though more for utility than aesthetics.

Sushi Roku

Japanese

A3

8445 W. 3rd St. (bet. Croft Ave. & La Cienega Blvd.)

Phone: 323-655-6767 — Mon – Sat lunch & dinner
Web: www.sushiroku.com — Sun dinner only
Prices: $$$

Don't be dissuaded by Sushi Roku's brick town-house exterior or the fact that it's part of a small chain. This is one of the most popular sushi spots in town. The décor of gray concrete, bamboo, and stone suits a fashionista crowd, who are served by a courteous waitstaff in black kimonos.

The fare is delectable, with an emphasis on fish. Innovative Cal-Asian dishes include black cod in sweet miso, Chilean sea bass with yuzu butter, King crab croquettes, and seared albacore with crispy wontons. Sushi reigns here, presented according to the market's best each day. For the chef's choicest selections, go for the omakase sampling, which will give you a comprehensive experience. For dessert, try the decidedly un-Japanese vanilla profiteroles.

Talésai

Thai XX

A2

9043 Sunset Blvd. (at Doheny Dr.)

Phone: 310-275-9724 — Mon – Fri lunch & dinner
Web: www.talesai.com — Sat – Sun dinner only
Prices: $$

Upscale, elegant, welcoming, and unpretentious, this may be the best Thai experience in town. (Not to mention that this stretch of Sunset holds some of LA's top pop-music venues.) Superior ingredients and top-notch preparation distinguish the delicately seasoned dishes, which include Thai curries, cashew chicken, classic pad Thai, crispy duck, spicy unagi, sea bass tamarind, and Thai dim sum, to name a few. Vegetarians are taken care of here with selections ranging from spicy eggplant with Thai basil and black-bean sauce to Eight Princes, eight types of Asian vegetables sautéed with light soy sauce. Oh, and then there's the excellent martini list.
For more casual fare, visit the Cafe Talésai in Beverly Hills *(9198 Olympic Bvd.)*.

Tasca

Mediterranean X

B3

8108 W. 3rd St. (at Crescent Heights Blvd.)

Phone: 323-951-9890 — Dinner daily
Web: www.tascawinebar.com
Prices: $$

The beautifully appointed wooden bar and small dining room were quickly staked out by a boisterous upscale crowd after opening in 2007. The main attractions include a menu of flavorful, well-executed small plates, large plates, and daily chalkboard specials; as well as a wine list featuring California and French labels along with Spanish, Chilean, and Argentinean vintages.
Come evening, you'll find a convivial buzz over delectably tasty starters like giant *gambas al ajillo*; a sweet tartare of Ahi tuna; a casserole of creamy brandade; or a lemony *ensalada de mariscos*. Larger dishes might include an herbaceous risotto *verde*, or on Tuesdays and Wednesdays, *paella Valenciana* for two.
Prices are reasonable here and the service gracious and attentive.

Taste

Contemporary

8454 Melrose Ave. (Bet. Orlando Ave. & La Cienega Blvd.)

Phone: 323-852-6888 — Tue – Sun lunch & dinner
Web: www.ilovetaste.com — Mon dinner only
Prices: $$

Snug in a Spanish Colonial-style bungalow next door to Lucques, this casual place shines a spotlight on bright flavors that reflect the best of Golden State cuisine: mostly light, chock-full of vegetables, ideal for alfresco dining on the covered sidewalk patio.

For lunch you might start with an Ahi tuna tartare, its finely diced fish mixed with avocado, crunchy jicama, and fresh herbs. Main courses include salads, sandwiches, and pasta dishes; but the pizzettas are always a popular choice. At dinner, the menu adds global entrées such as grilled chicken masala with Indian spiced tomato cream sauce; and a cumin-spiced pork chop with mojo.

After your meal, spend some time poking around in the high-end antique shops that fill the surrounding blocks.

Terroni

Italian

7605 Beverly Blvd. (at Curson Ave.)

Phone: 323-954-0300 — Lunch & dinner daily
Web: www.terroni.ca
Prices: $$

Located on the corner of Beverly and Curson, Terroni is a spacious Southern Italian restaurant (via Toronto) that offers sidewalk patio seating and an eclectic, casual feel to its largely local clientele. The warm dining room with wood floors and closely spaced tables offers a great view into the open kitchen.

This kitchen turns out rustically traditional cuisine. Pizzas are a popular option and an offering of about 15 seasonal pastas are furnished daily. On a spring evening you might find *maccheroncini geppetto,* tiny house-made rigatoni with dandelions, spicy sausage, fontina, Parmigiano, garlic, and olive oil. *Apristomaco, secondi,* and *dolci* round out the menu and a selection of Italian wines provides a good match to your meal.

Tinto

Spanish XX

C2

7511 Santa Monica Blvd. (at Gardner St.)

Phone: 323-512-3095 Mon – Sat dinner only
Web: www.tintotapas.com
Prices: $$

This tapas house is dedicated to the belief that the convivial act of sharing authentic, impeccably presented small plates is central to a good experience.

Comfortable stools make the bar as desirable as the small tables tucked into the room, in which couches, soft lighting, and exposed brick walls evoke the owners' Basque heritage. The menu, however, travels all over Spain; the *tabla de Ibéricos* presents four types of regional Spanish cured meats with Marcona almonds, white garlic, Vasque chile peppers, and Obregon olives. The *Don Quixote i Sancho Panza* classically pairs 16 month-old Serrano ham with manchego cheese.

The wine list is exclusively Iberian, mostly *tinto*. There are whites too and, of course, sangria ready to serve.

Tower Bar

Californian XX

B2

8358 Sunset Blvd. (bet. Crescent Heights Blvd. & La Cienega Blvd.)

Phone: 323-848-6677 Dinner daily
Web: www.sunsettowerhotel.com
Prices: $$$

This Moderne building once hosted Howard Hughes, John Wayne, Benjamin "Bugsy" Siegel, and other Tinseltown players. Beyond the lounge, the curving walnut-paneled dining room, jazz pianist, and old-school maitre d' evoke the era when stars bound for Europe booked passage on the *Normandie*.

The fashionable clientele reflects the West Hollywood upscale gay scene and the anything-goes mainstream movie world, so dress accordingly. Chef Dakota Weiss specializes in skillfully prepared Californian fare with a French-Italian twist. Starters include raw shellfish or shaved fennel; for entrées, consider a lobster Cobb Salad; roasted lamb T-bone; or an organic omelet with black truffles and caviar.

For the city-wide views, request a window table.

Vivoli Café

Italian

7994 Sunset Blvd. (at Laurel Ave.)

Phone: 323-656-5050 Lunch & dinner daily
Web: www.vivolicafe.com
Prices:

Cached away in a strip mall on Sunset, Vivoli is no longer a secret. The menu in this busy little place features authentic and simple dishes from every region of the Italian boot, complemented by daily chef's specials like homemade lasagna with ragù and béchamel. Osso buco is a signature here, along with thin-crust pizzas and favorite starters like calamari *fritti,* lightly fried and served with a lemony *arrabiata* sauce spiked with hot peppers, garlic, and herbs. A marinara sauce with capers and olives finishes the branzino *alla Livornese.*

The décor is unassuming but warm, with yellow walls and wine bottles on display. Portions are generous, prices affordable, and the Italian-speaking staff sets a friendly tone of relaxed hospitality.

WA

1106 N. La Cienega Blvd. (at Holloway Dr.)

Phone: 310-854-7285 Tue – Sun dinner only
Web: N/A
Prices: **$$**

Despite the location of this sushi bar on the second level of an aging shopping mall on the corner of La Cienega and Holloway Drive, WA is worth seeking out for its Japanese cuisine. The dingy feel extends to the interior, where a few tables by the front window look out on the gas station across the street, and the L-shaped sushi bar provides the rest of the seating.

What this place seriously lacks in ambience, however, it makes up for with its intriguing dishes. Traditional and contemporary sushi and sashimi preparations are balanced by an à la carte menu and nightly hot and cold specials (smoked jumbo clam; spicy baked crab dynamite; and grilled Chilean sea bass with eggplant) noted on a blackboard.

Added bonus: there's free parking in the mall's garage.

Xiomara on Melrose

Latin American XX

6101 Melrose Ave. (at Seward St.)

Phone: 323-461-0601 — Mon – Fri lunch & dinner
Web: www.xiomararestaurant.com — Sat dinner only
Prices: $$

Chef Xiomara Ardolina is a native Cuban whose creative and refreshing take on Latin flavors has consistently won raves from critics and diners alike. The upscale vintage décor, with a beautiful old wooden bar, wrought-iron staircase, and framed mirrors, is offset by white linens, candlelight, and a mix of soft jazz and Cuban music engendering a romantic mood.

Consider the charcuterie platter, a bevy of Spanish cured sausages, plus *dulce de membrillo* (quince paste), and Manchego cheese. A spicy, crusted lamb shank comes with a casserole of *malanga* (a root vegetable) and mojo; while saffron rice and twice-fried plaintains accompany tasty *nuevo cubano* chicken *patacones*. Mojitos are practically obligatory.

Yabu

Japanese XX

521 N. La Cienega Blvd. (bet. Melrose & Rosewood Aves.)

Phone: 310-854-0400 — Mon – Sat lunch & dinner
Web: N/A — Sun dinner only
Prices: $$

The original (and more casual) West L.A. location and its younger West Hollywood sibling serve superb sushi, tempura, and noodles in elegantly spare rooms. Their open kitchens offer ringside seating on the creation of sashimi and sushi served with miso and ponzu citrus sauce; and favorites like the baked scallop Dynamite roll and yellowtail carpaccio with jalapeño.

Udon and buckwheat soba noodles are made fresh here daily, and topped with organic tofu, Japanese yam, fresh seaweed, nameko mushrooms, and green onion. The tapas vogue has inspired innovations like spicy pan-fried lotus root, soft-shell crab and oysters, stir-fried eggplant with miso, broiled black cod, and homemade shrimp *shu mai*.

There is a good selection of fine Japanese sake.

Pasadena

Located less than 10 miles (via the Pasadena Freeway) from Downtown Los Angeles, Pasadena seems a world away from the bustle and sprawl of its neighbor to the southwest. The San Gabriel Mountains loom over this sunny city of 146,000, whose 22.5 square miles captured the nation's fancy long ago as proof of what California living could be.

Originally part of the vast lands encompassed by San Gabriel Mission—the fourth in California's mission chain—the area that would become Pasadena passed through several different owners as Mexican-era grant lands in the late 1800s. This acreage eventually came into Anglo-American hands, incorporating as the city of Pasadena in 1886.

In 1890, the city's elite Valley Hunt Club marked New Year's Day with a procession of flower-bedecked horses and carriages. The event quickly evolved into an annual tradition, now known as the **Rose Parade**.

A GENTEEL PAST

Pasadena became a winter resort for wealthy Easterners, whose homes account for scores of buildings listed on the National Register of Historic Places. None of them, however, surpass the Italian Renaissance **Tournament of Roses House** *(391 S. Orange Grove Blvd.)*, now the event's headquarters.

Pasadena's 23 parks impart a bucolic air, and there's a sense of yore in the **Old Pasadena Historic Area**. This quarter holds some 200 buildings from the late 1800s, including the Gamble House, a masterpiece of the American Arts & Crafts Movement. In the district's 22 blocks you'll find most of the city's best dining, entertainment, and nightlife.

California's official State Theater, **The Pasadena Playhouse** *(39 S. El Molino Ave.)*, is famed for its stellar casts. The **Rose Bowl Stadium**, home of the New Year's Day football classic, hosts the Southland's premiere flea market on the second Sunday of every month

RENOIR, ROSES, AND ROCKETS

Cultural offerings are ripe for the picking here. The **Norton Simon Museum** exhibits masterpieces from one of the world's choicest private art collections. In nearby San Marino, treasures at the **Huntington Library** include rare books and manuscripts, as well as a world-class collection of 18th- and 19th-century British art. The Huntington's Botanical Gardens nurture 15,000 plants from all over the world.

As for the local brain trust, faculty and alumni (including Albert Einstein) of the **California Institute of Technology** have won 31 Nobel Prizes. For space-exploration buffs, NASA's **Jet Propulsion Laboratory** *(4800 Oak Grove Dr.)* offers free tours once a week (advance reservations required).

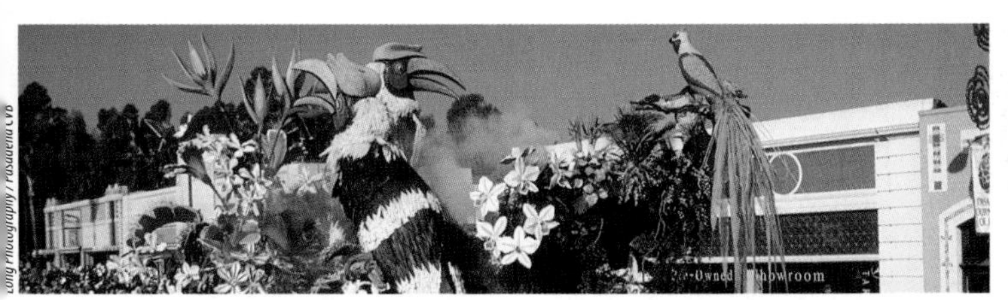

Long Photography / Pasadena CVB

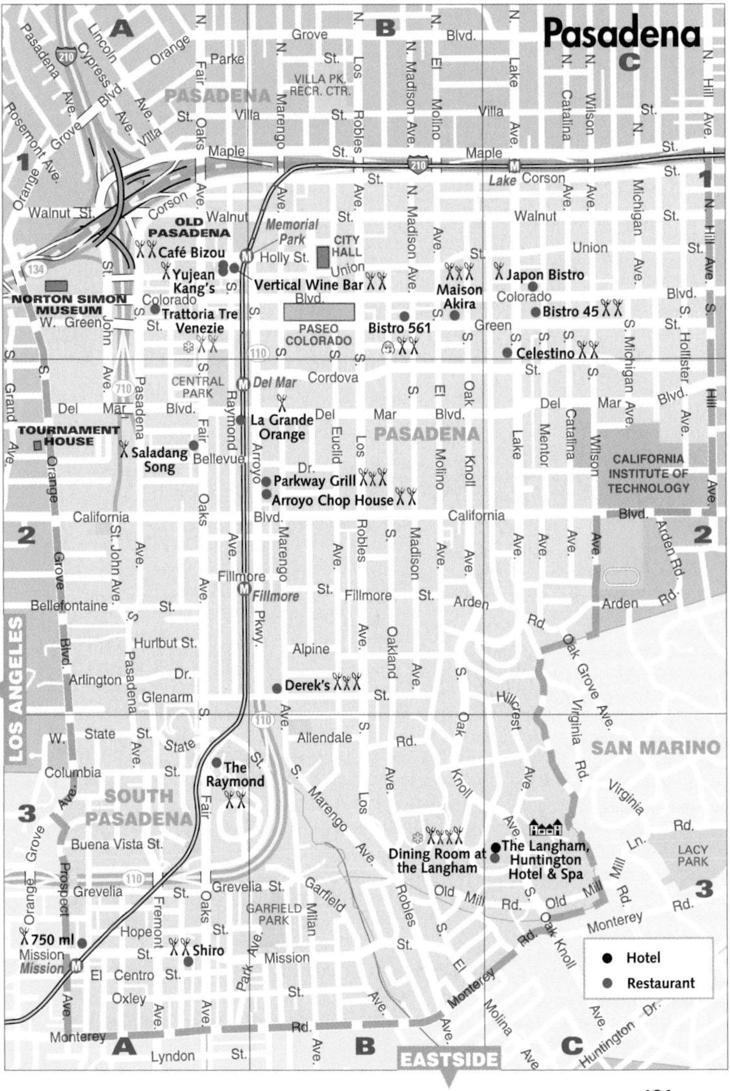
Pasadena
A
B
C
1
2
3
OLD PASADENA
Café Bizou
Yujean Kang's
Vertical Wine Bar
Trattoria Tre Venezie
Maison Akira
Japon Bistro
Bistro 45
Bistro 561
Celestino
La Grande Orange
Saladang Song
Parkway Grill
Arroyo Chop House
Derek's
The Raymond
Dining Room at the Langham
The Langham, Huntington Hotel & Spa
750 ml
Shiro
NORTON SIMON MUSEUM
TOURNAMENT HOUSE
CITY HALL
PASEO COLORADO
CENTRAL PARK
VILLA PK. RECR. CTR.
Memorial Park
CALIFORNIA INSTITUTE OF TECHNOLOGY
PASADENA
SOUTH PASADENA
SAN MARINO
LOS ANGELES
EASTSIDE
GARFIELD PARK
LACY PARK
Lake
Del Mar
Fillmore
Mission
Hotel
Restaurant

Arroyo Chop House

Steakhouse XX

536 S. Arroyo Pkwy. (bet. E. Bellevue Dr. & Pico St.)

Phone: 626-577-7463 — Dinner daily
Web: www.arroyochophouse.com
Prices: $$$$

With its white-linen tablecloths, wooden chairs, and dark slat blinds, the contemporary Craftsman interior of this ivied chophouse is classic Main Street, evoking scenes in film where pols knife into prime beef and each other as they decide how democratic things will be. The servers are attentive and affable, and a traditional paneled partition topped with etched glass sets most tables and booths apart from the chatter at the bar's leather stools.

A steakhouse-sized wedge of chilled heart of iceberg lettuce is topped with a creamy yet subtle blue-cheese dressing; a filet mignon is served with béarnaise sauce and a side of sugar-snap peas. It's all-American and it's serious food, backed by piano music softly playing under the conversation.

Bistro 561

Californian 

561 E. Green St. (at Madison Ave.)

Phone: 626-405-1561 — Mon – Fri lunch & dinner
Web: www.561restaurant.com
Prices: $$$

Staffed by students (with supervision) completing their training at the California School of Culinary Arts, this is a great place to play guinea pig. The subdued sage-green tones and exposed brick walls are tastefully simple, while large windows give the room a bright and airy feel.

Expect touches like an amuse-bouche of warm artichoke leaves with mushroom duxelles and great freshly baked bread. Menus change regularly, presenting acolytes with challenges like perfectly searing foie gras with a sweet apple *mostarda,* or accurately simmering homemade pappardelle served with veal. There are occasional lapses as this is, after all, a school. But in context they seem trifling and the quality overall quite commendable for these chefs-in-training.

Bistro 45

Californian

C1

45 S. Mentor Ave. (bet. Colorado Blvd. & Green St.)

Phone: 626-795-2478 — Tue – Fri lunch & dinner
Web: www.bistro45.com — Sat – Sun dinner only
Prices: $$

Three intimate dining rooms huddle inside this vintage Art Deco building, its little front garden scented by lavender and rosemary. The smartly casual interior and swanky red bar and lounge—even the sheltered patio—create a residential serenity bolstered by the welcoming staff.

Pure Golden State, the menu spotlights fresh produce, organic meats, farm-raised duck, and Pacific seafood. Regional favorites include shaved vegetable salad with heirloom tomatoes, mâche, peppered brioche, and a cucumber-mint dressing; or grilled diver sea scallops with lemon crème fraîche and artichoke *barigoule*. As for wine, a large selection of California pinot noir and cabernet sauvignon is first up at bat, with red Bordeaux ready in the bullpen.

Café Bizou

Californian

A1

91 N. Raymond Ave. (at Holly St.)

Phone: 626-792-9923 — Tue – Fri & Sun lunch & dinner
Web: www.cafebizou.com — Mon & Sat dinner only
Prices: $$

Call this a Californian bistro with a French heart. While you may see *bizou*, the kitchen is *très sérieuse*. Friendliness and courteous service are central to the popularity here and a lively crowd of diners enjoys the warm ambiance daily. It's easy in the dining room where large street windows light the classic bistro style, with banquettes, vintage posters, and exposed brick.

The cuisine runs from Golden State to Gallic, and French technique is applied to all dishes in expertly made sauces and careful presentations. A Scottish grilled salmon in citrus sauce with mashed potatoes and fresh vegetables is a classic display of skill.

The wine list is mostly Californian but includes good French labels. Regulars often bring their own, as corkage is a mere $2.

Celestino

Italian XX

C1

141 S. Lake Ave. (bet. Cordova & Green Sts.)

Phone: 626-795-4006 Mon – Fri lunch & dinner
Web: www.calogerodrago.com Sat dinner only
Prices: **$$**

This outpost of the Drago empire, located on lively Lake Avenue, offers authentic regional Italian fare. Sit on the front patio if you want to take in the scene, or opt for a table in the rustic dining room, with its sunny walls and open kitchen. The attentive brigade is uniformed in white aprons and black bow ties.

Italian recipes favor the North, with classic dishes like roasted rabbit with black olives; osso buco *alla Milanese* (with saffron risotto); lasagne bolognese (with meat ragù); and a buttery mozzarella cheese with arugula and cherry tomatoes. You'll wait 15 to 20 minutes for the risotto of the day, but the delay is worth it.

Desserts include standards like tiramisú and panna cotta.

Derek's

Californian XXX

B2

181 E. Glenarm St. (at Marengo Ave.)

Phone: 626-799-5252 Tue – Sat dinner only
Web: www.dereks.com
Prices: **$$$$**

Beef Wellington and rack of lamb bordelaise are among the signature dishes at Derek Dickinson's cozy establishment. The stylish wood and peach tones suit a contemporary à la carte menu mixing such classics with more innovative dishes, some with Asian touches, all backed by a strong wine list.

When the kitchen focuses on what it does best, out come pleasing entrées like a roasted spicy quail stuffed with wild mushroom and rice, presented in a savory thick Port wine reduction. A filet of pan-seared sea bass accented with a miso glaze is served with soba noodles infused with green tea.

The bar is convivial, the staff friendly, and desserts have a certain flair—this is quite the beloved place for many locals.

The Dining Room at the Langham ✿

Contemporary XXXX

1401 S. Oak Knoll Ave. (at Huntington Dr.)

Phone: 626-568-3900 — Tue – Sat dinner only
Web: pasadena.langhamhotels.com
Prices: **$$$$**

It takes guts to put on a jacket in perennially chill California, but that's how diners do it at the new at the Dining Room at the Langham Hotel, which took over the old Ritz-Carlton space last year.

The new Dining Room pretty much picks up where the old one left off, with a sweeping balcony that runs the length of the restaurant, and a formal, elegant interior with warm honey-toned wood panels; semi-veiled alcoves lined with cushy banquettes; and plush, blue-gray armchairs.

Chef Craig Strong remains in the kitchen, most likely because his brand of inventive contemporary cuisine never goes out of style. Start with the roasted calamari, stuffed with tender garlicky French bread, and paired with a tangle of fresh arugula; and then set your sights on a flaky wild sea bass, topped with an airy bouillabaisse, and served with an eggplant and roasted red pepper ratatouille.

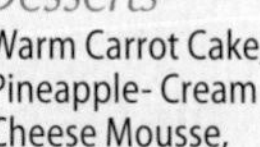

Appetizers

- Squash Blossom Tempura, Cod Purée, Romesco Sauce
- Liquid Polenta and Truffles, Poached Quail Egg, Serrano Ham
- Lobster and Foie Gras, Sunchoke Froth

Entrées

- Sea Bass on Provençal Style Eggplant, Cardoons, Bouillabaisse Sauce
- Muscovy Duck Breast, Basil-Potato Mousseline, Huckleberry Sauce
- Trio of Colorado Lamb

Desserts

- Warm Carrot Cake, Pineapple- Cream Cheese Mousse, Ginger Ice Cream
- Lemon Mousse, Toasted Meringue, Nutmeg Beignet, Pistachio Ice Cream
- "Spanish Virgin"

Japon Bistro

Japanese

C1

927 E. Colorado Blvd. (bet. Lake & Mentor Aves.)

Phone: 626-744-1751
Web: www.japonbistro-pasadena.com
Prices: $$

Tue – Fri lunch & dinner
Sat – Sun dinner only
Mon lunch only

Consistently good Japanese food draws a clutch of business diners to this bistro at lunch, whereas local families and couples take over the place at dinnertime. All appreciate the casual atmosphere and the friendly, laid-back service.

Once you sit down, your waiter will present a whiteboard listing the day's specials. If that's not enough to tempt you, you can choose from the main menu—which includes cooked dishes—or the list of sushi and house maki, like the bold Southwest roll, a combination of salmon, jalapeño, avocado, and cilantro, drizzled with red chili aïoli. If *tokubetsu junmai* means anything to you, you'll appreciate the fine sake selection here.

Look for validated parking nearby on Mentor Street, across from the Ice House comedy club.

La Grande Orange

American

A2

260 S. Raymond Ave. (at Del Mar Blvd.)

Phone: 626-356-4444
Web: www.lgostationcafe.com
Prices: $$

Lunch & dinner daily

This newcomer to Pasadena is located at the historic Del Mar train depot in an old California mission-style building with exposed high wood beam ceilings. The casual, family friendly spot includes an enclosed patio and bar on one side, an open kitchen through a tiled archway on the other, and a patio for alfresco dining in the California sunshine. In the main dining room, the décor is simple and jovial with simple wood tables and chairs, and brown leather banquettes. Festive and bright walls are painted green with orange and red-orange decorative accents.

The appealing menu offers simple and tasty American classics. Salads, sandwiches, burgers, and taco platters are bursting with freshness and flavor and are consistently well-prepared.

Maison Akira

French

713 E. Green St. (at Oak Knoll Ave.)

Phone: 626-796-9501 — Tue – Fri & Sun lunch & dinner
Web: www.maisonakira.com — Sat dinner only
Prices: $$$

As the name suggests, this casual fine dining eatery has its French gloves in the Asian cookie jar. But Chef/owner Akira Hirose's globe-trotting menu makes perfect sense for a Japanese chef who cut his culinary teeth with Joël Robuchon before honing his skills at two other French institutions. After wandering west to California, Hirose opened Maison Akira—a cozy, red brick cottage in Pasadena where he spins a classical French menu with Japanese influences.

Give yourself over to the gentle thrum of Mozart and Vivaldi playing softly in the distance, and dip your spoon into a sweet and creamy white corn soup, studded with a few garlicky croutons; or try the tender, white asparagus starter, perfectly grilled and squeezed between a *pâté feuilletée*.

Parkway Grill

Californian

510 S. Arroyo Pkwy. (at California Blvd.)

Phone: 626-795-1001 — Mon – Fri lunch & dinner
Web: www.theparkwaygrill.com — Sat – Sun dinner only
Prices: $$$

In a stand-alone red brick building, with exposed ceiling beams and track lights above, dark wood paneling, stained-glass panels, and cushioned chairs below, Parkway Grill boasts archetypal contemporary West Coast design: warm, spacious, solid, and comfortable.

The kitchen draws some of its spices, greens, and garnishes from the garden out back, and whips up creations like a crab cake soufflé presented atop a creamy avocado purée; or a grilled Pacific salmon atop a purée of cauliflower and garnished with sautéed slices of wild mushroom and crisp sugar-snap peas. The wine list is long, as is the comfy bar.

Wearing white shirts and black ties, well-trained servers lend an air of relaxed professional confidence that puts the room at ease.

The Raymond

A3 — Californian XX

1250 S. Fair Oaks Ave. (at Columbia St.)

Phone: 626-441-3136 Tue – Sun lunch & dinner
Web: www.theraymond.com
Prices: $$$

The Raymond Hotel closed in 1931, but its caretaker's cottage survives—amid flowering bushes and trees secluding a brick patio dining area with umbrella-shaded tables and comfy chairs. The elegant décor inside the three small dining rooms compliments the building's Craftsman architecture.
Cuisine here relies on seasonal, locally grown produce—thus an organic free range Jidori chicken breast with rosemary, potato purée, and a mushroom sauce. California's burgeoning culinary vocabulary is spoken fluently here, as in a seared Ahi tuna with oven-roasted tomatoes, green beans, red beet purée and black olive tapenade.
Come for afternoon tea on weekends.

Saladang Song

A2 — Thai 

383 S. Fair Oaks Ave. (bet. California & Del Mar Aves.)

Phone: 626-793-5200 Lunch & dinner daily
Web: N/A
Prices: ⓢⓢ

This restaurant became so popular that the owners opened a second next door (*song* means two in Thai). The modern concrete and steel space with its lovely patio doesn't compete for attention with traditional fare like *miang goong* (ground grilled shrimp flavored with lime, peanut, and ginger) and a range of flavorful noodle dishes. Carnivores will appreciate the skewers threaded with generous portions of beef balls or marinated pork.
The outdoor terrace seems especially suited for Thai breakfasts (a choice of porridges) and the modestly priced lunch options. Seasonal dishes are updated regularly. If you want the hot stuff, look for specials like spicy seafood curry, after which your palate can be soothed with creamy, sweet Thai iced tea.

750 ml

French

A3

966 Mission St. (at Meridian Ave.)

Phone: 626-799-0711 — Dinner daily
Web: N/A
Prices: $$

This charming wine bistro is a great find in the sleepy neighborhood of South Pasadena. The location couldn't be more convenient to the Gold Line metro station right across the street. In fact, you can see the trains racing by from the large bay windows in the spacious dining room, where thick brown paper covers the tablecloths to catch spills, and linen kitchen dishcloths serve as napkins.

The menu changes nightly, headlining a handful of appetizers, small plates, main courses, and desserts. You can expect bistro fare such as sweet-corn agnolotti enveloped in a luscious brown-butter parmesan sauce; and a daube of lamb served over a warm salad of summer beans. A single sheet lists the well-chosen artisan wines available by the bottle and the glass.

Shiro

Contemporary

A3

1505 Mission St. (at Fair Oaks Ave.)

Phone: 626-799-4774 — Wed – Sun dinner only
Web: www.restaurantshiro.com
Prices: $$$

Does French cuisine plus Japanese influences equal modern Californian? In Chef/owner Hideo Yamashiro's spacious, pleasant, and popular "South Pas" venue it does. The décor is simple and the setting economy-class, but what comes from the open kitchen is well made.

The fusion *Californie-Japonaise* produces appetizers like a shiitake mushroom salad with walnut oil dressing; pan-fried oysters with a Champagne curry sauce; foie gras sautéed on pineapple with Port wine sauce; or asparagus tips with a vibrantly flavored fresh tarragon dressing, pecans, and tomatoes. Entrées exhibit the same tasty melding of cuisines: a whole catfish (a house specialty) garnished with ginger, cilantro, and a ponzu-soy sauce.

Free parking is available in the adjoining bank lot.

Trattoria Tre Venezie

Italian

A1

119 W. Green St. (bet. Pasadena & De Lacey Aves.)

Phone: 626-795-4455 — Tue – Thu & Sat – Sun dinner only
Web: N/A — Fri lunch & dinner
Prices: **$$$**

A divine taste of authentic Northern Italy makes its way to California, by way of this Pasadena favorite. Duck into this charming little bungalow and you'll be greeted with a warm hello from the maître d'—the perfect way to begin an evening in a restaurant lovingly cloaked in homey charm, with copper pots hanging from the ceiling and shelves lined with cookbooks and framed pictures. Though it might look like Grandma's house, Trattoria Tre Venezie isn't mailing in the old spaghetti-and-meatball routine—not by a long shot.

Devoted to the cooking of the three Northeastern regions in Italy with historical ties to Venice, the wizard-like Chef Gianfranco Minuz channels the traditional seafood dishes of the area, whips up pastas from ancient organic grains, designs his own pastries, and produces his own liqueurs. Even crudo has recently snuck onto the daily specials list. Mario who?

Appetizers

- Cjalsons with Ricotta; Spices, Cocoa, Smoked Ricotta
- Baccala' mantecato, Polenta, Vegetable Julienne
- Apple and Celery Salad with Pestolato Cheese

Entrées

- Lamb Ravioli with Sautéed Zucchini
- Daily Fish cooked in Garlic and Vinegar with Soft Polenta
- Bollito Misto with Green Sauce, Mostarda and Horseradish Sauce

Desserts

- Crema del Gondoliere
- Presnitz; Baked Pastry with Dried Fruit and Nuts
- Dolce di Cioccolato Served with Vanilla Sauce

Vertical Wine Bar

Californian

70 N. Raymond Ave. (bet. Holly & Union Sts.)

Phone: 626-795-3999 Tue – Fri lunch & dinner
Web: www.verticalwinebistro.com Sat – Sun dinner only
Prices: $$

As the name suggests, wine takes center stage at this Old Town Pasadena establishment. Located up a flight of stairs (there's also an elevator), Vertical Wine Bistro is couched in a chic and contemporary space, with a large front lounge separated from the dining room by the focal point of the restaurant—a glass-enclosed wine cellar that's visible from both sides.

More than 100 wines by the glass are offered, along with featured wine flights. The wine selection is designed to pair deliciously with small plates such as a peppery arugula salad balanced by slices of sweet Bosc pear, toasted hazelnuts, and a piece of tangy goat cheese.

Regulars are encouraged to note their impressions of the wines, which the restaurant will file away for future visits.

Yujean Kang's

Chinese 

A1

67 N. Raymond Ave. (bet. Holly & Union Sts.)

Phone: 626-585-0855 Lunch & dinner daily
Web: N/A
Prices: ◎

Bright red with black trim walls and printed posters brighten this friendly dining room, whose tables host numerous local families feasting on the good quality Chinese cuisine.

All main courses are accompanied by an herby chicken salad with five-spice-baked tofu and cilantro vinaigrette, and a tangy hot and sour soup with sliced tofu, silky veils of egg, bamboo shoots, scallions, and strips of pork.

Assorted seasonal vegetables in many dishes are expertly wok-cooked to retain taste and textures and enliven recipes such as crispy beef Szechwan-style, lamb loin with baby bok choy in chili, scallion, and cilantro sauce, or red-braised black cod with soy sauce.

Desserts stray from the Asian canon to include cheesecake, albeit one layered with Mandarin oranges.

Santa Monica Bay

Malibu - Marina del Rey - Venice

Within its 8.3 square miles, bounded by Santa Monica Canyon, 26th Street, Montana and Centinela avenues, LA's Venice district, and the Pacific Ocean, Santa Monica is a city of about 94,000. Its populace ranges from beach layabouts to film folk, with a lifestyle-oriented sensibility overall.

LIVING WELL BY DECREE

Commerce crowds the main streets, but in City Hall, a Streamline Moderne gem dedicated in 1939 to "civic responsibility," quality-of-life issues prevail. In 1875 the city's developers offered "the Pacific Ocean, draped with a western sky of scarlet and gold... a frostless, bracing, warm, yet languid air, braided in and out with sunshine and odored with the breath of flowers... and the song of birds." They weren't exaggerating much. Year-round, locals idle in palmy **Palisades Park** on the city's ocean bluffs or on Santa Monica and Will Rogers state beaches below, and walk, jog, or pedal the South Bay Bicycle Trail.

Pedestrian-only **Third Street Promenade**, between Wilshire and the Santa Monica Place mall on Broadway, is chockablock with cinemas, restaurants, and stores catering to current tastes. Fine hotels rise along **Ocean Avenue**, while **Main Street** south of Pico is lined with bistros, boutiques, and galleries.

There's old-fashioned amusement-park fun on the 1909 **Santa Monica Pier**, where the Hippodrome shelters an antique carousel. At the other end of the sophistication spectrum is Southern California's largest art-gallery complex, Bergamot Station *(2525 Michigan Ave.)*, home to the **Santa Monica Museum of Art**.

A TOWN CALLED VENICE

Founded by tobacco tycoon Abbot Kinney in 1905, Venice featured canals, a 1,200-foot pleasure pier, and an arcaded Main Street built in the Venetian style. Today, **Ocean Front Walk** is a carnival of street artists, vendors, and body-builders pumping iron in the Muscle Beach weight pen. Many regard the restaurant, club, and gallery scene along Abbot Kinney and Grand boulevards and Main Street as among the most avant-garde in the LA Basin.

Santa Monica Bay Area
Malibu
Nobu
Tra di Noi
Malibu Beach Inn
Moonshadows
Cholada
Malibu Beach
Topanga Beach
Las Flores
Pacific Ocean
Topanga State Park
Will Rogers State Park
Riviera Country Club
Brentwood Country Club
VA Medical Center
West Los Angeles
Westside
Il Carpaccio
Amici
Caffe Delfini
Giorgio Baldi
Sam's by the Beach
Santa Monica
Rustic Canyon
Mélisse
Michael's
The Huntley
The Penthouse
Real Food Daily
Locanda del Lago
La Botte
Anisette
JiRaffe
Bar Pintxo
Border Grill
La Serenata de Garibaldi
The Lobster
Santa Monica Pier
Loews
Whist
Viceroy Santa Monica
One Pico
Capo
Shutters on the Beach
Casa del Mar
Catch
City Hall
Wilshire
Drago
The Ambrose
Le Petit Café
Bergamot Station
Violet
Lares
Valentino
Josie
Santa Monica Municipal
The Hump
Typhoon
Ocean Park
Chinois on Main
Via Veneto
Hidden
Chaya Venice
Mar Vista
Ocean Front Walk
Joe's
Axe
Primitivo Wine Bistro
Piccolo
3 Square Café & Bakery
Shima
Wabi-Sabi
Venice Beach
Venice
Venice Fishing Pier
Venice City Beach
The Ritz-Carlton, Marina del Rey
Jer-ne
Cafe del Rey
sugarFISH
Sapori
Marina del Rey
Santa Monica Bay
Hotel
Restaurant

Amici

Italian

B1

2538 San Vicente Blvd. (at 26th St.)

Phone: 310-260-4900 — Mon – Sat lunch & dinner
Web: www.tamici.com — Sun dinner only
Prices: **$$**

Brentwood is part of Los Angeles, but many within its putative boundaries consider it a separate city. So never mind that this charming trattoria bills itself as being in Brentwood, but is actually in Santa Monica. As some Malibu folks say, Brentwood is a state of mind. (The original Trattoria Amici is in Beverly Hills.)

The dining room is simple, yet stylish, with its Mexican tile floors, plank and beam ceilings, and surfeit of windows to suit the upscale, mostly local trade. The food is straightforward and generously served. You could easily make a meal out of a thick home-style cannellini bean and organic lentil soup alone, but the long list of pastas and the selection of meat, fish, and pizza will please even the pickiest ladies who lunch.

Anisette

French

A2

225 Santa Monica Blvd. (bet. 2nd & 3rd Sts.)

Phone: 310-395-3200 — Lunch & dinner daily
Web: www.anisettebrasserie.com
Prices: **$$$**

Locals have been salivating with anticipation at the thought of Chef Alain Giraud's new restaurant. Now that it's open—for breakfast, lunch, afternoon light fare, and dinner—Angelenos have been swarming the place; so expect to wait for a table (walk-ins are more often than not seated at the bar).

Charming and authentic in both ambience and menu, Anisette features a *bar à huitres* (oyster bar)—the origin of the towering seafood platters—as well as à la carte offerings. The likes of duck confit, *moules* frites, and beef tartare are made with fresh, local, and premium ingredients. Desserts go equally Gallic with profiteroles, chocolate mousse, and *Iles flottantes*—the classic "island" of meringue afloat in a pool of vanilla-bean-infused crème anglaise.

Axe

B3 **Californian**

1009 Abbot Kinney Blvd. (bet. Broadway & Brooks Ave.), Venice

Phone: 310-664-9787 Wed – Sun lunch & dinner
Web: www.axerestaurant.com
Prices: $$

The young, the socially conscious, and the free-spirited of Venice frequent Axe, whose name echoes a Yoruban salutation (pronounced ah-SHAY) that means: go with the power of the gods and goddesses.

Divine beings would no doubt count themselves blessed to feast on homemade breads, farm-fresh local produce, and other organically grown foods that compose Axe's internationally influenced dishes. One day's lunch offered a Mediterranean albacore tuna salad with a lemon-cayenne vinaigrette, the fish smoked and served atop grilled artisan bread and spicy young arugula leaves crowned with buttery chickpeas, red onion slices, and diced hard-boiled egg.

The atmosphere is no-frills and the feeling is communal, with sharing-size portions to match.

Bar Pintxo

A2 **Spanish** 

109 Santa Monica Blvd. (at Ocean Ave.)

Phone: 310-458-2012 Lunch & dinner daily
Web: www.barpintxo.com
Prices:

Pronounced "pin-cho", this cozy space feels like a native Spanish tapas bar. At its front counter, patrons order from a selection of classic tapas featuring quality Spanish ingredients. Further back, high-top tables under a wrought iron chandelier allow you to mingle surrounded by shelves holding a marvelous offering of Spanish wines.

Combined, these little dishes create memorable feasts. Top a slice of baguette with spicy chorizo and a soft-fried quail egg and let the yolk run. Follow with a succulent and smoky grilled shrimp over a slice of roasted piquillo pepper and tomato conserve. Next, a warm wedge of tortilla Espanola with a dollop of garlicky aïoli. Surely enjoy an order of decadent *jamón Ibérico* to accompany the briny olives.

Border Grill

A2

1445 4th St. (bet. Broadway & Santa Monica Blvd.)

Phone: 310-451-1655 Lunch & dinner daily
Web: www.bordergrill.com
Prices: **$$**

Convenient to Santa Monica shops and beaches, Border Grill has reigned as the flagship of Chefs Mary Sue Milliken and Susan Feniger since it graced L.A.'s dining scene in its original location on Melrose. Black floors and ceilings balance dark orange walls—the latter two painted with oversized animals, stars, and planets in vivid primary colors.

Boisterous and fun, Border Grill boasts a funky feel as well as excellent food. Flavors speak boldly here, in well-composed *bocaditos* and *platos especiales*, such as *conchinita Pibil*—achiote-marinated slow-roasted pork deliciously spiced with toasted cumin, smoked chiles, orange zest, and cinnamon.

Visitors and young urban locals pack this place nightly, so reserve ahead or be prepared to wait for a table.

Cafe del Rey

Contemporary XX

C4

4451 Admiralty Way (near Promenade Way), Marina del Rey

Phone: 310-823-6395 Lunch & dinner daily
Web: www.cafedelreymarina.com
Prices: **$$$**

Thanks to abundant large windows, diners at this Marina del Rey darling enjoy stellar vistas from every table. Boats berthed in the world's largest manmade small-boat harbor account for the great views outside, while the interior architecture sports a 70's condo-loft look.

Asian influences and American preferences fill the seasonal menu with maki of salmon, tuna, shrimp, and eel; appetizers of *kalbi*-style short ribs with radish salad, and shucked Kumamoto oysters. Fish courses make big waves here, and the availability of choice Hawaiian-caught fish, such as grouper, ono, and hapu'upu'u flown into nearby LAX, makes for interesting "day-boat" offerings.

One of the best restaurants in this area, Cafe del Rey's large bar and lounge is a popular after-work stop.

Caffe Delfini

Italian XX

A2

147 W. Channel Rd. (at Pacific Coast Hwy.)

Phone: 310-459-8823 Dinner daily
Web: N/A
Prices: $$$

Across the street from trendy Giorgio Baldi, Caffe Delfini offers a more low-key option for Italian food. The cafe-style menu in this charming neighborhood spot features a short list of main courses, a long list of pastas, and nightly specials that typically star seafood. The skilled kitchen presents simple pleasures like a creamy rigatoni gorgonzola, and linguine *mare*, swimming with shellfish. Desserts are lush.

The shingled taupe exterior has an inviting beach/cottage look, while the cozy dining room is crowded with rattan chairs and small linen-covered tables with votive candles and decanters of vinegar and olive oil. Windows look out onto the sidewalk, and Italian music plays softly.

Valet parking is essential on this busy street.

Capo

Italian XX

A3

1810 Ocean Ave. (at Pico Blvd.)

Phone: 310-394-5550 Tue – Sat dinner only
Web: N/A
Prices: $$$$

In a cottage hiding just off the Ocean Avenue sidewalk in Santa Monica, Capo's cabin-like interior of wood floors, truss-plank ceiling, and brick fireplace contrasts with the sophisticated décor—paintings, velvet drapes, European bistro chairs, backlit wooden wine cabinets, tabletop bud vases, and flickering oil lamps—all *molto romantico*.

Excellent ingredients are the boss here, dictating that Italian courses be prepared simply, while producing bold flavors with a rustic technique. Zucchini blossoms stuffed with goat cheese are served with roasted tomatoes and garlic; large grilled shrimp come with a medley of lightly seasoned Tuscan beans. And after such lovely dishes, savor a tangy Meyer lemon semifreddo drizzled with blueberry compote.

Catch

A3 — Seafood XX

1910 Ocean Way (at Pico Blvd.)

Phone: 310-581-7714 — Lunch & dinner daily
Web: www.catchsantamonica.com
Prices: $$$

Airy as an ocean breeze, this fairly recent addition to the Casa del Mar hotel *(see hotel listing)* combines a stunning location on the beach with a solid menu of delectable seafood. From the windows you can catch panoramas of the Pacific waves crashing on the white sand, but the best catch will be on your plate.

European technique is evident in the seafood entrées—as in a finely seasoned crispy skate wing entrée, caramelized and served on a bed of braised, vinegar-tangy savoy cabbage, the fish wearing a pesto-like strip of deep-green puréed herbs; or tender Gulf prawns atop *bucatini* pasta, accompanied by wild broccoli. Starters of sushi, sashimi, and *crudo* are fashioned at the mother-of-pearl sushi bar. All in all, an impressive show.

Chaya Venice

B3 — Fusion XX

110 Navy St. (at Main St.), Venice

Phone: 310-396-1179 — Lunch & dinner daily
Web: www.thechaya.com
Prices: $$$

Life in Venice, or Venice Beach as some call it, blends laid-back lifestyles with intense careerism. Many residents work in the arts or entertainment, and are drawn to Chef Shigefumi Tachibe's fusion of French and Japanese cuisine. Reflecting the area's casual style set on a foundation of determined discipline, Chaya makes for some of the neighborhood's best and most sophisticated dining.

Sushi bar patrons may order from the full menu, which features international seafood determined by the market. International is the key word; Mexican spices fire up a Tuscan-style bean soup; a Californian arugula pesto tops grilled wild Canadian salmon. There is a good and generous selection of wines by the glass, and the bar is noted for creative mixology.

Chinois on Main

B3 Asian

2709 Main St. (at Hill St.)

Phone: 310-392-9025
Web: www.wolfgangpuck.com
Prices: $$$$

Wed – Fri lunch & dinner
Sat – Tue dinner only

Made for meandering, Santa Monica's Main Street beckons with its artsy boutiques—but when you're ready for a break, consider this Wolfgang Puck institution. Asian shabby-chic describes the dining room, where service is friendly and informal. Bamboo wainscoting, Asian artwork, peacock statues, and a large central skylight merge in an Orient-meets-California-beach décor. At the back of the room, a sushi-style counter flanks the open kitchen.

Opened for more than two decades now, Chinois on Main fuses premium California products with classic cooking techniques. The resulting dishes (sweet Maine crab and pork *siu mai*; grilled Szechuan beef with spicy shallot-cilantro sauce) are sized to share and explode on your palate with expertly balanced flavors.

Cholada

C1 Thai 

18763 Pacific Coast Hwy. (near Topanga Beach Dr.), Malibu

Phone: 310-317-0025
Web: N/A
Prices:

Lunch & dinner daily

The crowd at this popular Malibu restaurant is about as diverse as they come. Surf rats, wealthy Palisades mothers, swimsuit-clad teenagers, powerful industry types—come to think of it, is there anyone who doesn't rub elbows at Cholada's close-knit tables? Not many, because one step into this homespun, funky little Thai beach shack and you're a lifer. If the unpretentious charm doesn't win you over, the fat portions of super-fresh food, humming with bold flavors of ginger, lemongrass, and basil, certainly will.

After the noodle and curry parade, save room for a simple, rustic Thai dessert: a mound of sweet sticky rice that's sinful enough on its own, but gets even more decadent with a blanket of warm, gooey coconut sauce and toasted sesame seeds.

Drago

Italian 

B2

2628 Wilshire Blvd. (bet. Princeton & 26th Sts.)

Phone: 310-828-1585 — Mon – Fri lunch & dinner
Web: www.celestinodrago.com — Sat – Sun dinner only
Prices: $$$

Born in 1991, Drago spawned a mini-empire of restaurants for chef-entrepreneur Celestino Drago, who stakes his fortune on premium products, skillful preparation, and polished service. Food and family figure prominently in his epicurean philosophy, which is no surprise since the chef originally hails from Sicily. You can taste his heritage in dishes such as *panzanella*, a rustic salad of toasted bread cubes, mozzarella, heirloom tomatoes, and olives; a pumpkin *tortelloni* bathed in a fragrant sage cream; and, for dessert, ricotta-filled cannoli dipped in chopped pistachio nuts and orange marmalade.

Expensively conservative, the dining room abounds with leather and suede in muted colors, attracting a sophisticated business crowd for lunch.

Giorgio Baldi

Italian XX

A2

114 W. Channel Rd. (off Pacific Coast Hwy.)

Phone: 310-573-1660 — Tue – Sun dinner only
Web: www.giorgiobaldi.com
Prices: $$$$

This gleaming white cottage at the seaside mouth of Santa Monica Canyon resembles a Hamptons' hideaway and caters to an equivalently affluent local crowd, including celebrities drawn from Malibu and the posh residential heights above.

Chef/owner Giorgio Baldi pulls out all the stops, serving a fluffy crêpe topped with fine slices of smoked salmon in a pool of melted butter. A whole roasted lobster (an evening special) is a case study in rustic perfection: the meat removed, cut into bite-size lumps and tossed with sweet, roasted Italian plum tomatoes and leaves of freshly torn oregano and basil, then drizzled with olive oil. Then back into the shell, onto a platter, and placed before you.

Parking is scarce, so let the valet deal with it.

Hidden

International XX

3110 Main St. (at Marine St.)

Phone: 310-399-4800 — Tue – Sun lunch & dinner
Web: www.hiddenrestaurant.com
Prices: $$$

This hip newcomer really is hidden, or say protected, within a commercial complex. Seating is found in a few different areas: the tree-shaded courtyard set with tables and cabanas; the white-brick dining room; or the counter with a view over an open kitchen. A DJ spins clubby lounge music, adding to the cool vibe.

This menu spans the world, featuring foods from Italy to Vietnam, and Japan to Spain, with anything from thin-crust pizza to kobe beef mini tacos. Globally-inspired tapas provide a world tour, encouraging discovery by sampling an assortment of small plates among a group of friends. There's nonstop exotica like a spicy spider maki stuffed with an expertly-fried soft shell crab, or creatively-presented lemongrass short ribs singing with aromas.

The Hump

Japanese 

3221 Donald Douglas Loop S. (off Airport Ave.)

Phone: 310-313-0977 — Tue – Fri lunch & dinner
Web: www.thehump.biz — Sat – Mon dinner only
Prices: $$$$

Talk about a destination spot. Three stories above Santa Monica Airport's bustling tarmac, you'll find sushi so good that private pilots have been known to fly in just for dinner. The Hump takes its name from an old World War II flier's code for the Himalayas, paying homage to those brave enough to cross the once-forbidden mountain range. You don't have to be quite so brazen to grab a seat on the Hump's terrace, or in its stylish dining room. The passing planes might be all the entertainment you need, but over at the lively sushi bar, there's another kind of genius taking flight.

In front of a beautiful, etched-glass panel of a pilot entering the Himalayas, the chefs' slice and dice their way through the day's catch, spinning fresh fish into bright, new culinary creations.

Il Carpaccio

Italian XX

A1

538 Palisades Dr. (at Sunset Blvd.), Pacific Palisades

Phone: 310-573-1411 Dinner daily
Web: www.ilcarpaccioristorante.com
Prices: **$$$**

Little sister to Santa Monica's La Botte, this encore by Chef Antonio Murè offers traditional dishes with almost everything made in-house. Just off Sunset, in the Palisades Highlands Plaza, its dark ceilings, bright walls, wood chairs, framed mirrors, and cozied-up white cloth-covered tables create a domestic intimacy. Everything, from the *crudi* to *carpacci*, or pasta to *secondi*, is good.

Consider a starter of *carpaccio di manzo*, thinly-sliced filet presented classically with a mustard sauce, nutty Parmigiano, and peppery arugula. Follow with *tortelli di patate*, envelopes of pasta filled with creamed potato topped with sautéed arugula and tangy pecorino. Finish with a rich slice of *pastiera*, a traditional ricotta cake enhanced with lemon zest.

Jer-ne

Contemporary XXX

C4

4375 Admiralty Way (bet. Bali & Palawan Ways), Marina del Rey

Phone: 310-823-1700 Mon – Sat lunch & dinner
Web: www.ritzcarlton.com Sun dinner only
Prices: **$$$$**

Off the hotel's marbled lobby, the dining room and outdoor terrace overlook boats moored in the marina. Contemporary inlay wood floors, burgundy armchairs, soft lighting, and candles create a soothing sense of casual luxury.

Ingredients are superb and presentations striking. The warm fluffy meat of crispy golden brown lobster cakes is accented by fresh chives, minced herbs, and citrus zest, and served with a grace note of tangy-garlicky aïoli over a bed of sweet jicama-cilantro slaw. The kitchen makes smart use of the local fish markets. Desserts are, well, the Ritz. A chocolate mint *soufflé glacé* with *fleur de sel* cookie crumble and strawberry and basil sauces ventures out well beyond the marina's culinary shallows. The wine list is well-chosen.

JiRaffe

A2 Californian XX

502 Santa Monica Blvd. (at 5th St.)

Phone: 310-917-6671 Dinner daily
Web: www.jirafferestaurant.com
Prices: $$$

Raphael Lunetta was a dedicated surfer before catching his life's big wave as Chef/owner of JiRaffe. That's as Californian as you can be, and so is his casual-chic bistro on the last blocks of Route 66. Big windows flood the airy main floor and loft with light, and the chef's affable presence fills it with bonhomie.

At JiRaffe, Lunetta's cuisine always has personality, but see-saws occasionally in execution. Old World recipes marry exotic ingredients here, as in rack of New Zealand lamb with samosas and curried vegetable moussaka; and purple Peruvian potato gnocchi with Florida rock shrimp. Menus change often—nightly specials showcasing seasonal produce from the nearby farmers' market.

Intimate and charming, the dining room is staffed by friendly servers.

Joe's

B3 Californian XX

1023 Abbot Kinney Blvd. (bet. Main St. & Westminster Ave.), Venice

Phone: 310-399-5811 Tue – Sun lunch & dinner
Web: www.joesrestaurant.com
Prices: $$$

Contemporary and comfortable, the atmosphere inside this single-story stucco building matches this low-key residential neighborhood. An exposed wood ceiling lends a rustic feel to an airy main room cloaked in neutral tones. On a warm evening, though, the partially covered dining patio out back is by far the most coveted place to dine.

Farmers' market finds dictate Chef Joe Miller's reasonably priced seasonal menu. High-quality products are spotlighted in dishes such as an elegantly presented salad of frisée and sunflower sprouts topped with a trio of rabbit preparations: poached liver, roasted tenderloin, and rich confit. All this, plus a prix-fixe menu and a more ambitious chef's tasting, make Venice denizens happy that they eat at Joe's.

Josie

American XXX

C2

2424 Pico Blvd. (at 25th St.)

Phone: 310-581-9888 Dinner daily
Web: www.josierestaurant.com
Prices: $$$$

The street fronting Josie's honors Pío Pico (1801-94), last governor of Mexican California. His Los Angeles dram shop sold drinks in hollowed-out ox horns with false wooden bottoms. By the 1850s he was one of the province's wealthiest, known for posh living and devil-may-care ventures that eventually returned him to the ranks of the poor. Josie's elegant shades-of-gray dining room, formally-set tables, and efficient waitstaff would have suited Don Pio in his heyday.
As would the refined menu, citing appetizers like sautéed frogs' legs, or a tagine of short ribs as an entrée, the ribs braised Moroccan style and served over cous cous with a dollop of spicy yogurt. Josie enjoys a reputation it may not always live up to, but its regulars remain loyal.

Lares

Mexican 

C2

2909 Pico Blvd. (bet. 29th & 30th Sts.)

Phone: 310-829-4559 Lunch & dinner daily
Web: www.laresrestaurant.com
Prices:

To step into the tiled downstairs dining room is to go back in time to the *cantinas* of old, reincarnated here with Mission-style furniture, an ornate carved bar, colorful paintings, sunny plaster walls, and a beamed ceiling. To be welcomed by pretty *señoritas* in flowing skirts and embroidered off-the-shoulder blouses, perhaps also by a flamenco guitarist, completes the journey.
In Old California, supper-table hospitality was the measure of any hacienda, however humble. But here even the most humble dishes are proud. Homey Maclovio enchiladas are wrapped in tender white-corn tortillas filled with pinto beans—they ooze with melted cheese. A zesty tomato-red chile sauce and yet more melted cheese puts the gilding on the lily. You should feel welcome.

La Botte ✿

Italian

620 Santa Monica Blvd. (at 6th St.)

Phone: 310-576-3072 — Sat – Thu dinner only
Web: www.labottesantamonica.com — Fri lunch & dinner
Prices: $$$

Stefano De Lorenzo

No one—not your Mom, not your sweetheart, not even your childhood puppy—was ever as excited to see you as manager of La Botte. "*Buona sera*!" is the now-famous greeting—and just like that, you know you're welcome. And lest all that good-natured exuberance freaks you out, the interesting thing is that La Botte is also a sexy, intimate restaurant—all warm woods and romantic candlelight. The place is designed to feel like an Italian wine cellar, with built-in wine storage shelves lining the walls and dark, smoky ceilings.

And if that weren't enough to secure the award for most well-rounded, there's this too: the food is bold, bright, and lovely—like a silky fan of Mediterranean sea bass carpaccio, drizzled with fruity olive oil and dotted with creamy, neon-bright sea urchin; or a tangle of perfectly al dente spaghetti, swirled with tender brown lentils, smoky roasted tomatoes, and wilted fresh spinach.

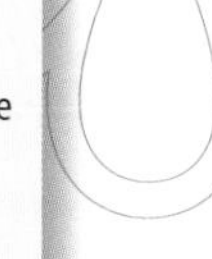

Appetizers

- Stuffed Calamari with Roasted Red Pepper Sauce, and Arugula
- Shaved Artichoke Hearts and Celery with Arugula and Parmesan
- Cauliflower Soup with Capers & Croutons

Entrées

- Homemade Pistachio Pappardelle with Braised Lamb Ragout
- Risotto Mantecato, with Burrata and Santa Barbara Spot Prawns
- Ricotta Cavatelli "alla Lina"

Desserts

- La Pastiera Napoletana-Ricotta Cheese and Grain Pie
- Apple Strudel with Vanilla Ice Cream
- Chocolate Tortino with an Oozing Center

La Serenata De Garibaldi

Mexican XX

A2

1416 4th St. (at Santa Monica Blvd.)

Phone: 310-656-7017 — Lunch & dinner daily
Web: www.laserenataonline.com
Prices:

A great choice for a casual meal, La Serenata is well located near Third Street Promenade. Old Mexico comes to life in the hacienda-style interior, with its warm gold and orange tones, and elaborate wrought-iron accents. Real flower-filled window boxes festoon faux windows painted on one wall of the charming dining space.
Fresh ingredients light up dishes like comforting lima-bean soup, and *tacos blandos*, topped with shredded roasted chicken, crisp lettuce, creamy guacamole and piquant garlic-tomatillo sauce.
Although street parking is limited in this area, you will find several parking garages nearby. La Serenata, part of a small group of local eateries, has two other locations in LA *(1842 E. 1st St. and 10924 W. Pico Blvd.)*.

Le Petit Café

French 

C2

2842 Colorado Ave. (at Stewart St.)

Phone: 310-829-6792 — Mon – Fri lunch & dinner, Sat dinner only
Web: www.lepetitcafebonjour.com
Prices: $$

Appealing French provincial décor (nobody really notices) and simple French cafe food (everybody really notices) sum up the story of Chef/owner Robert Bourget's cheery cottage-like restaurant, set off by itself in a commercial neighborhood. Painted Provençal plates decorate the walls; chalkboards list the choices; and small tables draped with flower-patterned cloths fill the room. Farther back is an open kitchen, then a line of hallway tables leading to a rear dining area.
Dishes are *très Français*, with appetizers citing pâté, and *plats principaux* including duck confit and steak au poivre. A chicken breast well-seasoned with pepper and fresh Provençal herbs is served in a creamy Dijon mustard sauce. Fresh berry tarts proclaim that spring has arrived.

The Lobster

Seafood

1602 Ocean Ave. (at Colorado Ave.)

Phone: 310-458-9294 Lunch & dinner daily
Web: www.thelobster.com
Prices: $$$

Looking at the non-descript exterior of this restaurant, you would never guess what extraordinary panoramas await you on the cantilevered dining deck. Expansive glass panels in the dining room afford views of the pier, the lovely stretch of beach, and the Palisades coastline—and every table enjoys a great view.

Yet this pierside place does not have to rely on its views to attract diners. Great American seafood fills the menu with whole live Maine lobsters—steamed or grilled by the pound—and much of whatever else crawls or swims beneath the sea. The restaurant's namesake crustacean flavors many of the dishes: a lobster chowder with Manila clams; a lobster and avocado salad; a lobster BLT club. Landlubbers can resort to grilled chicken or steak.

Locanda del Lago

Italian 

231 Arizona Ave. (at 3rd St.)

Phone: 310-451-3525 Lunch & dinner daily
Web: www.lagosantamonica.com
Prices: $$$

If you're wondering which *lago*, it's Northern Italy's Lake Como. The menu showcases recipes from the lakeside city of Bellagio and environs. Take a seat in this bistro on the busy pedestrian-only Third Street Promenade, with its rustic wood tables and warm golden walls, and you could be in Lombardy.

Watch the chefs in the open kitchen prepare such Lago di Como traditions as *trota alla Comasca*, fillet of rainbow trout marinated in lemon juice, salty capers and fresh parsley, and served atop potato slices draped in melted cheese. This is hearty fare, like the *ribollita*, a Tuscan soup of chicken broth, smoky cannellini beans, *cavolo nero,* and minced vegetables, topped with Parmesan cheese and croutons. The wine list favors fine Italian vintages.

Mélisse ✿✿

French 

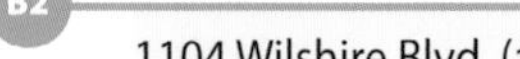

B2

1104 Wilshire Blvd. (at 11th St.)

Phone: 310-395-0881 Tue – Sat dinner only
Web: www.melisse.com
Prices: **$$$$**

Ranking among the best restaurants in L.A., Mélisse owes its existence to Chef/owner Josiah Citrin, who founded this place with his wife, Diane, in 1999. Since then, those who know food in the City of Angels flock here for exquisite French fare.

The kitchen's style is classically French, producing dishes that require meticulous attention to detail and laborious techniques. Flavors balance beautifully in a lamb course that shows off its main ingredient in three preparations: a petite chop, a thick stew, and an herb-encrusted leg tenderloin. A timbale of chopped courgettes provides the finishing touch. Sumptuous desserts are their own reward, but don't overlook the tableside cart of domestic and imported cheeses.

The extensive wine list at Mélisse (French for lemon balm) highlights California whites and French reds, including some rare—and pricey—labels.

Appetizers

- Maine Lobster Thermidor
- Egg Caviar, Poached Egg, Lemon-Chive Crème Fraîche, American Osetra Caviar
- Seared Foie Gras, Apricots, Pain d'Epice, Sauternes Reduction

Entrées

- Almond Crusted Sole, Chanterelles, Butter Jus
- Spring Lamb, Courgettes, Garlic, Olive-Lamb Jus
- Duck Breast, Glazed Radish, Spinach, Cherry Sauce

Desserts

- Toffee Pudding, Mocha Malt Ice Cream, Berry Consommé
- Red Berries "Gratin," Mousse de Lait
- Passion Fruit Parfait, Coconut Sorbet, Lemongrass

Michael's

American

1147 3rd St. (at Wilshire Blvd.)

Phone: 310-451-0843 Mon – Fri lunch & dinner
Web: www.michaelssantamonica.com Sat dinner only
Prices: **$$$$**

Going on 30, this survivor has seen many contemporaries fail to launch. But founder Michael McCarty believed that a smart gallery look (including A-list art), a seasonal menu of "modern American cooking" with high-quality ingredients, a well-trained staff, and smart promotion would boost his namesake into orbit. It did, and the restaurant, its interior little changed, enjoys a long-standing, well-heeled following of regulars who know to ask for a table on the tented garden patio.

Starters run the gamut: yellowtail sashimi; a fig and goat-cheese salad cradling a balsamic-vinegar-based fig confiture; and an artisan foie gras. Main courses span the 50 states—from Maine diver scallops and lobster to a Sonoma County duck breast, or an Alaskan halibut.

Moonshadows

American

20356 Pacific Coast Hwy. (west of Big Rock Dr.), Malibu

Phone: 310-456-3010 Lunch & dinner daily
Web: www.moonshadowsmalibu.com
Prices: **$$$**

The chatterbox crowd at this oceanfront Malibu veteran often suggests a reunion of recent college grads. Look again and you'll see a range of people, all of whom come for the delicious food, the exhilarating panorama, and soothing rush of surf below the open-air deck. The place recalls a '70s hangout, with its cobalt blue bar and dated architecture, but the kitchen is first-rate, using the finest local products to turn out inspired cuisine.

While fish from near and far are featured, the fare is solidly American—as in filet mignon; pork chops; short ribs; free-range chicken; and a Kobe beef burger layered in slices of caramelized onion and ripe tomato.

At night, the young elite show up to toast to the amazing sunsets.

Nobu

Japanese 

B1

3835 Cross Creek Rd. (off Pacific Coast Hwy.), Malibu

Phone: 310-317-9140 Dinner daily
Web: www.noburestaurants.com
Prices: **$$$$**

Set in a back corner of a low-slung complex of shops, galleries, and restaurants, this convivial local favorite is much more laid-back than its chi-chi new sibling in West Hollywood. Even so, it retains a loyal crowd of local regulars and a handful of low-key celebrities.

Nobu is, of course, another jewel in the crown of acclaimed sushi master Nobu Matsuhisa. The menu balances sushi and raw fish with cooked dishes; all are executed with precision and skill. Yellowtail sashimi, for instance, calls for superbly fresh fish sparked by thin slices of green jalapeño and sprigs of cilantro; seared Kobe beef is complemented by tangy ponzu sauce.

Sit at the sushi bar or at tables on the screened and tented patio. Either way, reservations are recommended on weekends.

One Pico

Californian

A3

1 Pico Blvd. (at Ocean Ave.)

Phone: 310-587-1717 Lunch & dinner daily
Web: www.shuttersonthebeach.com
Prices: **$$$$**

Completely remodeled within the last year, One Pico now sports a beachy-chic look. The former lodge-like room at Shutters on the Beach (*see hotel listing*) has been replaced by a bright, airy space thanks to a new white- and beige-toned palette. Iron lanterns now form light fixtures; ocean-blue fabric upholsters chairs; and nautical accents abound. Of course, the huge windows still steal the show with stellar ocean vistas.

Vying with the view, delicious seasonal California fare here is not contrived, allowing superior ingredients to state their case. As such, lobster salad tossed with pesto mayonnaise is sandwiched between slices of tender brioche in a Maine lobster BLT for lunch; while Mediterranean snapper might be spit-roasted whole at dinner.

The Penthouse

Contemporary XX

1111 2nd St. (at Wilshire Blvd.)

Phone: 310-393-8080 Lunch & dinner daily
Web: www.thehuntleyhotel.com
Prices: $$$

If heaven had a members-only club, it might look like this restaurant in The Huntley Hotel *(see hotel listing)*, where white fabric and leather dominate and views sweep across the Santa Monica Bay. Come evening, the night-club ambience is palpable with its pulsing music, and throngs of A-listers and chic wannabes vying for seats at the circular bar.

Without the kitchen's culinary prowess you couldn't pull off a "Green Crunch" salad of fresh raw asparagus, snap peas, greens, and edamame. You might botch the fruity pomegranate vinaigrette, and probably wouldn't get a roasted Kurobuta pork shank with sweet roasted yams and cherry sauce just right.

You'll be more at ease, up here on the 18th floor, if you dress with a bit of style.

Piccolo

Italian 

5 Dudley Ave. (off Speedway), Venice

Phone: 310-314-3222 Dinner daily
Web: www.piccolovenice.com
Prices: $$$

The healthy fare at this small neighborhood haunt sacrifices no flavor for its lightness. Chefs here are journeymen steeped in native skill. Fine slices of a duck prosciutto get a garnish of gorgonzola cream and olive oil, the meat's flavors drawn out by cracked pepper and sea salt. *Pesce* vary with the day, but the preparation is consistently excellent, as in a baked black cod with a crust of reduced balsamic vinegar and dry mustard, covered with diced sweet tomatoes and torn arugula. Furnishings are simple, and Italian is spoken in the open kitchen, resonating off the red tile floors.

Take Rose Avenue to the beach and park in the public lot. Allow yourself the time to linger, since seating is on a first-come, first-served basis.

Primitivo Wine Bistro

Mediterranean XX

1025 Abbot Kinney Blvd. (near Main St.), Venice

Phone: 310-396-5353 — Mon – Fri lunch & dinner
Web: www.primitivowinebistro.com — Sat – Sun dinner only
Prices: $$$

Tapas make up the menu at this urban-bohemian Venice bistro. The location accounts for the thirty-something crowd who, come evenings, create a noisy mixer with the added fun of sampling wines from all points of the compass rose.

The house bets on pairing wine with tapas; given that the list of both is long and that the former includes a wide selection of flights, the odds favor the house. Since these dishes evolved into mini-entrées in the States, tapas have gotten fancy. You might see a steak carpaccio sprinkled with sliced shallot and capers, Medjool dates wrapped in bacon, sautéed Tiger shrimp in a garlic-scented broth, or a seared sea bass topped with a butternut-squash purée. For those who find menu choices difficult, this is a forgiving place.

Real Food Daily

Vegan 

A2

514 Santa Monica Blvd. (at 5th St.)

Phone: 310-451-7544 — Lunch & dinner daily
Web: www.realfood.com
Prices:

All organic, no animal products is the rule here (with a second, West Hollywood location). Yet no dish in this multi-level, sparely furnished place shorts flavor.

It's a buzzing place and if you arrive during primetime, expect to give your name and wait out front on the sidewalk for a bit. The casually-dressed, health-conscious clientele ranges from the entertainment business set to free-thinking activists. The menu is mouthwatering, vast, and playfully written. Its substantial offering is supplemented by specials which might include items like a velvety roasted butternut squash bisque or kung pao tempeh.

When possible, baked goods are made with minimal fats or sugars, thus desserts invite you to indulge yourself with healthy abandon.

Rustic Canyon

Californian XX

1119 Wilshire Blvd. (bet. 11th & 12th Sts.)

Phone: 310-393-7050 Tue – Fri lunch & dinner
Web: www.rusticcanyonwinebar.com Sat – Mon dinner only
Prices: $$$

The real Rustic Canyon is a wild, deep groove in the nearby Santa Monica Mountains, where the ruins of an early 20th-century artist colony remain. Rustic Canyon, the restaurant, is a neighborhood favorite that has established itself with Santa Monica's stylish and affluent thirty-something set, who come with friends to sample wines and share small plates.

With its regularly changing menu of dishes that pair well with the extensive selection of wines, Rustic Canyon affords a new experience each time one dines here. Fresh and simple combinations show off the kitchen's talent in the likes of a chopped free-range chicken salad with buttery cannellini beans, California-made Fra'Mani salami, salty shavings of fontina, and a tangy red wine vinaigrette.

Sam's by the Beach

International XX

108 W. Channel Rd. (off Pacific Coast Hwy.)

Phone: 310-230-9100 Tue – Sun dinner only
Web: N/A
Prices: $$$

In an unassuming cottage, steps from where the Santa Monica Canyon meets the Pacific Coast Highway, this cozy, casual-chic citizen of the world serves Mediterranean food with influences from California, the Continent, and the Middle East.

The skillful melding works well here. Calamari is coated with a piquant spice-rub of cayenne pepper, paprika, cumin, garlic, sumac, and turmeric, grilled to marvelous tenderness, and presented alongside spicy watercress dressed in olive oil and lemon juice. Desserts, like a phyllo "bird nest" filled with rosewater-scented milk pudding, sprinkled with roasted chopped pistachios, may adopt a Middle Eastern flair.

Valet parking is your only option on this heavily trafficked street.

Sapori

Italian

13723 Fiji Way (in Fisherman's Village), Marina del Rey

Phone: 310-821-1740 — Lunch & dinner daily
Web: www.sapori-mdr.com
Prices: **$$**

Beyond the promenade skirting this cheery, friendly spot in Marina del Rey's Fisherman's Village, boats glide gracefully by. The Village draws tourists, so among strollers, cyclists, and skaters at ease here, you'll likely hear foreign tongues and the occasional sidewalk musician.

The restaurant serves tasty rustic seafood, meat, and pasta dishes. A dramatic Caprese Napoleon—slices of red tomato and fresh mozzarella drizzled with fruity olive oil, basil pesto, and a sweet balsamic reduction, is artistically presented between layers of cracker bread. Tender potato gnocchi, well-seasoned and pillowy, are skillet-baked in a bath of tomato and fresh basil, covered with melted bubbling mozzarella.

On balmy days, the patio is sublime.

Shima

Japanese 

1432 Abbot Kinney Blvd. (at Milwood Ave.), Venice

Phone: 310-314-0882 — Tue – Sat dinner only
Web: N/A
Prices: **$$$**

It's easy to walk right by Shima and not realize that inside this two-level town house sits an excellent sushi restaurant. Look for the white piece of paper typed with the establishment's name and taped to an orange wooden gate in front; this will be your only clue to Shima's presence. Inside, bright molded-plastic chairs and bar stools add splashes of color to the neutral palette in this loft-like space, while floor-to-ceiling windows bathe the room in natural light.

Attention to detail reigns supreme in the preparation and presentation of the freshest ingredients. This is made clear in the taste of silky-smooth house-made tofu as well as the signature brown-rice sushi. Venice regulars ignore the standard menu items in favor of the list of daily specials.

sugarFISH

Japanese

C4

4722 1/4 Admiralty Way (bet. Mindanao & Fiji Ways), Marina del Rey

Phone: 310-306-6300 Lunch & dinner daily
Web: www.sugarfishsushi.com
Prices: $$

Notorious Chef Kazunori Nozawa earned his reputation as the "sushi nazi" at his Studio City digs, where his strict adherence to tradition means that he refuses to serve California rolls and spicy tuna. In his new super-casual place in Marina del Rey, he sticks to his omakase-only style with three menu options: Trust Me #1, Trust Me #2, and Trust Me #3. With this level of confidence, you might as well do as the chef suggests: "Don't think, just eat."

What you'll eat may be slices of deep-red tuna drizzled with ponzu, and nigiri of albacore and yellowtail served on mounds of tender rice. Where you'll eat is either at the long sushi bar (there are no chefs behind the bar; dishes arrive from the small kitchen), or at the few booths along the wall.

3 Square Café & Bakery

Bakery

B3

1121 Abbot Kinney Blvd. (at San Juan Ave.), Venice

Phone: 310-399-6504 Lunch & dinner daily
Web: www.rockenwagner.com
Prices: $$

Venice has plenty of casual dining spots, but this one is a step above the rest. Among the baked goods here are the wonderful signature pretzel rolls studded with coarse salt. It's this roll that accounts for the popularity of the pretzel burger, topped with melted Swiss and caramelized onions.

This airy cafe has floor-to-ceiling windows and tables whose planks extend through openings in a glass wall to the patio. The owner's German roots influence the menu—hence apple pancakes with crème fraîche and *leberkäs* (Bavarian breakfast meatloaf) made with eggs, Bavarian mustard and, of course, a pretzel roll.

This isn't a place to count calories; the likes of a luscious vanilla-bean cheesecake are too good to pass up.

Tra di Noi

Italian XX

B1

3835 Cross Creek Rd. (off Pacific Coast Hwy.), Malibu

Phone: 310-456-0169 Lunch & dinner daily
Web: N/A
Prices: $$

Amidst art galleries and boutiques, this casual, inviting Italian restaurant is located in the Malibu Country Mart. In front, a large patio overlooks a small grassy park and residents walking their dogs under shade trees. Families can dine under the large umbrellas, offering relief from the unrelenting California sunshine, while their children play in clear view at the playground just a few steps away.

Inside, orange-hued tile floors, bright yellow tablecloths, and woven wicker cafe chairs add to the warm, homey atmosphere. A spot frequented by wealthy Malibu couples and families, conversations easily erupt between the closely set tables.

The menu features classic Italian dishes prepared simply with traditional flavors and fresh ingredients.

Typhoon

Asian X

C3

3221 Donald Douglas Loop S. (off Airport Ave.)

Phone: 310-390-6565 Sun – Fri lunch & dinner
Web: www.typhoon-restaurant.com Sat dinner only
Prices: $$

Windows frame the Santa Monica Airport and sea, the take-offs and landings of airplanes diverting attention from the open kitchen where chefs meld Thai, Chinese, Vietnamese, and Korean cuisines and techniques. Concrete floors and simple furnishings suit the convivial room, a favorite of retired pilots.

Ingredients are premium and fresh, preparations quite flavorful, and portions typically generous. A heaping plate of *pad Thai* is prepared perfectly, topped with large, sweet prawns, and the requisite garnishes. A fragrant soy-oyster sauce accents a unique version of Mongolian beef, accompanied by savory, pan-fried pastries.

Typhoon offers some Asian delicacies such as chicken-stuffed water bugs and Singapore-style scorpions for more adventurous palates.

Valentino 

Italian 

C2

3115 Pico Blvd. (bet. 31st & 32nd Sts.)

Phone: 310-829-4313 — Mon – Thu & Sat dinner only
Web: www.welovewine.com — Fri lunch & dinner
Prices: $$$$

Valentino Restaurant Group

In a town peppered with Italian restaurants, Valentino laid the bricks. More interestingly: over three decades after it broke onto the scene, Piero Selvaggio's Santa Monica flagship (he owns two more in Las Vegas) still remains a worthy competitor for the new kids on the block, with a reputation that has stood the test of time.

The wine list—as big as a phone book and sporting over 2,500 labels—is the stuff of legend, and would be worth a visit alone; but the beautifully prepared cuisine is what really keeps this place booked. Tuck into a warm *caprino* cheese flan, made to order and garnished with wild mushrooms and fava beans; or a premium, milk-fed veal loin touched with garlic, and served with wilted greens and aromatic porcini mushrooms.

Save room for the much-lauded desserts, like a trio of canolli, filled with a delicately sweet ricotta and garnished with almond.

Appetizers

- Lasagnetta Bolognese, Quail Reduction Sauce
- Duckling and Tomato Crespelle, Mosto Cotto Reduction
- Sweet White Corn Tortelloni, Farmer's Market Vegetables

Entrées

- Sautéed Cod, Red Pepper Sauce, Sichuan Pepper
- Lamb Osso Buco, Wilted Greens, Chanterelles
- Braised Veal Cheeks, Red Wine Sauce, Root Vegetables

Desserts

- Bianco e Rosso: White Chocolate Mousse, Raspberry-Cherry Center
- Italian Rice Pudding, Strawberries, Balsamic Sorbet
- Amaretto-flavored Peaches in Phyllo

Via Veneto

Italian XX

3009 Main St. (bet. Marine St. & Pier Ave.)

Phone: 310-399-1843 — Dinner daily
Web: www.viaveneto.us
Prices: $$$

If you can find a more romantic place, go there. Glimmering candles (the primary light source), a high ceiling, wooden wine racks, and gilt-framed mirrors on faux-finished, earth-tone walls take you halfway there. Charming Italians serving tasty dishes with traditional flavor combinations do the rest, or nearly so.

This is authentic cuisine: strips of earthy, roasted portobello mushrooms topped with shaved salty-sharp aged Parmesan; a salt-crusted baked sea bass seasoned with sprigs of rosemary. As sweets for your sweet, a ricotta-cheese tart is dotted with plump, sweet raisins and finished with a dusting of powdered sugar.

After a wedding, bring your party back to the upstairs balcony room, which affords privacy to small groups.

Violet

American XX

3221 Pico Blvd. (at 32nd St.)

Phone: 310-453-9113 — Tue – Fri lunch & dinner
Web: www.violetrestaurant.com — Sat & Sun dinner only
Prices: $$

Boldly painted walls adorned with earth-tone canvasses brushed with graffiti-like scrawlings set an edgy urban tone in this otherwise bistro-style dining room. The effect is tattoo-parlor chic, a nod to the style of the young, talented chef, Jared Simmons. With his buff bod and trendy haircut Simmons may look like a rocker, but his skills in the kitchen strike no false chords.

The kitchen is right on key with uncontrived small plates that might include roasted baby red and gold beets capped with creamy homemade cheese and slices of tangy pickled fennel; or a braised short rib over savory vanilla-bean-infused risotto. Seven might turn out to be your favorite number Tuesday through Thursday, when you can choose among 7 dishes priced at $7 before 7:00 P.M.

Wabi-Sabi

B3-4

Japanese

1635 Abbot Kinney Blvd. (at Venice Blvd.), Venice

Phone: 310-314-2229 Dinner daily
Web: www.wabisabisushi.com
Prices: **$$**

Industrial décor meets contemporary Japanese food at this boho-chic space on Venice's signature boulevard of shops and cafes. The gallery-style look (polished concrete floor, brick walls, track lighting, framed art) suits the neighborhood and the restaurant's name—a reference to the key physical and philosophical elements of traditional Japanese beauty, which seeks perfection while accepting its impossibility.

Sushi and sashimi, along with small plates and hot food, are crafted using traditional and modern approaches. That permits a sushi roll of baked warm crab meat to be paired with chunks of creamy avocado and a sweet rice-wine sauce; or shrimp potstickers to be served on a pool of carrot-ginger purée—a fine fusion of East and West.

Whist

A3

Californian

1819 Ocean Ave. (at Pico Blvd.)

Phone: 310-260-7511 Lunch & dinner daily
Web: www.viceroysantamonica.com
Prices: **$$$**

Neo-English décor and formal staff, not to mention a name that refers to an 18th-century card game, belie the fun of fine dining at the hip Viceroy Hotel. What the chef calls "New American" cuisine amounts to seafood, steak, and specialties made with familiar ripe, seasonal, and flavorful ingredients in innovative combinations. A celebrity hotspot, the Viceroy is a stylish retreat, including Whist's cozy booths and outdoor poolside patio tables and intimate cabanas, rendered romantic by candlelight.

There's show biz in a pan-seared fillet of King salmon placed atop a bed of wilted bok choy, roasted shiitakes, udon noodles, and miso broth; so, too, in a Black Angus tenderloin with portobello fries. There's star-gazing as well—both sideways and straight up.

Wilshire

Californian 

2454 Wilshire Blvd. (at 25th St.)

Phone: 310-586-1707
Web: www.wilshirerestaurant.com
Prices: **$$$**

Mon – Fri lunch & dinner
Sat dinner only

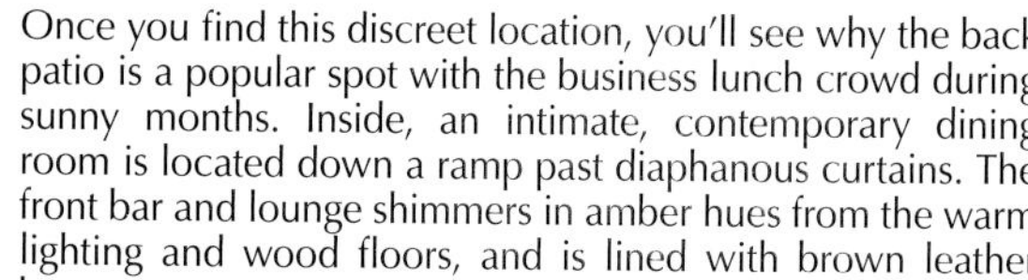

Once you find this discreet location, you'll see why the back patio is a popular spot with the business lunch crowd during sunny months. Inside, an intimate, contemporary dining room is located down a ramp past diaphanous curtains. The front bar and lounge shimmers in amber hues from the warm lighting and wood floors, and is lined with brown leather banquettes.

Superbly fresh and seasonal dishes are created for a "New urban cuisine". The menu makes ample use of locally procured and organic ingredients to promote sustainable sensibilities. Dishes like hamachi sashimi with ponzu, or a lobster cobb salad offer light and flavorful enjoyment.

Wilshire has settled into its rhythms still with service that is friendly, informal, and efficient.

Hotels and restaurants change every year, so change your Michelin Guide every year!

ubiubi
Discover. Indulge. Impress.
www.ubiubi.mobi
ubi
VENTO
MICHELIN
Menu

Ventura Boulevard

Agoura Hills - Calabasas - Westlake Village

Even though Los Angeles voters rejected a 2002 bid to let nearly two dozen unincorporated communities within the San Fernando Valley's 235 square miles form a separate city, most view "The Valley" as distinct from LA. Indeed, the Census Bureau finds the 1.75 million people living between the Sierra Madre, Santa Monica and San Gabriel mountains more affluent, more foreign-born, and more likely to find parking.

The Tongva were here for at least 2,000 years before the Spanish founded **Mission San Fernando** in 1797, and cattle ranchos with haciendas like the De La Osa Adobe at **Los Encinos State Historic Park** in Encino. By the 20th century, the valley's Mediterranean clime was producing a cornucopia of fruits, nuts, and vegetables. Photoplays of Hollywood stars on rustic ranch-style spreads added cachet. Between 1945 and 1960, the exodus to the suburbs, along with booms in aerospace and other industries, quintupled the area's population.

FROM SYCAMORES TO SITCOMS

Part of El Camino Real, the old mission road that Highway 101 now follows west past Agoura Hills. Ventura Boulevard runs some 17 miles from Calabasas (named for its native wild pumpkins) through Woodland Hills—where in 1922 Victor Girard planted over 120,000 pepper, sycamore, and eucalyptus trees—to the Cahuenga Pass near Universal City. Along the boulevard's busy lanes you'll now find the Valley's densest collection of small businesses, including popular Sushi Row in **Studio City**, as well as restaurants serving a world of diverse cuisines.

Also in 1922, the area's first golf links opened at Ventura and Coldwater Canyon. Just east of Laurel Canyon Boulevard were

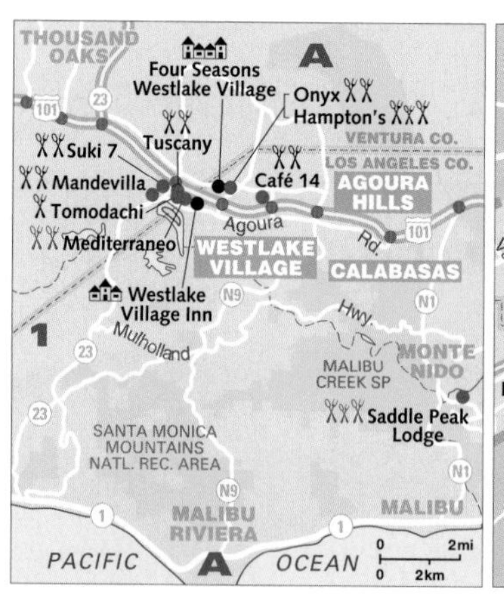

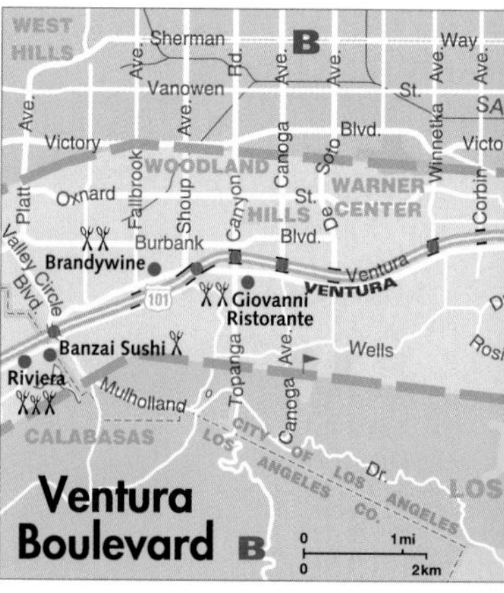

Mack Sennett's Keystone Studios, a silent-movie laugh factory whose two-reelers featured Fatty Arbuckle, W. C. Fields, Stan Laurel and Oliver Hardy, and the Keystone Kops. The lot became Republic Pictures in 1935, where John Wayne and Roy Rogers created their cowboy personas. Today it hosts **CBS Studio Center** *(closed to the public)*, where TV sitcoms and dramas are produced.

Long used for filming street scenes, Ventura Boulevard—and the Sherman Oaks Galleria mall—gained iconic status in 1982 when Frank and Moon Unit Zappa's hit single "Valley Girl" ("On Ventura, there she goes...") introduced America to the dialect ("Like, *totally* awesome!"). Countering the boulevard's lowbrow stigma are offbeat communities like North Hollywood's **NoHo Arts District** just north of **Universal Studios**. With more than 20 live theaters and dozens of galleries, dance studios, recording venues, and clothing and specialty shops, Ventura is *totally* fun.

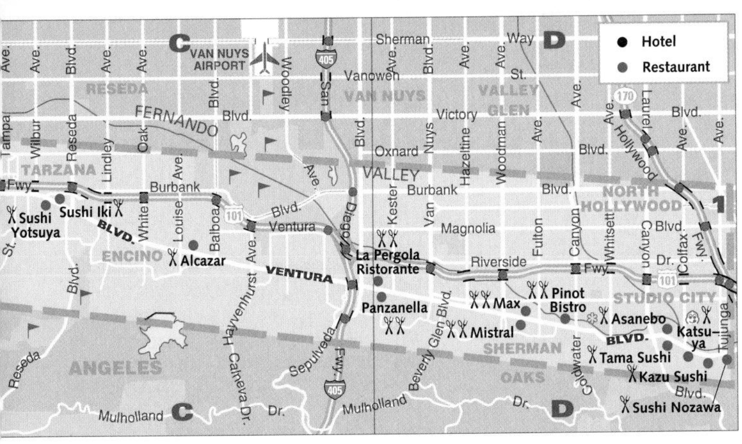

Alcazar

C1 **Lebanese**

17239 Ventura Blvd. (at Louise Ave.), Encino

Phone: 818-789-0991 Tue – Sun lunch & dinner
Web: www.al-cazar.com
Prices: $$

Loyals cherish the Oriental décor at Alcazar as an authentic paean to life at the far eastern reach of the Mediterranean. An extensive menu of Lebanese and Middle Eastern dishes is offered here with a definitive selection of traditional cold and hot *mezza* (appetizers). You can dine well on *mezza* alone, sampling classics like *hummos* or *s'feehah*, a baked meat pie; or choose one of the set-price *mezza* menus offering a taste of the best options. Main courses like the combination dish of Lebanon's famed grilled meats, rich with savory spices, are also an alternative.

Desserts are bold and there are plenty to choose from. *Halawet eljeben* fills a cheese and farina dough with rosewater cream and tops it with crushed pistachio nuts and rosewater syrup.

Banzai Sushi

B1 **Japanese**

23508 Calabasas Rd. (at Valley Circle Blvd.), Calabasas

Phone: 818-222-5800 Mon – Fri lunch & dinner
Web: www.banzaisushi.com Sat – Sun dinner only
Prices: $$

Located in the heart of Old Town Calabasas, this casual, popular spot offers a wide selection of innovative, boldly flavored specialty rolls. Chefs behind the L-shaped bar, where locals hover waiting for seats to open up, make sushi that's contemporary and fun, along with meals combining sushi, teriyaki, and sashimi.

The Hawaiian roll, a Banzai specialty, is a California roll of shredded crab meat dressed in light mayonnaise, with creamy avocado and batons of cucumber, topped with sesame- and soy-accented deep-red tuna. Wrap large lumps of steamed lobster with those little green batons and steamed asparagus, garnish with crunchy beads of *tobiko* caviar, and you have the house lobster roll.

There's a pleasant tree-shaded patio up front.

Asanebo ✿

Japanese

D1

11941 Ventura Blvd. (at Radford Ave.), Studio City

Phone: 818-760-3348 — Tue – Fri lunch & dinner
Web: N/A — Sat – Sun dinner only
Prices: $$$

On the face of it, Asanebo isn't much to look at. Set in a predictable strip mall on Ventura Boulevard in the heart of Studio City, with a warm but simple interior, there's not much scenery to cluck over in a city packed with over-the-top décors. But looks can be deceiving, and what looks like a boring neighborhood sushi spot, in this case hides a culinary gem.

Don't trust us, though: find a seat at the lively, laid-back sushi bar, where the waiters get just as involved as the sushi masters, and indulge in the very reasonably priced omakase. Though it changes daily, it might include a luscious wedge of creamy, homemade sesame tofu sporting a dollop of wasabi and radish for garnish; little butter lettuce cups, stuffed taquito-style with Mishima beef; Chilean sea bass; or three plump little Hama Hama oysters, served over half a lemon and perched in a pool of tangy vinegar sauce.

Appetizers

- Japanese Beef with Butter Leaf, House-blended Miso
- Halibut, Shrimp, Shiitake and O-ba Leaf Fried Seafood Stick
- Spinach with Sautéed Portobello Salad

Entrées

- Halibut Sashimi, Black Truffle and Hot Olive Oil
- Konpachi Sashimi, Serrano Pepper and Yuzu Sauce
- Seared Toro, Daikon, Wasabi, Sweet Miso-Vinegar Sauce

Desserts

- Homemade Black Sesame or Roasted Brown Tea Ice Cream

Brandywine

European XX

B1

22757 Ventura Blvd. (at Fallbrook Ave.), Woodland Hills

Phone: 818-225-9114 — Tue – Fri lunch & dinner
Web: N/A — Mon & Sat dinner only
Prices: $$$

Nothing, including the small pink cottage sheltering this tiny low-ceilinged dining room, is modern here. Not the pink-saturated décor suggesting a Victorian great-aunt's parlor, not the dried pink carnations, the rickety bookshelves holding old tomes, nor the vintage tableware. Call it charmingly old-fashioned.

The bill of fare (chalked on a blackboard) is the thing. Dishes are made with quality ingredients and simply presented, yet with a dash of ambition—a Mediterranean seafood bouillabaisse; a breast of duck roosting on a mound of mashed potatoes; a Meyer lemon pudding soufflé curtsying in a seasonal fruit compote. Expect only traditional continental European dishes at this old-fashioned place.

Café 14

A1

30315 Canwood St. (at Reyes Adobe Rd.), Agoura Hills

Phone: 818-991-9560 — Dinner daily
Web: www.cafe-14.com
Prices: $$$

A gourmet surprise, tucked into the back corner of Reyes Adobe Plaza, Café 14 is more refined than its name or location implies. A tented L-shaped patio wraps from the front to the side of the building, and the dining room is set about with muted taupe walls, framed mirrors, vintage posters, and finely set tables.

Skillfully prepared, internationally influenced dishes use premium and savory seasonal ingredients. Those international accents flavor a salad crafted from crispy duck and ripe, sweet nectarines, accented with Thai basil and a drizzle of hoisin-infused vinaigrette. They also show up in salmon seared in the fat rendered from andouille sausage, then roasted and served with a sweet-potato sausage hash and Cajun butter sauce.

Giovanni Ristorante

B1 — Italian XX

21926 Ventura Blvd. (at Topanga Canyon Rd.), Woodland Hills

Phone: 818-884-0243 — Tue – Fri lunch & dinner
Web: www.giovanniristorante.com — Sat – Sun dinner only
Prices: $$

Fond memories of a patriarch's 1929 odyssey from Southern Italy to America inspire the menu in this quaint, family-friendly spot in Woodland Hills. Dishes are straightforward and generous, shining a spotlight on pasta. The dining room's pale gold walls and white-linen-draped tables create a homey ambiance; while a covered patio adds a sense of ease in a neighborhood that's lean on good dining choices.

Pastas are presented with the option to mix any of them with a variety of vegetables and traditional sauces. Hearty favorites satisfy, as in lasagna oozing with melted cheese and an herb-rich tomato sauce spiked with meat. A huge piece of oven-browned focaccia brushed with olive oil and sprinkled with fresh rosemary is perfect for sopping up any leftover sauce.

Hampton's

A1 — Californian XXX

2 Dole Dr. (at Via Rocas), Westlake Village

Phone: 818-575-3000 — Tue – Sat dinner only
Web: www.fourseasons.com/westlakevillage — Sun lunch only
Prices: $$$

European-style abounds at Hampton's in the Four Seasons Westlake Village *(see hotel listing)*. You see it in the entry lined with cabinets filled with wine bottles, and in the semi-circular paneled dining room where windows look out on water splashing over boulders in the hotel gardens. Gold sofas and red tapestry armchairs ease up to spacious linen-topped tables—their deep colors matched by drapes and carpeting. Service is professional and attentive.

Culinary mastery is obvious in morel mushrooms sautéed in butter and rendered pork fat, served with crispy cubes of pork belly roasted until the fat is gone; as well as in a meaty snapper roasted in olive oil with baby artichokes, and garnished with a pale green olive-oil foam. A meal here is memorable.

Katsu-ya

D1 **Japanese**

11680 Ventura Blvd. (at Colfax Ave.), Studio City

Phone: 818-985-6976
Web: www.sushikatsu-ya.com
Prices: $$

Mon – Sat lunch & dinner
Sun dinner only

The sushi bar is the place to be at this little Studio City spot, the firstborn in an L.A. mini-chain. Equally popular with locals, twenty-somethings, celebrities, and entertainment-industry types, Katsu-ya wows diners with its contemporary Japanese flavor combinations.

Opened by Chef/owner Katsuya Uechi, this is not a place for sushi purists. Concentrate instead on the sparkling sushi and innovative specialty dishes here. Everyone's reading the handwritten menu of daily specials, which on any given night encompasses a host of sushi, sashimi, cold and hot dishes: a baked crab cut roll wrapped in soy paper; or perhaps crispy rice with spicy tuna.

Don't be intimidated by the hungry stares of those hovering around waiting for your spot at the counter.

Kazu Sushi

D1 **Japanese**

11440 Ventura Blvd. (at Ridgemoor Dr.), Studio City

Phone: 818-763-4836
Web: N/A
Prices: $$$

Mon – Fri lunch & dinner
Sat dinner only

With an unassuming strip-mall storefront, Chef Kazu's place is small and modest, and he is sometimes alone behind his black-granite sushi bar, but his traditional sushi and sashimi offerings are fresh, simple, and very good, an argument for taking the more expensive omakase option.

The notion of "simple" sushi may seem redundant, but natural taste is the goal: a thin slice of *toro* (fatty tuna belly prized in Japan) is served on tender mounds of rice without garnish or sauce, letting its silky texture and buttery flavor speak for itself. A smear of wasabi on sushi rice offsets the sweetness of a cooked butterflied prawn. A small yuzu citrus garnish tops halibut sushi. For a stronger taste experience, ask the maestro for a spicy tuna hand roll.

La Pergola Ristorante

Italian XX

D1

15005 Ventura Blvd. (at Lemona Ave.), Sherman Oaks

Phone: 818-905-8402 — Mon – Fri lunch & dinner
Web: www.lapergolaristorante.net — Sat – Sun dinner only
Prices: $$$

Rustic and simple, with a charming Italian countryside décor of beamed ceilings, a tile floor, and a cadre of Italian-American regulars, La Pergola grows a large portion of the vegetables, fruits, and herbs in the owner's adjoining *giardino organico*—the roasted figs and sun-dried tomatoes on your baguette likely traveled a mere 30 paces to your table. This garden adds farm-fresh spontaneity to the ever-changing fish, pasta, meat, and poultry specials chalked up daily, which tend to trump the extensive printed menu. Either way, let the kitchen show off its skill at cooking fish, and save room for dessert.

If you've been admiring the lovely Italian pottery that decorates La Pergola, you can purchase pieces at the restaurant's ceramic shop.

Mandevilla

International 

A1

951 S. Westlake Blvd. (bet. Hampshire & Townsgate Rds.), Westlake Village

Phone: 805-497-8482 — Mon – Fri lunch & dinner
Web: www.mandevillarestaurant.com — Sat – Sun dinner only
Prices: $$$

At Mandevilla, hearty and flavorful dishes—the pastas in particular—have a strong Italian character, but also show American and international influences. The dining rooms' tawny walls, soft lighting, and touches like the brick-faced kitchen and exposed wine racks distance you from the modern shopping area outside. A tented and screened patio, with its green garden décor, takes you a bit farther.

A daily fish special supplements other seafood, poultry, and meat entrées. Classics like an appetizer of oversized prawns perched on the rim of a cocktail glass, served with a horseradish cream and a tangy, tomato-based sauce—not to mention a New York-style cheesecake—add a touch of steakhouse flair to the old-school trattoria ambiance.

Max

Fusion XX

D1

13355 Ventura Blvd. (bet. Dixie Canyon & Fulton Aves.), Sherman Oaks

Phone: 818-784-2915 Dinner daily
Web: www.maxrestaurant.com
Prices: $$$

The smartly conceived "Pan-Asian" mix of Far East, western, and southern California cuisines at this friendly, laid-back streetside enterprise, along with its sidewalk terrace tables, softly-lighted banquette and alcove seating, savvy bartending, and competently attentive service account for the loyal patronage here.

The chef's daily inspirations supplement a concise menu of creations like a softly fried crab cake with a thin nut crust adding a sweet crunchy texture, served with a pineapple and mango relish. A thick filet of broiled miso-marinated cod arrives with sautéed Asian vegetables and sticky rice in a mushroom sake broth. There are many Western touches here too, starting with a Caesar salad and a seared foie gras in puff pastry.

Mediterraneo

Italian XX

A1

32037 Agoura Rd. (bet. Lakeview Canyon & Lindero Canyon Rds.), Westlake Village

Phone: 818-889-9105 Lunch & dinner daily
Web: www.med-rest.com
Prices: $$$

Located on the grounds of the Westlake Village Inn, Mediterraneo is popular with both hotel guests and well-to-do locals. Surrounded by a lake, trickling streams, fountains, and manicured gardens, the patio is perfect for alfresco dining in the relaxing environment. The u-shaped bar and roaring fire pit are comfortable spots to enjoy a cocktail with live music on weekends. Inside, a dramatic, contemporary-chic dining room sets the stage for the palatable Italian-infused cuisine.

Flavorful dishes like crab *fritella* with a three bean ragú or Olivia's orecchiette with Italian sausage, tomatoes, and Swiss chard are a serious step up from the bland fare often found nearby. The lunch menu expands to include salads, pizzas, and panini for a lighter bite.

Mistral

French XX

D1

13422 Ventura Blvd. (at Greenbush Ave.), Sherman Oaks

Phone: 818-981-6650
Web: N/A
Prices: $$$

Mon – Fri lunch & dinner
Sat dinner only

Step into Mistral and you'll forget you're in Los Angeles. Once inside this Sherman Oaks eatery, it's easy to imagine you're in Paris, between the dark wood paneling, the brass accents at the bar, and the authentic brasserie food. Peppered with elegant touches—linen tablecloths, crystal chandeliers—the décor strikes a complimentary chord between a rustic ambience and an elegant dining experience.

French dishes fill the menu, from escargots and steak au poivre to a classic frisée salad, sprinkled with crispy *lardons* and crowned with a soft-poached egg whose yolk, once pierced, melts into the light mustard dressing.

It all goes to show that there are other reliable dining options along Ventura Boulevard if you're not in the mood for Japanese cuisine.

Onyx

Japanese XX

A1

2 Dole Dr. (at Via Rocas), Westlake Village

Phone: 818-575-3000
Web: www.fourseasons.com
Prices: $$$

Dinner daily

A 2,000-gallon saltwater aquarium behind the front bar, translucent wall panels of semi-precious stone, bamboo floors, and other striking Asian details render Onyx's space in the Four Seasons Westlake *(see hotel listing)* dramatic. A small sushi bar and a terrace dining area overlooking the hotel gardens and waterfall just gild the lily.

Diners well beyond hotel guests are attracted to Chef Masa Shimakawa's specialties. His inspirations include a Hawaiian "poke" martini of diced tuna drizzled with red-chili oil, creamy avocado cubes, and micro greens with truffle oil, garnished with wasabi-spiked flying-fish roe. A triumph of nuance, green-tea sea salt and a soy-based dipping sauce season sweet-potato tempura. Mild top-quality *toro* sushi is indeed a gem.

Panzanella

D1 Italian XX

14928 Ventura Blvd. (at Kester Ave.), Sherman Oaks

Phone: 818-784-4400 Dinner daily
Web: www.panzanellaristorante.com
Prices: $$$

Typical fare at this member of Giacomino Drago's restaurant family runs to *scaloppini a piacere,* with a rich and tasty Marsala demi-glace, served with mashed potatoes and a bevy of delicately cooked small vegetables. Some get no further than the antipasti, making a meal of prosciutto and dried figs; beef carpaccio; marinated swordfish; goat-cheese-filled eggplant rolls; or a truffle-accented mushroom soufflé. Italian wines are well represented. Desserts, as in a golden brown-butter tart filled with blackberries and served with vanilla ice cream, are (old-country) rich.

Come evening at Panzanella, a casual-chic clientele of couples and young families arrives. As always on Ventura, you must, as they say, valet.

Pinot Bistro

D1 French XX

12969 Ventura Blvd. (at Coldwater Canyon Ave.), Studio City

Phone: 818-990-0500 Mon – Fri lunch & dinner
Web: www.patinagroup.com Sat – Sun dinner only
Prices: $$$

Imagine a provincial French farmhouse—on commercial Ventura Boulevard. Inside at least, the Patina Group pulls it off with rooms and alcoves paneled in dark wood, where cabinets display decorative ceramics, black banquettes line some walls, and a fireplace adds to the ambience.

At midday the vaulted room fills with a mix of retirees and young film executives from nearby Studio City, who come here to discuss their latest project over the likes of a slow-roasted pork sandwich with braised red cabbage, steak frites, or a lovely roasted trout sprinkled with diced bacon and smoky almonds. At dinner, the menu trades sandwiches for heartier fare.

Locals go Sunday nights for the weekly changing Sunday supper, a steal at three courses for under $35.

Riviera

Italian XXX

B1

23683 Calabasas Rd. (bet. Calabasas Pkwy. & Mulholland Dr.), Calabasas

Phone: 818-224-2163 — Mon – Fri lunch & dinner
Web: www.tuscany-restaurant.com — Sat – Sun dinner only
Prices: $$$

When sunlight floods the front curtains, the gold walls, high-backed blue-and-beige-striped upholstered chairs, fine pale linens, shaded table lamps, and deep-blue carpeting produce a peculiarly European mood in this contemporary dining room. You can't help but dream of foreign lands.

Consistency and flavor are winning cards here, and the house plays a skillful hand of classic Italian dishes using the finest ingredients. Tradition trumps tinkering. Thus an earthy medley of minced mushrooms stuffs a fillet of orange roughy. A salad special of *insalata caprese* (butter lettuce, beefsteak tomato, and fresh mozzarella) may withhold the basil, but the herb's role is fulfilled by a tangy balsamic vinaigrette spiked with creamy chive dressing.

Saddle Peak Lodge

American XXX

A1

419 Cold Canyon Rd. (at Piuma Rd.), Calabasas

Phone: 818-222-3888 — Wed – Fri dinner only
Web: www.saddlepeaklodge.com — Sat – Sun lunch & dinner
Prices: $$$$

Just west of San Fernando Valley, a ways down Ventura Highway, you'll find Saddle Peak Lodge—a century-old hunting lodge set among the woody slopes of Las Virgenes Canyon. Most folks would make the drive out just to soak in the adorable rustic charm of the log interior, stocked with hunting trophies, countrified hurricane lamps, and a glowing fireplace—but what really keeps this place bumping most nights is the game-driven American menu, like grilled California squab, delicately roasted and tucked into leaves of crispy cabbage filled with tender artichoke and dancing with vinaigrette.

Guests can choose from two chef's tasting menus, paired with or without wine—or just order à la carte.

Suki 7

A1 Japanese XX

925 Westlake Blvd. (bet. Hampshire & Townsgate Rds.), Westlake Village

Phone: 805-777-7579 Mon – Fri lunch & dinner
Web: www.suki7lounge.com Sat dinner only
Prices: **$$$**

Dramatic, contemporary Japanese ambiance sets the stage for pretty dishes of sushi, sashimi, and *robata*-grilled items here. Modish green armchairs provide nontraditional seating at the U-shaped sushi bar, while pulsing music and attractive servers play to a hip audience. It's anybody's guess whether the cool crowd comes for the bold décor or the delicious food.

The draw for most is the tasty food. Impeccable hand rolls make assertive use of flavor accents like spicy radish sprouts or red chili laced with sesame oil and chives. A signature miso-paste-glazed black cod is served on a swirl of creamy miso sauce and scallion-infused oil atop Swiss chard. Consider musty-sweet *shochu*, a barley-based traditional spirit, as an alternative to sake.

Sushi Iki

C1 Japanese X

18663 Ventura Blvd., Suite 106 (at Yolanda Ave.), Tarzana

Phone: 818-343-3470 Tue – Fri lunch & dinner
Web: N/A Sat – Sun dinner only
Prices: **$$**

This place serves oversized pieces of sushi from a short menu that's long on quality. Upping the ante on the run-of-the-mill sushi bar, the dining room boasts comfortable cushioned chairs, cloth napkins, and table runners. Sushi chefs chat and joke with customers as if they were old friends.

Fresh as can be is the overall impression. Neatly pressed rectangles of sushi rice with a thin layer of wasabi cushion large slices of albacore tuna and hamachi *toro* tarted up with grated yuzu zest. The tuna roll is spiced by mixing the minced fish with a dab of red-chili paste, sesame oil, and scallions—the whole shebang rolled up with cucumber batons in toasted nori.

Parking options include a front lot and a garage in back of the shopping plaza.

Sushi Nozawa

D1 Japanese

11288 Ventura Blvd. (at Eureka Dr.), Studio City

Phone: 818-508-7017 Mon – Fri lunch & dinner
Web: N/A
Prices: **$$$**

To be granted one of the nine chairs before Chef/owner Kazunori Nozawa's sushi bar, you must accept his omakase offering. This is a no-nonsense sushi experience for the purist, technical perfection without fancy presentation. Nozawa's no-frills autocracy discourages chit-chat. A sign commands "Don't Think/Just Eat." The full omakase is served rapidly in about 20 minutes. Then you go, which can be unsettling for those seeking communion with the master.
That said, this small Monday-Friday only strip mall space offers some of the best sushi in the city. Baby tuna sashimi seasoned with ponzu is followed by expertly-assembled *nigiri* with slightly sticky warm rice. Finally come hand rolls of toro, crab, and shrimp wrapped in perfectly toasty nori.

Sushi Yotsuya

C1 Japanese

18760 Ventura Blvd. (at Burbank Blvd./Crebs Ave.), Tarzana

Phone: 818-708-9675 Mon – Fri lunch & dinner
Web: N/A Sat dinner only
Prices: **$$$**

Traditional excellence defines Masa Matsumoto's small sushi bar, where the affable chef will describe his creations for you. Traditional means just that: no spicy tuna or California roll, no popularized concoctions. Excellence includes devotion to craft and the freshest ingredients possible, the best argument for choosing Matsumoto's omakase menu, which changes daily.
What to expect? *Toro* (choice cuts of tuna belly), perhaps with onion shoots; a bite-sized piece of *hamachi* (yellowtail) with wasabi; konpachi (a kind of yellowtail) paired with a fresh mint leaf; raw salmon covered with sweet miso-marinated kelp and toasted sesame seeds; and sticky rice scented with seasoned Japanese vinegar. Trust the master.

Tama Sushi

Japanese

D1

11920 Ventura Blvd. (at Carpenter Ave.), Studio City

Phone: 818-760-4585
Web: www.tamasushi.net
Prices: $$

Mon – Sat lunch & dinner
Sun dinner only

Chef/owner Katsu Michite's status among his peers rests partly on superior ingredients, giving this elegantly spare establishment an edge among the many sushi venues in Los Angeles. That's apparent in the omakase sashimi, chirashi, and sushi menus, which offer the best of the freshest at good prices.
There are contemporary "Americanized" specialty rolls, tempura selections, teriyaki combinations, gyoza, tofu, and salads, but traditional skills are most splendidly demonstrated when the chefs do the choosing. They may present you with a plate of scallop, hamachi, tuna, halibut, and toro, some splashed with lemon juice and a dash of volcanic gray salt; others smeared with wasabi, or accented with tangy pickled daikon.
And, there's parking here!

Tomodachi

Japanese

A1

2779 Agoura Rd. (at Village Glen), Westlake Village

Phone: 805-777-7578
Web: www.sushitomodachi.com
Prices: $$

Mon – Fri lunch & dinner
Sat – Sun dinner only

A casual place where families are welcome, Tomodachi could be easily overlooked in this sprawling shopping strip, hidden amid groceries and coffeeshops. To miss it, though, would be a mistake.
Exceptionally fresh fish and intriguing specialty rolls augment traditional offerings such as tempura and teriyaki. Buttery yellowtail sashimi, for instance, is fanned out on a large plate and sprinkled with slivers of jalapeño, sprigs of pungent cilantro, and shavings of daikon. The signature Tomodachi roll combines a bit of everything—crispy shrimp tempura, lump crab, and various vegetables—inside nori and rice mounded with spicy tuna and slices of avocado.
The décor may have no frills, but this Westlake Village restaurant is a great find in the area.

Tuscany

A1 **Italian** XX

968 S. Westlake Blvd. (bet. Agoura & Townsgate Rds.), Westlake Village

Phone: 805-495-2768 Mon – Fri lunch & dinner
Web: www.tuscany-restaurant.com Sat – Sun dinner only
Prices: **$$$**

Tuscany sits in a pleasant shopping center, and its simple bar and dining room, with gold walls, tabletop lamps, and colored glass light fixtures, evokes a casual ease. A small patio is sheltered by potted plants and wrought iron fencing, where a fountain trickles and the overhead trellis provides shade.The extensive menu of this neighborhood favorite leans Italian though the kitchen hits its high notes in the daily specials. The minestrone, offered daily, features perfectly-cooked vegetables swimming in a light tomato aromatic of garlic, bay leaf, oregano, and basil. Specials like a panko-crusted butterfish bathed in roasted garlic cream sauce with *cappellini* display more creativity.
At lunch, salads and sandwiches offer lighter bites.

Park your car without a problem when you see for valet parking.

Westside

Brentwood - Century City - Culver City - West LA - Westwood

To many Angelenos "West LA" means everything within the city limits west of La Cienega Boulevard to the Pacific, running from the Santa Monica Mountains south to Los Angeles International Airport. Most use the blanket term "Westside" to include everything regardless of municipal borders. All agree, however, that aside from its traffic jams, life on the sundown side of the Big Pueblo is something to be desired.

WESTSIDE REDUX

Brentwood and Pacific Palisades were once part of the 33,000-acre Mexican land grant known as *Rancho San Vicente y Santa Monica*. Parceled off after Mexico ceded California to the U.S. in 1848, the area's rolling woodlands and ocean breezes attracted developers taking cues from Beverly Hills by bordering streets with date palms and letting them follow the contours of the land. The aesthetic they instilled responded when the Depression shut down the Pacific Electric Railway's San Vicente Boulevard route—popular for seafood-dinner excursions to Playa del Rey—by replacing the tracks with its present grassy median of groomed coral trees running four miles from central Brentwood's restaurant row to the sea. The only downside to the Westside's sylvan nature—most accessible at **Will Rogers State Historic Park**, the humorist's former polo estate above Sunset in Pacific Palisades—became apparent in 1961 when the Great Bel-Air–Brentwood Fire, the worst in Los Angeles history, destroyed 484 homes.

A BLEND OF CULTURES

Though the residential enclaves within upscale northern districts like Century City, Holmby Hills, Westwood, and Brentwood are less diverse, overall the Westside is cosmopolitan. It includes a Japanese-American community along northern Sawtelle Boulevard, Latino neighborhoods in Palms, and Brentwood as well as Westwood share a large Persian population. Each has restaurants that highlight cooking from the neighborhood's origin on the compass rose.

Anchored by **UCLA**, the Westside also boasts the **Getty Center**, whose hillside terraces afford a matchless panorama of nearly the entire 525-square-mile LA Basin.

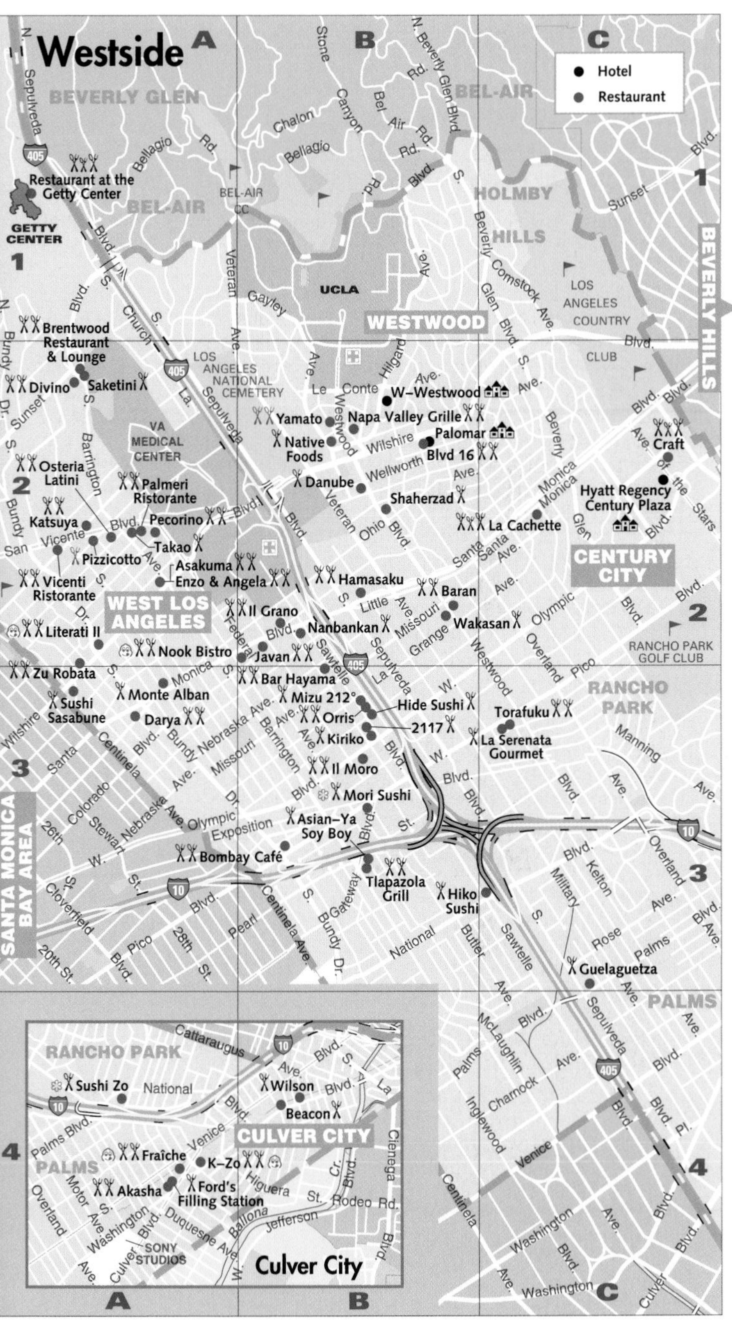
Westside
Hotel
Restaurant
Restaurant at the Getty Center
GETTY CENTER
BEVERLY GLEN
BEL-AIR
UCLA
WESTWOOD
HOLMBY HILLS
LOS ANGELES COUNTRY CLUB
BEVERLY HILLS
Brentwood Restaurant & Lounge
Divino
Saketini
LOS ANGELES NATIONAL CEMETERY
VA MEDICAL CENTER
W-Westwood
Yamato
Napa Valley Grille
Native Foods
Palomar
Blvd 16
Craft
Hyatt Regency Century Plaza
Osteria Latini
Palmeri Ristorante
Danube
Shaherzad
Katsuya
Pecorino
Takao
La Cachette
Pizzicotto
Asakuma
Enzo & Angela
CENTURY CITY
Vicenti Ristorante
Hamasaku
Baran
WEST LOS ANGELES
Il Grano
Nanbankan
Wakasan
Literati II
Nook Bistro
Javan
RANCHO PARK GOLF CLUB
Zu Robata
Bar Hayama
Monte Alban
Mizu 212°
Hide Sushi
RANCHO PARK
Sushi Sasabune
Darya
Orris
Torafuku
2117
Kiriko
La Serenata Gourmet
Il Moro
Mori Sushi
Asian-Ya Soy Boy
SANTA MONICA BAY AREA
Bombay Café
Tlapazola Grill
Hiko Sushi
Guelaguetza
PALMS
Sushi Zo
Wilson
Beacon
CULVER CITY
Fraîche
K-Zo
Akasha
Ford's Filling Station
SONY STUDIOS
Culver City

Akasha

American XX

A4

9543 Culver Blvd. (at Watseka Ave.), Culver City

Phone: 310-845-1700 — Mon – Fri lunch & dinner
Web: www.akasharestaurant.com — Sat dinner only
Prices: $$

American, that is, with strong international influences, particularly Asian, Indian, and Italian, and a commitment to sustainable agriculture, organic ingredients, and natural products. Servers wear organic cotton, and the airy, contemporary dining room was renovated with recycled materials.

A Green philosophy, however, doesn't inhibit the flavors from the kitchen or the adjoining bakery. A creamy hummus of canellini beans, flavored with cumin and topped with minced parsley and olives dripping in oil, comes with a flat pizza-like cracker bread topped with sweet caramelized onions. You can imagine the earthy taste of the pan-fried black lentil and bean burger, served on a hearty whole wheat roll with sautéed onions and house made onion rings.

Asakuma

Japanese XX

A2

11701 Wilshire Blvd. (at Barrington Ave.)

Phone: 310-826-0013 — Lunch & dinner daily
Web: www.asakuma.com
Prices: $$

Large portions of flavorful, high-quality Japanese food at good prices draw a capacity lunch crowd of local business people to the dining rooms and long sushi bar at this location, one of several. Lunch and dinner combination specials are tasty and hearty, and the exposed wood of traditional Japanese framing, and a muted color scheme of beige and black carpet, black banquettes, beige table linens, and grey wallpaper create a calming environment.

Deft touches enhance home-style traditional dishes here. A bowl of nutty, salty, mild miso soup is additionally flavored with strips of fried tofu skin, scallions, seaweed, and silken tofu cubes. Flaky bite-sized pieces of sweet mirin and miso-marinated black cod are served over steaming sticky rice.

Asian-Ya Soy Boy

Korean

B3

11660 Gateway Blvd. (at Barrington Ave.)

Phone: 310-312-3861 Thu – Tue lunch & dinner
Web: N/A
Prices:

The menu is not extensive and the décor won't win awards, but this no-frills newcomer in a strip mall offers deliciously flavorful dishes at very good prices.

You'll be served an assortment of *banchan* after ordering, perhaps some tangy spiced cabbage or daikon kimchi, or a salad of cucumber and seaweed. Beef *bulgogi* is served sizzling; the thin strips of meat wonderfully full of sweet-garlic-soy flavor, accented by scallions and caramelized onions. *Soon tofu,* a traditional spicy Korean soup with tofu, beef, and seafood easily makes a satisfying entrée. It's traditional for the server to crack a raw egg on the surface of the hot broth, which is flavored with garlic, soy, onion, and lots of chili oil.

Lunchtime combination meals are a great value.

Baran

Persian 

B2

1916 Westwood Blvd. (at Missouri Ave.)

Phone: 310-475-4500 Lunch & dinner daily
Web: www.baranrestaurant.com(coming soon)
Prices:

Fine Persian dining in one of the world's largest expatriate communities is not as common as you'd expect. That's a key reason why this relative newcomer was quickly noted for its classic dishes mixing foreign flavors in interesting ways.

Baran's food is pleasantly mild, not overly spiced. The notion of a salad of diced raw cucumber, white onion and tomato, accented with chopped fresh mint and parsley, surprises with its refreshing crunchiness. What looks familiar, like a grilled chicken kabob, tastes exotic, flavored with onion, parsley, and saffron. The marvelous sweet-tart taste of cherry rice (tender basmati cooked with tangy pitted cherries, rendering it pale violet in color) probably can't be done justice even in Farsi.

Bar Hayama

B2-3 **Japanese** XX

1803 Sawtelle Blvd. (at Nebraska Ave.)

Phone: 310-235-2000 — Mon – Fri lunch & dinner
Web: www.bar-hayama.com — Sat – Sun dinner only
Prices: $$$

This new name on Sawtelle Avenue's restaurant row offers traditional sushi, fusion plates, a selection of macrobiotic offerings, and a stellar sake list. The setting is lovely: a corner cottage trimmed with dark wood beams, and a front courtyard behind a high wood fence and bamboo plants, with an eating bar embracing a fire pit. Inside, a 12-seat sushi bar and dining room are found.

Freshness and presentation rule here in dishes like bonito sashimi (*katsuo*) served with a salty-citrus ponzu sauce, garnished with daikon ribbons, shaved cucumber, and a fragrant *shiso* leaf. Creamy soft scallops top warm sushi rice drizzled with a sweet soy glaze. *Maguro* (tuna sushi) is finished with a glaze of honey and mustard for an interesting twist.

Beacon

Asian

3280 Helms Ave. (at Washington Blvd.), Culver City

Phone: 310-838-7500 — Tue – Sat lunch & dinner
Web: www.beacon-la.com — Sun dinner only
Prices: $$ — Mon lunch only

High ceilings and tall windows give a loft feel to the former Beacon Laundry, a tenant of the renovated 1930s Helms Bakery complex. There's a sushi bar and an umbrella-shaded patio.

A range of small plates encourages sharing dishes like skewered chicken and pork, spring rolls, and crispy fried oysters. A sugar snap pea salad mixes radish, goat cheese, and cashews in a delicate *ume-shiso* vinaigrette. Come dinner, large-plate offerings include miso-braised shortribs and grilled chicken with a marinated green papaya salad. A *bento* box lunch in a lacquered container, and a mid-week prix-fixe menu, offer a good sampling of the tastes and textures coming out of the display kitchen here.

Blvd 16

Contemporary XX

10740 Wilshire Blvd. (at Selby Ave.)

Phone: 310-474-7765 Lunch & dinner daily
Web: www.hotelpalomar-lawestwood.com
Prices: $$$

It may be in the Hotel Palomar (*see hotel listing*), but Blvd 16 has the potential to become a stand-alone dining destination. This welcome newcomer to the Westwood area offers an inspired contemporary American menu, using local ingredients in thoughtfully composed savory courses. A short rib *raviolo* with fennel marmalade and lemongrass emulsion shows creativity. Tender Brandt Farm's skirt steak sided with merlot-soaked cherries, celery root dumplings, and Point Reyes blue cheese is full of flavor.

The dining room is soothing with its repeating wood surfaces, warm brown fabrics, and monochromatic color scheme, enhanced by colorful canvases. An informal alternative, the front lounge caters to a mix of hotel guests and the local business crowd.

Bombay Café

Indian 

B3

12021 W. Pico Blvd. (at Bundy Dr.)

Phone: 310-473-3388 Lunch & dinner daily
Web: www.bombaycafe-la.com
Prices: $$

With handmade naan, a hearty selection of appetizers, Indian beverages, and daily specials, the menu here hovers above typical Indian fare. The list of starters includes exotica like a salad of diced cucumber, tomato, and red onion; and *sev puri*, handmade crackers topped with smoky tomato chutney and beads of fried chickpea-flour batter. Pungently spiced lamb, stewed with sautéed onion slices, is cooled with a cucumber and yogurt *raita*. Memorably lush desserts encompass almond-flour *badaam* cake soaked in citrus-scented milk and served in a pool of spiced caramel.

In the skylit yellow room, rattan chairs, royal-blue wainscoting, and a mirrored wood-and-brass bar evoke the Raj. Foliage shades the front windows, buffering the rush of traffic.

Brentwood Restaurant & Lounge

A2 — American XX

148 S. Barrington Ave. (at Sunset Blvd.)

Phone: 310-476-3511 — Dinner daily
Web: www.brentwoodrestaurant.com
Prices: $$$

Typically busy, with a bar catering to a young upscale crowd and a dining-room clientele spanning many generations, Brentwood's unassuming exterior belies its popularity and its good food.

American fare here goes multicultural, allowing tender yellow corn tortillas to be served open-face with slices of roasted Maple Leaf duck breast and drizzled with a pomegranate reduction, minced white onion, and sprigs of cilantro. Almost as American as apple pie are the warm doughnuts with vanilla pastry cream and dark-chocolate dipping sauce.

The folks who frequent this hangout often congregate around the lively bar area. Know that the noise level can make conversation difficult, and a pen light could make you popular in the dimly lit dining room.

Craft

C2 — Contemporary XXX

10100 Constellation Blvd. (at Ave. of the Stars)

Phone: 310-279-4180 — Mon – Fri lunch & dinner
Web: www.craftrestaurant.com — Sat – Sun dinner only
Prices: $$$$

This 300-seat extravaganza is the local entertainment industry's newest place to be seen. The impressive modernist design bathes the stylish crowd in a naturally neutral palette, allowing flattering light in through its soaring windows. A glass wine cellar sections off private dining areas and an 80-seat patio terrace offers dining alfresco.

Craft cooks with superbly fresh and well-sourced ingredients displaying ambition (not always successfully) in its artisinal, seasonally-influenced menu. Mushrooms, always a strength at Craft, are simply roasted or braised, depending on the variety, accented with a touch of garlic butter and a bit of salt. Braised black chicken gains smokiness from fantastic quality bacon with a little help from seasonal vegetables.

Danube

Bulgarian

B2

1303 Westwood Blvd. (at Wellworth Ave.)

Phone: 310-473-2414 Lunch & dinner daily
Web: N/A
Prices:

In a storefront space off Wilshire Boulevard, Danube's décor is high émigré, with prints of traffic on the Danube, elbow-to-elbow tables draped in humble fabric, and cushioned wood chairs. There's a familial air here, with the staff chatting in Bulgarian and homeland music videos blaring from an overhead flat screen (a nod to expatriate regulars).

They must feel at home to find perfectly made *dolmas* flavored with olive oil and lemon, sautéed onion, and fresh herbs. To be able to dine on spicy *kufta* (falafel-sized patties of seared ground beef with garlic, white onion, and red-chile flakes) served with white rice saturated with salted butter, and finsh with a chocolate-layered *garash* cake, must make even the most stoic expat sigh.

Darya

Persian

A3

12130 Santa Monica Blvd. (at Bundy Dr.)

Phone: 310-442-9000 Lunch & dinner daily
Web: www.daryarestaurant.com
Prices: $$

Though it may seem gaudy to some, Darya's grand dining room, with its columns, crystal chandeliers, and gilded mirrors is opulent in a style more associated with days gone by in a cherished Persian homeland.

Richly flavored, authentic, and nostalgic dishes please patrons from West Los Angeles' large Persian community. Charbroiled on a skewer, a marinated chicken breast takes on a bright yellow hue from turmeric and saffron. Imagine it served with *albolo polo*, basmati rice cooked with stewed black cherries and cherry juice. Baklava, saturated in sweet floral rosewater syrup, is irresistibly delicious.

Located off busy Santa Monica Boulevard in a commercial strip, Darya is more easily accessed from the parking lot behind the restaurant.

Westside

Divino

Italian XX

A2

11714 Barrington Ct. (bet. Barrington & Sunset Aves.)

Phone: 310-472-0886 Lunch & dinner daily
Web: N/A
Prices: $$$

Nestled in Brentwood Village, Divino divides its space between a spacious, airy dining room and a little outdoor terrace. Though the latter overlooks the parking lot, flower boxes and pots of flowering plants perk up the ambience.

Redolent with fresh high-quality ingredients, savory pastas, thin-crust pizzas, and chicken dishes—especially the *pollo Portofino* (a boneless breast of chicken served with a sauce made with tomatoes, capers, and olives)—headline here. Don't ignore the daily specials, which complement the classics with the likes of seared salmon picatta served in a butter sauce made tangy by the addition of lemon juice and capers.

Service is friendly, informal, and efficient; and Divino regulars are on a first-name basis with the staff.

Enzo & Angela

Italian XX

A2

11701 Wilshire Blvd. (at Barrington Ave.)

Phone: 310-477-3880 Mon – Fri lunch & dinner
Web: www.enzoandangela.com Sat – Sun dinner only
Prices: $$

The scarcity of interesting space in Los Angeles leaves many restaurateurs with site choices that don't measure up to their visions. Here again is a jewel tucked into a strip mall, just off Wilshire Boulevard. Inside, however, the bright dining room recalls a beachfront Adriatic hotel, in which white linens and seascape paintings buffer the tension of traffic and commerce. Excellent home-style dishes banish it altogether.

A house minestrone filled with al dente vegetables relies on the subtle taste of its ingredients. Artistic selections like *spigola con checca* (flaky Mediterranean sea bass layered with fresh ripe red tomatoes and herbs, and doused with lemon juice, white wine, and capers) open a visceral connection to the Old Country.

Ford's Filling Station

Gastropub

9531 Culver Blvd. (at Washington Blvd.), Culver City

Phone: 310-202-1470 — Lunch & dinner daily
Web: www.fordsfillingstation.net
Prices: $$

Initial buzz concerned the chef, actor Harrison Ford's son Benjamin. But his skills quickly won over the neighborhood the old-fashioned way, interpreting pub classics using prime seasonal ingredients. The beam and plank ceiling, red brick, wood floors, rustic furnishings, and open kitchen add a homey, casual warmth.

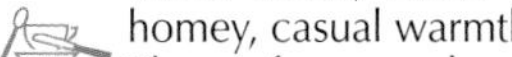

There's fancy, such as a salad of curried, earthy black lentils on a bed of fresh frisée sprinkled with roasted pecans, creamy goat cheese, halved cherry tomatoes, and a bit of olive oil and vinegar. There's simple: fish n' chips using moist flaky fingers of battered, deep-fried Atlantic cod served with tangy pickled carrots and thick potato wedges. A house burger is a long-running hit. On nice days the outdoor patio is a delight.

Fraîche

Mediterranean

9411 Culver Blvd. (bet. Cardiff Ave. & Main St.), Culver City

Phone: 310-839-6800 — Tue – Fri lunch & dinner
Web: www.fraicherestaurantla.com — Sat – Sun dinner only
Prices: $$

On an appealing stretch of Culver Boulevard's burgeoning gourmet row, this upscale house serves excellent food at excellent prices. A talented open kitchen, wood floors, cushioned comfort, and a spacious sidewalk patio elegantly tented in cooler months evoke a bistro atmosphere.

During any month you're likely to find the house filled with stylish types, many drawn from nearby studios. It is no wonder when you have choices like house-cured *branzino*, a fennel-spiced European sea bass in a rich sauce gribiche of hard-boiled eggs, capers, shallots, vinegar, and fresh herbs; or short rib ravioli, the braised beef cooked in red wine and shredded to fill perfectly round envelopes of fork-tender pasta, finished in a bit of rosemary-infused butter.

Guelaguetza

Mexican

11127 Palms Blvd. (at Sepulveda Blvd.)

Phone: 310-837-1153 — Lunch & dinner daily
Web: N/A
Prices:

Situated in a Palms district shopping center, this modest room is filled with locals seated at plastic-covered tables as heat blasts from the kitchen in a symphony of hot air, overhead TV, and Mexican music. But all find solace in the traditional Oaxacan cooking, specifically the moles, made with uncompromising authenticity.

First, treat yourself to tortilla chips drizzled with red mole *Coloradito*. Next, partake in a thick, fragrant green mole smothering stewed chicken breasts, green beans, potato, and *chayote*. Accompany your feast with a *Horchata con Tuna y Nuez;* the popular house version of this sweet rice beverage is garnished with cantaloupe slivers, chopped walnuts, and purée of cactus fruit. And you thought Mexican food holds no more surprises.

Hamasaku

Japanese

11043 Santa Monica Blvd. (at S. Bentley Ave.)

Phone: 310-479-7636 — Mon – Fri lunch & dinner
Web: www.hamasakula.com — Sat dinner only
Prices: $$$

Despite the friendly, helpful staff at this pricey celebrity hot spot in a strip mall, the busy buzz makes some patrons feel rushed. That's new. What hasn't changed is the chef's imaginative use of unusual ingredients to produce contemporary sushi rolls with inspired flavor combinations.

So you'll see thick slices of fresh albacore atop crispy-seared warm caramelized rice, drizzled with a salty-tangy ponzu sauce and garnished with minced jalapeño. Or the Intuition roll of soy paper wrapped around baked crab and raw spicy tuna, and topped with a sprinkle of velvety thick, smoky-sweet eel sauce and creamy chili-aïoli. The Luca roll (some are named for patrons) wraps baked lobster in sticky rice and mild soy paper for the eel sauce treatment.

Hide Sushi

Japanese

B3

2040 Sawtelle Blvd. (bet. La Grange & Mississippi Aves.)

Phone: 310-477-7242 Tue – Sun lunch & dinner
Web: N/A
Prices:

Couched amid authentic Japanese grocery and hardware stores, gift and magazine shops, nurseries, and restaurants, this modestly decorated sushi and sashimi restaurant stands out above the competition on this stretch of Sawtelle Boulevard for pairing high-quality ingredients with notably low prices.
Cooked items are limited here. The memorable fare flows from the skill behind the ten-seat sushi bar. So if you stick with the raw-fish dishes, you won't be disappointed. Service is efficient, if a bit frantic; the restaurant always seems to be packed with local regulars who wait patiently for a seat.
Although Hide Sushi takes cash only, there's an ATM inside, just in case you forget. Parking is in the back lot, accessible through a narrow alley.

Hiko Sushi

Japanese 

C3

11275 National Blvd. (at Sawtelle Blvd.)

Phone: 310-473-7688 Mon – Fri lunch & dinner
Web: N/A
Prices: **$$**

Before you park, be aware of a few rules at Hiko Sushi. Of course, cell phones are forbidden. Not surprisingly, the sushi bar is for omakase only. Otherwise, sit at a table, but there's a four-item minimum.
If you're still interested, the pay-off is exceptionally fresh sushi, wonderfully accented by whatever ingredients strike the chef's fancy, which you are best to follow. If you go with an omakase, you may find before you a mound of diced baby tuna, surrounded by a pool of tangy-salty ponzu, enhanced by a sprinkling of toasted sesame seeds. Next might be red snapper sashimi or halibut drizzled with a citrus ponzu. A decadent finish is the hand roll of finely shredded lobster mixed with creamy, sweet aioli enveloped in perfectly-toasted nori.

Il Grano

B2 Italian XX

11359 Santa Monica Blvd. (bet. Corinth & Purdue Aves.)

Phone: 310-477-7886 Mon – Fri lunch & dinner
Web: N/A Sat dinner only
Prices: $$$

Affable Chef/owner Sal Marino's locally trend-setting leap into the world of *crudo*, fish served raw like sashimi but seasoned with, say, virgin olive oil or a daikon and Meyer lemon garnish, won him an enduring following in Westwood.

His modern and casually elegant cooking features fresh organic seafood prepared with heart-healthy technique and presented in a nearly all-white room with banquettes of butter-hued leather. Marino's innovative boldness produces occasional lapses. But when it works it produces memorable dishes like a lasagna with tomato coulis, mozzarella, chopped mushroom, ricotta cheese, and spinach; or a sautéed cod served with a hint of lemon and parsley in a creamy corn purée. A well-chosen list offers Italian wines by the glass.

Il Moro

B3 Italian XX

11400 W. Olympic Blvd. (at Purdue Ave.)

Phone: 310-575-3530 Mon – Fri lunch & dinner
Web: www.ilmoro.com Sat – Sun dinner only
Prices: $$$

Enter this highrise from a side street and walk through a modern bar/lounge to find a spacious, soaring room, beautifully appointed with floor-to-ceiling windows. Outdoor tables set in a palm-studded garden with a trickling stream enhance the restaurant's commercial setting.

Chef Davide Ghizzoni, who hails from Northern Italy, presided over Il Moro's debut in 1994, drawing inspiration from his native region. So, thin slices of shaved artichoke hearts on a bed of arugula are tossed in lemon juice and fruity olive oil, and capped with shaved aged parmesan. Roasted wild boar marries well with wide, flat ribbons of pappardelle pasta and a rich, tomato ragù flavored with garlic, onion, and salty pecorino cheese. This is how it's done in the Emilia Romagna.

Javan

Persian XX

B2

11500 Santa Monica Blvd. (at Butler Ave.)

Phone: 310-207-5555 Lunch & dinner daily
Web: www.javanrestaurant.com
Prices: ₴₴

Prompt and attentive service, fresh quality ingredients, pride in Persian cuisine and a mastery of its techniques number among the strong points of this warmly lit dining room, which looks out on a busy commercial neighborhood. Naturally, you'll find many patrons from the local Persian community here, but the flavorful dishes have won it a wider audience.

Chicken *koobideh*, ground and seasoned with saffron and other spices, roasted on skewers over an open fire, then served with steamed basmati rice and a roasted tomato, is a close cousin to other meat dishes, particularly lamb and beef. Stews such as *fesenjun* (sautéed walnuts cooked in pomegranate sauce and mixed with chicken) and other specials are offered only on specific days of the week.

Katsuya

Japanese XX

A2

11777 San Vicente Blvd. (bet. Gorham & Montana Aves.)

Phone: 310-207-8744 Mon – Fri lunch & dinner
Web: www.sbeent.com/katsuya Sat – Sun dinner only
Prices: $$

The delicious food here is artistically presented amid designer Philippe Starck's pale wood surfaces, white furnishings, and neutral colors, which set the cool of this see-and-be-seen "it-list" watering hole.

A special "liquid" kitchen features drinks made with fresh-squeezed fruit and vegetable juices. The dining room holds a *robata* grill, a third kitchen prepares sushi, a fourth—hot dishes. From these come crowd-pleasers like seared tuna, its center red and cool; the soy paper and cucumber-wrapped Katsuya roll of tuna, salmon, eel, and avocado; and a miso-mirin glazed black cod roasted in a *hoba* leaf. To all this, a recurring motif of a woman's lush red lips gives a kiss of approval.

A namesake *sans robata* buzzes at *6300 Hollywood Boulevard.*

Kiriko

Japanese

B3

11301 W. Olympic Blvd. (at Sawtelle Ave.)

Phone: 310-478-7769 — Tue – Fri lunch & dinner
Web: www.kirikosushi.com — Sat – Sun dinner only
Prices: $$

The omakase (chef's choice) selections and daily specials are the best bets at this homespun little place, where the décor is rustic. Superbly fresh ingredients are the trump cards here, though some dishes may not evidence what the skilled chefs are capable of.

When they're on, there are pleasures like a generously-sized block of thick, custard-style homemade tofu, dense and nutty, in a small pool of sweet soy, and garnished with dried smoky bonito flakes and toasted sesame seeds. A fresh Dungeness crab spring roll is wrapped Vietnamese-style in white rice dough and a pungent *shiso* leaf. Surprises run through dishes like a grilled house-smoked wild King salmon collar, a tasty rival to the standard filet cut.

There is street and validated parking.

K-Zo

Japanese

A4

9240 Culver Blvd. (at Venice Blvd.), Culver City

Phone: 310-202-8890 — Mon – Fri lunch & dinner
Web: www.k-zo.com — Sat dinner only
Prices: $$

Traditional and contemporary sushi, sashimi, and hot food courses, fresh, flavorful, and delicious, are expertly prepared and artistically presented by Chef/owner Keizo Ishiba. The industrial space's concrete floor and columns are warmed by touches like bud vases. There is a sake bar in front, a sushi bar in the back, and outdoor tables on a sidewalk patio.

The cuisine reflects Ishiba's training in Japan and France. Hence, the refinement of dishes like *Kinpira Gobo*, a cold salad of sautéed burdock and carrots accented with soy sauce and sesame oil; or a salmon collar broiled until caramelized and served with a small dipping sauce bowl of salty-citrus ponzu sauce. Daily specials add to the choice of specialty rolls, sushi, sashimi, and hot plates.

La Cachette

French

10506 Little Santa Monica Blvd. (at Thayer Ave.)

Phone: 310-470-4992 — Mon – Fri lunch & dinner
Web: www.lacachetterestaurant.com — Sat dinner only
Prices: $$$$

This hideaway of bright Gallic off-whites, beiges, and yellows, with a back-alley entrance, hosts a midday crowd of Hollywood deal-makers, validated by the serious food, old-world elegance, and made-to-order desserts like a thin crispy cinnamon tart or a chocolate soufflé.

Chef Jean-Francois Meteigner weaves Californian touches through his dishes, as in a sautéed venison chop with a dried cocoa bean crunch and cabernet game sauce, served with celery root purée, blueberry jam, and sautéed polenta. It works the other way, too, as in a *très* American grilled Black Angus New York steak topped with melted blue and goat cheeses in a sauce of brandy and crushed peppers. Desserts include a crème brulée trio of chocolate, vanilla, and coffee custards.

La Serenata Gourmet

Mexican 

10924 W. Pico Blvd. (at Kelton Ave.)

Phone: 310-441-9667 — Lunch & dinner daily
Web: www.laserenataonline.com
Prices:

Fresh, well-prepared, and flavorful food is the draw here. Service is adequate, the busy streetside location unromantic. The front room is essentially a bar with high-top tables suited for dining.

The menu is straightforward. Of course there are corn tortilla chips, served here with a sprinkle of shredded cheese and a spicy, smoky red chile salsa. Appetizers can be hearty, as are the green corn tamales studded with kernels of sweet corn flavored with cinnamon—the sweetness muted by lime crema (lime-infused sour cream). There is nothing Americanized about dishes like *chorizo sopes*, the griddled circular cakes of masa crispy-browned yet tender inside, cradling pinto beans, browned bits of spiced chorizo, shredded lettuce, and tomatillo salsa.

Literati II

A2 — Californian XX

12081 Wilshire Blvd. (at Bundy Dr.)

Phone: 310-479-3400 — Lunch & dinner daily
Web: www.literati2.com
Prices: **$$**

Fresh, superior ingredients prepared without complication and presented in a room of neutral walls, and on a tented patio, make this a popular respite from the urban rush. Attentive service starts with touches like artisan breads with an eggplant and roasted bell pepper tapanade. The frequently changing menu draws inspiration from Mediterranean technique and local farmers' markets. This produces unusual twists on the familiar, like a pale green gazpacho with grilled shrimp placed around a scoop of creamy *burrata*, the flavors of smoke and cheese boosted by fresh parsley. Tender flakes of sand dabs fried in a thin crispy batter are livened up with parsley and lemon, and tartar sauce made tangy with finely diced cornichon and pickled red onion.

Mizu 212°

B3 — Japanese X

2000 Sawtelle Blvd. (at La Grange Ave.)

Phone: 310-478-8979 — Lunch & dinner daily
Web: www.mizu212degrees.com
Prices: **$$**

Although guests are required to cook their own meals here, this Sawtelle establishment rivals the best locations in Little Tokyo. The reason? A wonderfully fresh and great variety of vegetables and a choice of vegetarian, chicken, beef, pork, seafood, and shrimp versions of the do-it-yourself meal called shabu shabu.

A platter heaped with ingredients such as tofu, mushrooms, cabbage, fish balls, Kabocha squash, and udon noodles is presented along with a platter of finely sliced meats. A large pot of kombu-scented water is placed on your table and heated to 212 degrees. Diners cook both meat and vegetables in the hot broth. Bowls of ponzu sauce and peanut-sesame sauce are provided for dipping. This may be the best meal you ever made at a restaurant.

Monte Alban

A3 Mexican

11927 Santa Monica Blvd. (at Brockton Ave.)

Phone: 310-444-7736 Lunch & dinner daily
Web: N/A
Prices: ⓈⓈ

Located in a strip mall off Santa Monica Boulevard, Monte Alban nestles between several small ethnic eateries and a Mexican grocery store. Saltillo tiles, Oaxacan textiles, murals of the Mexican countryside, and a blue-sky ceiling with painted clouds infuse the two dining rooms with a beguiling South of the Border feel.

The owners' loyalty to Oaxacan specialties, using traditional ingredients, is such that their pungent flavors are not tempered for the American palate. Thus, a delicious *clayuda con cesina* translates as a thin, crispy, handmade corn tortilla that owes its flavor of smoky corn to slight charring. The tortilla is spread with smooth black-bean purée and topped with strips of spicy pork leg that have been marinated in red chile paste.

Nanbankan

B2 Japanese

11330 Santa Monica Blvd. (at Corinth Ave.)

Phone: 310-478-1591 Dinner daily
Web: N/A
Prices: ⓈⓈ

The mix of raw fish and cooked hot food at this Westside institution, whose plain façade is easily missed, satisfies almost everyone. The chatty manner of the chefs who grill skewered food at the *robata* grill, and roll and cut sushi and sashimi belie their considerable skills and pride in carefully preparing each course.

In addition to daily specials, there are rolls galore (as in spicy tuna pumped up with sesame oil and hot chili and wrapped with radish, bean sprouts, carrot, and cucumber). The *robata* grill turns out skewers of eggplant or shiitake mushrooms, chicken, or beef. To watch the chefs work close-up is most rewarding—especially when you see something unfamiliar that looks utterly delicious.

There's street parking, as well as a small rear lot.

Mori Sushi ✿

Japanese

B3

11500 W. Pico Blvd. (at Gateway Blvd.)

Phone: 310-479-3939
Web: www.morisushi.org
Prices: $$$

Mon – Fri lunch & dinner
Sat dinner only

There is but one thing you are expected to concentrate on at Mori Sushi—Chef Morihiro Onodera's wildly fresh, expertly prepared sushi. Everything else about this restaurant is skillfully designed to take a backseat to the food—from the professional but never overbearing staff, to the simple, white-washed dining room, dressed in unsheathed wood tables and big, sun-streaming windows.

Japanese food arrives in many divine forms here—in small plates à la carte, or checked off of a list with a pencil—but none quite so indulgent as the wonderful omakase, which might include a Santa Barbara prawn, split whole and lightly grilled with intact roe and a pinch of salt; or octopus sashimi, fresh off a plane from Japan. If it's available, don't miss the silky abalone, delicately battered in tempura, and served with seaweed salt, ginko nuts, and a shake of tempura shishito pepper.

Appetizers

- Mori's Homemade Tofu with Mori's Blend Soy Sauce and Fresh Wasabi
- Nasu Dengaku, Eggplant with two types of Miso
- Osuimono, Traditional Clear Soup

Entrées

- Sushi
- Abalone Tempura with Lemon and various Sea Salts
- Yumegokochi Rice exclusively cultivated for Mori Sushi

Desserts

- Yokan, Homemade Jelly Cake in Red Bean or Persimmon
- Homemade Ice Cream in Sesame or Pumpkin
- Seasonal Fresh Japanese Totti Pear or White Peach

Napa Valley Grille

Californian XX

B2

1100 Glendon Ave. (at Lindbrook Dr.)

Phone: 310-824-3322 Lunch & dinner daily
Web: www.napavalleygrille.com
Prices: $$$

California's northern and southern halves are so distinct there's always talk of dividing the Golden State in two. No need. This grill brings a taste of the northern Wine Country to Westwood with its fresh California produce and Napa wines. Even the outdoor patio makes a heroic effort to emulate the bucolic gardens found at Napa's most hospitable wineries.
Italians played an important role in the Wine Country's development, and the menu pays them homage. So, heirloom tomato bruschetta means grilled sourdough with minced fresh garlic, basil, and olive oil; while artichoke ravioli topped with herbed tomato sauce, shredded parmesan, and kalamata olives crosses the Bear Flag with the *Tricolore*.
There's even a late-hour bar menu for night owls.

Native Foods

Vegan X

B2

1110 1/2 Gayley Ave. (at Lindbrook Dr.)

Phone: 310-209-1055 Lunch & dinner daily
Web: www.nativefoods.com
Prices: 

The innovative food, wholesome and flavorful, is the point in this hole-in-the-wall, whose health-conscious patrons amble in mainly from the nearby UCLA campus. Vegetable and fruit bins clutter the walkway downstairs, barring access to wheelchairs. A steep stairway leads to a small balcony seating area.
Chalkboards proclaim house manifestos such as "Save the Earth" and "Eat Different." Easy to do the second here. A hearty cup of crumbled soy meat chili, flavored with onion, tomato, peppers, spices, and garlic, is topped with scallions and red bell peppers. A burger of blackened soy tempeh is grilled with spices and paired with a creamy chipotle sauce to supplement the subtle flavor of the meat-like soy.

Nook Bistro

Contemporary 

11628 Santa Monica Blvd. (at Barry Ave.)

Phone: 310-207-5160 — Mon – Fri lunch & dinner
Web: www.nookbistro.com — Sat dinner only
Prices: $$

Aptly named, tucked in a strip mall's corner, this little gem offers skillfully prepared dishes featuring fresh ingredients and unusual flavor combinations at prices far below LA standards. Its stylish interior has a New York loft look, with polished concrete floors, green accent walls, and exposed joists and ductwork. Friendly, knowledgeable black-clad servers are quick to offer suggestions.

Among them might be Kurobuta pork belly, crispy and caramelized on the thick fatty side, smoky and tender on the meatier, the rich meat balanced by a tangy, pungent, herb-accented green chile salsa; or a roasted Arctic char on a bed of smooth, buttery sweet potato purée. You can enjoy the menu at home as well, for Nook does a booming take-away business.

Orris

2006 Sawtelle Blvd. (at La Grange Ave.)

Phone: 310-268-2212 — Tue – Sun dinner only
Web: www.orrisrestaurant.com
Prices: $$

Clearly the focal point in this fun, hip dining room is the long exhibition kitchen, source of the "world cuisine" tapas on the constantly changing menu. The décor is sleek and simple with standard flatware and bright placemats injecting blasts of vivid color. Orchids at the bar and votive candles here and there add a soft elegance.

Chef Hideo Yamashiro's view is that the best cuisine is found collectively at all points of the compass. So don't try to trace the origin of red snapper carpaccio—which here is lightly browned, accented with olive oil, a bit of ginger, and a bit of lime zest. Halibut tempura sounds Japanese, but in a pool of chunky pomodoro sauce, seasoned with fresh, woodsy rosemary and spicy oregano, all bets are off.

Osteria Latini

Italian XX

A2

11712 San Vicente Blvd. (at Barrington Ave.)

Phone: 310-826-9222 — Mon – Fri lunch & dinner
Web: www.osterialatini.com — Sat – Sun dinner only
Prices: $$

Come evening, Chef/owner Paolo Pasio works the tables, greeting regulars and pitching specials like suckling pig, osso buco, and calamari stuffed with lump crabmeat. His first-name familiarity creates a convivial air, as does the dining room, decorated with greenery, rosewood floors, and wine-storage racks that double as partitions.

Born in Trieste, Pasio worked his way to the City of Angels, where he now oversees the skilled crew and top-flight ingredients that rule this kitchen. You taste his talent in a creamy roasted mushroom soup made without dairy; or a bowl of al dente *bombolotti* pasta tossed in an herbed tomato sauce and deliciously paired with roasted chicken breast. The wine list features a wide-ranging collection of Italian labels.

Palmeri Ristorante

Italian XX

A2

11650 San Vicente Blvd. (at Bringham Ave.)

Phone: 310-442-8446 — Mon – Sat lunch & dinner
Web: N/A — Sun dinner only
Prices: $$$

A pleasant place in Brentwood, with an open kitchen, counter seating, a comfy sidewalk terrace, and rear parking. The luminous dining room is more West L.A. chi-chi than Old Country, but the friendly, courteous waitstaff includes natives of Italy and Macedonia well-versed in food and wine, who draw knowledgeably from an exposed cellar of well-selected vintages.

The menu hews to traditional fare, things like a salad of *buratta* cheese wrapped in prociutto over a bed of arugula drizzled with basil oil; or a lasagna Bolognese in its namesake sauce, cloaked in melting mozzarella with a thin, fresh house-made pasta. The standard menu is supplemented by daily specials. The desserts are classical, well suited to the house's dark and creamy espresso.

Pecorino

Italian XX

A2

11604 San Vicente Blvd. (bet. Bringham & Mayfield Aves.)

Phone: 310-571-3800 — Mon – Fri lunch & dinner
Web: www.pecorinorestaurant.com — Sat – Sun dinner only
Prices: $$$

Vines climb over the façade of this discreet yet elegant Italian spot on Brentwood's restaurant row—San Vicente Boulevard. In the dining room, brick walls, exposed wood beams, wooden wine-storage racks, and wrought-iron fixtures with candle-shaped lights boost the rustic European vibe.

Daily specials, such as fried zucchini blossoms stuffed with ricotta cheese, reflect the seasonal harvest; while the signature penne pecorino is tossed with house-made tomato sauce. Main courses run the gamut from veal Milanese to oven-roasted branzino.

Before they leave the open kitchen, each plate is checked by one of the three partners before it is presented to the guest. Servers, many of whom are Italian, glow with obvious pride as they deliver the dishes to the table.

Pizzicotto

Italian X

A2

11758 San Vicente Blvd. (at Barrington Ave.)

Phone: 310-442-7188 — Mon – Sat lunch & dinner
Web: N/A — Sun dinner only
Prices: $$

Known primarily for traditional pizza, this self-described "Italian market bistro" promotes that feel with its display of Italian food products, and the braids of garlic and clusters of dried chile peppers that hang over the service counter.

The open kitchen can spin a mean pizza, but also start you out with little joys like an aged prosciutto di Parma, topped with earthy truffled honey. Sprinkle cantaloupe melon balls, fresh fig quarters, and a chiffonade of fresh basil on this and you sense the repertoire here goes well beyond pies. Even so, the pizzas are terrific—with thin crusts and crispy edges, finely seasoned sauces, fresh everything and lots of it.

For dessert, the likes of a lusciously moist lemon pine-nut cake hits the sweet spot.

Restaurant at the Getty Center

Californian XXX

A1

1200 Getty Center Dr. (off Sepulveda Blvd.)

Phone: 310-440-6810 — Tue – Thu, Sun lunch only
Web: www.getty.edu — Fri – Sat lunch & dinner
Prices: **$$$**

Perched on a hilltop overlooking Los Angeles and the Pacific Ocean, the architecturally stunning Getty Center is a must-see on any visitor's list. The experience of wandering the museum's galleries is only enhanced by a lunch or a weekend sunset dinner at the restaurant. With its lofty skylit ceilings and glass walls flooding the minimalist space with changing light, the restaurant boasts sublime views from inside or out on the terrace.

Californian cuisine encompasses a world of possibilities. You see a sampling of these on the weekly changing menu, say, in an autumn heirloom-squash salad tossed with dates, aged Jack cheese, and toasted pumpkin seeds in a brown-butter vinaigrette.

Reservations are recommended. Park in the Center's garage.

Saketini

Asian X

A2

150 S. Barrington Ave. (at S. Barrington Pl.)

Phone: 310-440-5553 — Mon – Sat lunch & dinner
Web: www.saketini.com — Sun dinner only
Prices: **$$**

This petite Brentwood favorite features Japanese sushi and Korean barbeque, with cameo appearances by other Asian cuisines. Reasonably-priced *bento* box combinations pack its few tables at lunch. Come evening, mostly locals crowd the long and narrow dining room, decorated with carved wood tables, plank floors, red and gold seat cushions, and Asian wall hangings.

Deft touches, such as adding sliced scallions, cubes of silken tofu, woodsy threads of enoki mushroom, and rich, fermented nutty yellow miso paste to miso soup, enhances the flavors of familiar dishes like a made-to-order spicy tuna roll—its fresh meat mixed with a potent red chili sauce. Reservations are recommended. There is street parking and a public lot nearby.

Shaherzad

Persian

B2

1422 Westwood Blvd. (at Wilkins Ave.)

Phone: 310-470-3242 Lunch & dinner daily
Web: N/A
Prices:

Not mere Persian cuisine, proclaims the neon outside, but "royal" Persian cuisine. That must strike a harmonious chord in the Westside's Iranian-American community, for this longtime Westwood favorite is usually thronged with Farsi speakers, many arriving arm-in-arm from nearby neighborhoods.

From the bricks of the traditional *tanour* oven come baskets of slightly charred *tanouri* flatbread, served to you promptly upon being seated. This is a traditional place that makes liberal use of cardamom, rosewater, and saffron—the last mixed with yogurt and fragrant basmati rice into casserole-style *tahchin* with a layer of tender shredded chicken in the center. Portions are large, requiring willpower to save room for dessert. If you do, the reward is a plate of delicious baklava.

Sushi Sasabune

Japanese 

A3

12400 Wilshire Blvd. (bet. Carmelina Ave. & McClellan Dr.)

Phone: 310-820-3596 Mon – Fri lunch & dinner
Web: N/A
Prices: **$$$**

Located in a bustling Wilshire business district on the ground floor of a large office building, this no-frills enterprise bows to traditional flavor combinations using fresh, premium-quality fish for its sushi, sashimi, and grilled fish dishes.

A small team of chefs work behind the big U-shaped sushi bar, rolling and chopping, fanning thin slices of raw albacore in a mixture of tangy soy sauce and rice-wine vinegar, and sprinkling them with slices of sharp scallion. Using warm sweetened sushi rice, they offer a chef's assortment, some garnished with smoked-eel sauce, others with a citrus-infused ponzu, soy, and vinegar sauce; or pickled daikon radish.

Street parking is scarce, but you can use the building's underground garage.

Sushi Zo ✿

Japanese

A4

9824 National Blvd. (at Castle Heights Ave.)

Phone: 310-842-3977
Web: N/A
Prices: $$$$

Mon – Fri lunch & dinner
Sat dinner only

MICHELIN

There is no menu presented, and the server is quick to inform you that there will be no cut rolls or Americanized sushi tonight. And just like that, you get it: this no-frills operation might look like any old strip mall sushi den, but something very exciting is brewing behind Sushi Zo's innocent facade. Namely a nightly omakase dinner guaranteed to knock the socks off of L.A.'s most discriminating sushiphiles.

Utilizing whatever ingredients are freshest, Chef Keizo Seki's menu might include a fresh, raw, Kumamoto oyster dancing in a light ponzu sauce and topped with pickled daikon; or a buttery monkfish liver with a caramelized shell. He might offer a generous mound of creamy, super-fresh uni over warm, grainy rice; sake-and-soy soaked *ikura* (salmon roe), loosely piled on a mound of nori-wrapped rice; or three tiny, raw shrimp, perfectly fresh, translucent, and sweet.

Appetizers
- Raw Kumomoto Oyster with Daikon
- Nigiri Sushi Assortment
- Konpachi Sashimi with Jalapeño and Lemon

Entrées
- Seared Monkfish Liver on Warm Rice
- Butterfish with Miso and Vinegar
- Broiled Anago

Desserts
- Yuzu Shooter

Takao

Japanese       

A2

11656 San Vicente Blvd. (at Darlington Ave.)

Phone: 310-207-8636
Web: N/A
Prices: $$

Mon – Sat lunch & dinner
Sun dinner only

What Takao's plain black tile floors and taupe walls lack in eye appeal is made up for with warm service and fresh, simple, high-quality fare. Sushi and sashimi get top billing in the small L-shaped dining room and at the sushi bar, but cooked dishes are also offered.

On weekdays, the popular business lunch might be a deluxe sushi sampler with a California roll of crab and avocado, along with raw tuna, yellowtail, white fish, salmon, prawns, and red snapper. Check the board for daily specials, featured seasonal ingredients, and the chef's latest inspirations. Chef/ owner Takao is a fixture behind the counter, overseeing the preparation of his straightforward food.

The busy street makes self-parking problematic; let a valet handle it.

Tlapazola Grill

Mexican

B3

11676 Gateway Blvd. (at Barrington Ave.)

Phone: 310-477-1577
Web: N/A
Prices: $$

Tue – Sat lunch & dinner
Sun – Mon dinner only

Uninspiring as most are, LA's strip malls offer restaurateurs a place to start, with a few free parking spaces thrown in. This grill's owners use traditional dance masks and whimsical paintings to transform their dining room into an appealing salute to their native Oaxaca.

That requires classic dishes like *carne asada* (a ribeye steak), grilled trout tacos, *barbacoa de borrego* (braised lamb), masa pancakes with smoky achiote shrimp, and a nopalitos cactus salad. Chalk up the lobster enchiladas to native inspiration, and trust the friendly waitstaff to explain the many daily specials.

If you're a tequila fan, be sure to sample the extensive collection of tequilas, either here or at the second location on Lincoln Boulevard in Marina del Rey.

Torafuku

Japanese XX

C3

10914 Pico Blvd. (bet. Veteran Ave. & Westwood Blvd.)

Phone: 310-470-0014 — Mon – Sat lunch & dinner
Web: www.torafuku-usa.com — Sun dinner only
Prices: **$$**

Delicious, authentic food accounts for Torafuku's mostly Japanese clientele, who line its large square tables and exhibition kitchen. Traditional techniques paired with authentic ingredients result in classic home-style dishes.

This is the first US outpost of a small Japanese chain known for its centuries-old *kamado* method of cooking rice, one requiring a 500-pound iron pot to be placed in a stone and earthenware oven in order to create a unique consistency and flavor profile. Torafuku's homemade tofu, served in the bamboo container it is steamed in, is silky and slightly nutty. Sushi and sashimi share the menu with various cooked dishes; and a sake list runs the gamut from honey overtones to hints of pear, melon, or apple.

2117

Fusion X

B3

2117 Sawtelle Blvd. (at Mississippi Ave.)

Phone: 310-477-1617 — Tue – Sat lunch & dinner
Web: N/A — Sun dinner only
Prices: **$$**

The European-Asian dishes here rely on good organic ingredients. The narrow dining room is decorated with large modern paintings, draped ceiling cloth, and framed wine labels. Tables are close, but attentive friendly service promotes an intimate air inside and on the pleasant tented patio. Very reasonable prix-fixe lunch specials draw a midday crowd.

Dishes are simple. A butternut squash soup is made without cream from purée thinned with vegetable stock. Fresh jumbo scallops, pan-sautéed to a golden brown sear and seasoned with salt and pepper, come with toasty-tasting crispy brown rice, steamed yellow wax beans, and florets of cauliflower and broccoli, all drizzled with a fragrant lemongrass sauce. Valet service augments limited parking.

Vincenti Ristorante

Italian XX

A2

11930 San Vicente Blvd. (at Montana Ave.)

Phone: 310-207-0127 Mon – Thu & Sat dinner only
Web: www.vincentiristorante.com Fri lunch & dinner
Prices: $$$$

Stylish Westsiders come here for dinners in the Italian family tradition. Despite the bar's convivial buzz, the place is peaceful, votive candles providing a soft light. Wood floors, leather chairs and banquettes, and suspended light fixtures are elegantly simple. A glass partition frames the display kitchen. When the wood-burning rotisserie fires up, it offers an appetizing display of roasting meat.

The chef's daily special will make good choices on your behalf. Otherwise you have to choose between alluring dishes like a house-made pappardelle cooked al dente in Bolognese-style minced meat; or perhaps a risotto with beets, lobster, calamari, and roasted bell peppers. Fine wines are available by the glass, and desserts are typically luscious.

Wakasan

Japanese 

B2

1929 Westwood Blvd. (bet. La Grange & Missouri Aves.)

Phone: 310-446-5241 Wed – Mon dinner only
Web: N/A
Prices: $$

This popular little Westwood spot has developed a loyal Japanese ex-pat following, which is always a good sign. The downside is that tiny Wakasan—with only a few places to sit—is always hopping. They're likely piling in for the *izakaya* (a type of Japanese pub that serves more substantial fare than other bars) atmosphere, and reasonably priced omakase dinners—rendered here, most nights, as a series of ten or more simple, but deliciously authentic, small plates.

Grab a seat at one of the few wooden tables, or squeeze onto the bustling communal table, and dip into plates of crunchy oyster fritters with creamy aioli; tender snow crab in sweet rice vinegar; or a piping hot egg custard, studded with shrimp, ginko nuts, and Japanese fish cake.

Wilson

International

8631 Washington Blvd. (at Sherbourne Dr.), Culver City

Phone: 310-287-2093 Mon – Sat lunch & dinner
Web: www.wilsonfoodandwine.com
Prices: $$

Behind the arresting concrete checkerboard façade of Culver City's Museum of Design Art and Architecture (MODAA), you'll discover thought-provoking exhibitions that explore the interstices where art and design meet. But that's not all. Stick around to taste the internationally inspired dishes served at Wilson on the museum's ground floor.

Like the museum, the food is eclectic, the flavors bold. Choose a seat on the back patio and dig into a grilled and raw asparagus salad with truffled beet tartare, a rabbit Sloppy Joe, tagliolini carbonara with prosciutto, or a BLET—a bacon, lettuce, and tomato sandwich updated with barbecued eel and garlic aïoli. Lunchtime attracts an entertainment-industry crowd, while dinner brings in local residents.

Yamato

Japanese

B2

1099 Westwood Blvd. (at Broxton & Kinross Aves.)

Phone: 310-208-0100 Lunch & dinner daily
Web: www.yamatokura.com
Prices: $$

Given the ornate old flatiron bank building it occupies in Westwood Village, you may be surprised by the reasonably-priced menu. Moreover, the postmodern interior and furnishings, arched mezzanine, and 50-foot-high vaulted ceiling give great ambiance bang for your buck.

Hot dishes are delicious here, like chrysanthemum-shaped *shu mai* filled with fragrant and gingery ground pork and shrimp. But the real strength is found in the sushi. A crispy soft shell crab roll, wrapped with crunchy cucumber, creamy avocado, crisp shredded carrot, and daikon, provides a satisfying mouthful that's easily an entrées' worth of bites.

The sake collection is one of the finest in Los Angeles, including fine American surprises like California-brewed Ozeki.

Westside

Zu Robata

A2

12217 Wilshire Blvd. (bet. Amherst & Wellesley Aves.)

Phone: 310-571-1920 — Mon – Fri lunch & dinner
Web: www.zurobata.com — Sat – Sun dinner only
Prices: **$$**

This sophisticated take on a *robatayaki* is atmospherically impeccable. The contemporary beige/brown palette and low light produce a relaxed club-like feel, though awkwardly low tables might cramp your style.

The attraction is skillfully prepared char-broiled small plates ideal for sharing. A *kabocha* squash grilled with a thick tangy-sweet glaze of floral honey and nutty miso absorbs the smokiness of the charcoal perfectly.

You can't miss the back wall display of jumbo jars of house-infused *shochus*, which pack a powerful punch. Order a Pineapple Punch and the bartender will mix *shochu* infused with fresh pineapple with cranberry juice, and set before you a light, fruity, and very potent drink. Zu Robata has the perfect recipe for dinner and drinks.

The sun is out – let's eat alfresco! Look for a terrace .

Where to **stay**

© Tim Pannell/Corbis

Alphabetical list of Hotels

Avalon

B4

9400 W. Olympic Blvd. (at Cañon Dr.)

Phone: 310-277-5221 or 800-535-4715
Fax: 310-277-4928
Web: www.avalonbeverlyhills.com
Prices: $$$

84 Rooms
4 Suites

Kor Hotel Group

The relaxed "patio lifestyle" of mid-20th-century southern California is the theme of the Avalon's homage to chic design from then to now. Three distinctive buildings dating from 1949 and thoroughly updated, cluster in a residential area near fine art galleries, high-end boutiques, and A-list dining.

The main Olympic building, with 43 rooms and suites, hosts the hourglass-shaped pool, a fitness center, and a poolside restaurant—blue on blue—offering California fare and weekend brunch. Neighborhood views abound from the taller Beverly building's 26 rooms and two studio penthouses, but screenwriters in residence might prefer one of the 8 with kitchenettes in the 15-room Cañon, four with private patios. George Nelson lamps, Isamu Noguchi tables, Charles Eames-inspired chairs, and Italian linens add beauty and comfort. Movie and music players are state-of-the-art.

Service is attentive and fast, valet parking organized and friendly. Of course, the Avalon is totally connected, with DSL and wireless, which means you can send script revisions even from the discreetly tented poolside cabanas. Come join the fun Monday through Friday, when you can "kick the blues" at happy hour by the pool.

Hotel Bel-Air

A3

701 Stone Canyon Rd. (off Sunset Blvd.)

Phone: 310-472-1211 or 800-648-4097
Fax: 310-476-5890
Web: www.hotelbelair.com
Prices: $$$$

91 Rooms
39 Suites

Hotel Bel-Air

Nearly hidden by trees and meticulously groomed gardens, the Bel-Air sits on a dozen acres in a narrow canyon. What you glimpse as you enter suggests a Spanish Colonial estate. Cross the stone bridge over the swan-filled pond to the reception cottage, and you enter an inviting maze of flower-lined brick paths and columned arcades. Turn a corner and there's an expansive oval pool flanked by teak lounges and curtained cabanas. Walk on and there's an outdoor dining terrace, a fitness center, and another garden.

Of the property's 91 spacious guestrooms, more than a third are suites. Soon after you're in your room, which feels like a hideaway, a tea service arrives along with fresh fruit and a small pastry. Shortly after comes another knock to check that all's in order, offer ice for the mini-bar, or light your fireplace.

The décor and furnishings are classically grand, stopping tastefully short of grandiose. Fabrics and linens are the finest, the bathrooms cozy and sumptuous. Come evening, you can dress up a bit and stroll back down that path to The Restaurant at Hotel Bel-Air *(see restaurant listing)*, where there's live music in the clubby lounge, and dining inside and out.

The Beverly Hills Hotel & Bungalows

B3

9641 Sunset Blvd. (at Crescent Dr.)

Phone: 310-276-2251 or 800-283-8885
Fax: 310-887-2887
Web: www.thebeverlyhillshotel.com
Prices: **$$$$**

145 Rooms
59 Suites

Spa

On the slope of the wealthiest heights in zip code 90210, surrounded by estates and an air of supremacy among the city's most luxurious hotels, this palmy pink palace and its tropical gardens shelter a 12-acre world of ease. A thick red carpet runs from the porte-cochere valet-parking area into a palatial circular lobby with gilded pink armchairs, pale green sofas, and the signature pink-and-green carpet—the palm leaf is a recurring motif. Winding paths lead through a manicured jungle to the 22 private bungalows—what tales they could tell!—to the fabled pool lined by lounges, cabanas, and lighted tennis courts.

Guestrooms, some with private patios, are spacious and elegantly old-fashioned. Beige carpets, downy bedcovers, swoopy curtains, and wood furniture leave no doubt that these rooms are primarily for leisure. Still, there is a spacious desk, a fax machine, and high-speed Internet access. Bathrooms feature a jetted soaking tub with shower, plush linens and mats, and a separate toilet room. Service matches the promise of all this. The Polo Lounge *(see restaurant listing)* offers live music and fine dining inside as well as on the garden terrace.

Beverly Hilton

A2

9876 Wilshire Blvd. (at Santa Monica Blvd.)

Phone: 310-274-7777
Fax: 310-285-1313
Web: www.beverlyhilton.com
Prices: **$$$**

469 Rooms
101 Suites

Gensler/The Beverly Hilton

Lucy and Desi were in their heyday when this 570-room landmark opened a short stroll from Rodeo Drive. Nine of the 101 suites are luxury penthouses, party central during the Golden Globe Awards and other recurring events that fill up the three ballrooms here.

A recent $80-million makeover enhanced the iconic hotel's half-century of good will by adding contemporary luxury, moving the beloved but dated Trader Vic's Restaurant to the pool area where it reopened as Trader Vic's Lounge, and unveiling nearby Circa 55, a pricey morning-to-night venue featuring American cuisine.

Guestrooms in the Wilshire Tower overlook the boulevard. Poolside cabana rooms open out onto the pool deck or balconies above. Oasis rooms offer more privacy and quiet. All are spacious, with neutral earth tones intended to foster tranquility. The furniture is contemporary and functional; chairs match the height of desks large enough for serious work. Bathrooms feature cushy linens, high-end toiletries, large counters, roomy showers, and separate alcoves for the loo. White Frette linens, down comforters, bedside Bose stereos and a big-screen plasma TV make turning in early an attractive option.

Beverly Wilshire

9500 Wilshire Blvd. (at Rodeo Dr.)

Phone: 310-275-5200 or 800-332-3442
Fax: 310-275-5986
Web: www.fourseasons.com/beverlywilshire
Prices: **$$$$**

254 Rooms
141 Suites

Robb Gordon/Beverly Wilshire Four Seasons

Its imposing Italian Renaissance height and iron-gated auto entrance off El Camino Drive suggest officialdom within. There is indeed an official air about the place, especially when flagstaffs along its Wilshire Boulevard façade display the colors of foreign nations. If downtown Beverly Hills has a Ministry of Shopping and Pampering, this is it.

Arriving by car, you enter the lobby from valet parking between the front Wilshire wing and the rear Beverly wing. Some rooms are a bit sedate, some perhaps a trifle small (the hotel was completed in 1928), and the pool is more suited to dipping than swimming laps, but there is no stinting on amenities. Quiet beige-carpeted hallways lead to guestrooms with cushioned chairs, table desks, feather beds, marble baths with tubs and separate showers, and ample counter space. Plush terry robes and slippers wait in the closet.

The rear Beverly Wing houses a well-equipped fitness center and a full-service spa with an A-list clientele. You needn't venture outside for excellent food and people-watching. Wolfgang Puck's steakhouse Cut *(see restaurant listing)* and The Blvd *(see restaurant listing)* are located in the front Wilshire Wing.

Four Seasons Los Angeles at Beverly Hills

C4

300 S. Doheny Dr. (bet. Burton Way & 3rd St.)

Phone: 310-273-2222 or 800-332-3442
Fax: 310-385-4927
Web: www.fourseasons.com
Prices: $$$$

187 Rooms
98 Suites

Spa

Far from Beverly Hills' see-and-be-seen hustle, among apartment houses and homes, this European-style hotel attracts people who see such separation as a plus. A circular drive from the palm-lined street lands you among bellmen who usher you into a lobby with an inlaid marble floor and vases of fresh flowers. Then it's upstairs and along thickly carpeted hallways to elegantly appointed guestrooms with classically inspired birch-tone furnishings.

You can cocoon here, spinning CDs and watching movies, emailing friends over a high-speed connection at a marble-topped desk, losing yourself in a book while plopped into a cushy armchair in the hotel's plush terry robe and slippers, or soaking in the tub in the beige marble bathroom. At bedtime comes turn-down service, followed by a dive under a down comforter.

You can be just as happily indolent outdoors by the big pool, in a cabana if you want more privacy than the potted greenery provides. Either way, towel and drink attendants will find you. On the fourth floor there's a well-equipped fitness center and a full-service spa.

Just off the lobby, Gardens *(see restaurant listing)* serves delicious contemporary fare.

Maison 140

140 Lasky Dr. (bet. Charleville & Wilshire Blvds.)

Phone: 310-281-4000 or 866-891-0945
Fax: 310-281-4001
Web: www.maison140beverlyhills.com
Prices: $$

43 Rooms

Kor Hotel Group

Silent-film star Lillian Gish once owned this 1939 building, transformed by Kelly Wearstler (designer of the nearby Avalon, another Kor Hotel Group creation) into a hip amalgam of Chinoiserie with lots of red, black, and gray accents. Touches drawn from the Jazz Age and Seventies Modernism conjure up the ambience of a Left Bank Parisian inn with a pronounced Far Eastern flavor.

Mandarin rooms span 300 square feet, Parisian rooms are smaller (200 square feet), but all share amenities. Here this means dormers, potted topiaries, red-lacquered doors, one-of-a-kind antiques, original commissioned artwork, customized furniture and fabrics, down comforters, Italian linens, terrycloth robes, in-room spa services, and pool privileges at the Avalon. Flat-screen TVs and CD/DVD players are at hand, of course, along with Internet connections and two-line phones. A fitness room with free weights and cardiovascular equipment is open 24/7. You park your car in a pay lot on the premises.

Downtown Beverly Hills is around the corner, but the hotel's lounge Bar Noir holds its own as a nightspot, and also hosts a self-serve breakfast to guests from early to mid-morning.

Mosaic

A2

125 S. Spalding Dr. (off Wilshire Blvd.)

Phone: 310-278-0303 or 800-463-4466
Fax: 310-278-1728
Web: www.mosaichotel.com
Prices: **$$$**

44 Rooms
5 Suites

Mosaic Hotel

The lobby of this well-located four-story establishment is small, but the 49 rooms and suites on its upper three levels are large, quiet, and pleasingly decorated in a contemporary European motif of earthy browns, mossy greens, heather, and beige. Botanical prints and an occasional potted orchid, feather beds and bedding, plush carpets, a large overstuffed ottoman, and shaded lamps offer the comforts of a cozy pied-à-terre. Windows open onto a tree-shaded courtyard or a residential street. One- and two-bedroom suites have 42-inch plasma TV screens, DVD players, and oversized glass-enclosed showers.

Mosaic panels and partitions accent the common areas. Blacks and browns dominate small, chic Tastes restaurant, which serves regional European fare. Its French doors open onto the courtyard and a heated lap pool.

Well-trained and professional, the youthful staff dresses casually in Beverly Hills style. There's a day spa, and a state-of-the-art gym with free weights and a variety of exercise machines. Business travelers will appreciate high-speed in-room Internet connections, commodious desks, cordless phones, and a lobby office printer accessible to guests.

The Peninsula

A2

9882 South Santa Monica Blvd. (at Wilshire Blvd.)

Phone: 310-551-2888 or 800-462-7899
Fax: 310-788-2319
Web: www.peninsula.com
Prices: **$$$$**

160 Rooms
36 Suites

The Peninsula Beverly Hills

Given its amenities, including a rooftop spa and a pool with private cabanas, nightly live entertainment and the popular Belvedere *(see restaurant listing)*, this hotel could have been claimed by the young club-hopping Hollywood crowd that fancies itself uniquely qualified to judge everything. Somehow, it escaped that distinction, winning a following among wealthy professionals and leisure guests.

Sixteen of its 196 rooms are private villas, 36 are suites. All are spacious and appointed in classic European style, with ecru walls, crown moldings, canopied feather beds, and carved wooden nightstands matching the headboard and entertainment armoire. For serious work, there's a desk and a fax machine; a sitting area, a mini-bar, and a wide, flat-screen television foster relaxation when the work is done.

Spacious baths of beige and rose marble include a soaking tub and a separate shower, as well as ample counter space. You'll appreciate thoughtful touches like Molton Brown bath products, high-quality towels and linens, and a comfy bathrobe and slippers. At night a warming fireplace adds romantic magic to the casual Roof Garden cafe.

Raffles L'Ermitage

9291 Burton Way (bet. Foothill Rd. & Maple Dr.)

Phone: 310-278-3344 or 800-800-2113
Fax: 310-278-8247
Web: www.raffles-lermitagehotel.com
Prices: **$$$$**

103 Rooms
16 Suites

Proclaiming itself a "sanctuary," Raffles strikes a chord with people who count privacy among the luxuries that separate good hotels from great ones. Details include a private entrance for those wishing to avoid the public eye, and elevators accessible only with a room key. That means no paparazzi on the rooftop sun deck and pool area, or in the fitness center, and all room service preceded by a call.

Service sets the bar high at this tranquil Euro-Asian hotel, yet the atmosphere is subdued—designed around soothing neutral tones. Off the lobby, Jaan restaurant features a lush patio in addition to its domed, gold-and-white dining room.

Spacious rooms reflect the East-West duality in the light-toned, polished-wood panels, the beige carpets, and walls and linens that create a spa-like serenity. All guest quarters have private balconies. King-size feather beds are set low in the Japanese style; you control the lights from a bedside panel. Plush armchairs with a footrest offer a place to read or watch the big-screen TV. Marble bathrooms are unstinting, with a soaking tub, a separate shower, a double sink, and a walk-in closet with dressing room. Yes, this is how stars live.

Omni

251 S. Olive St. (bet. 2nd & 3rd Sts.)

Phone: 213-617-3300 or 888-444-6664
Fax: 213-617-3399
Web: www.omnihotels.com
Prices: **$$**

453
Rooms

The Omni Hotel at California Plaza

When young novelist John Fante, who is to Los Angeles what James Joyce is to Dublin, checked into the Alta Vista hotel on Bunker Hill during the Depression years it was a down-at-the-heels bump on the Downtown landscape. Everything has changed, including the hill itself, crew-cut long ago for highrises like the Wells Fargo Center. Where Fante and his fictional alter-ego Arturo Bandini wandered hungry, the Museum of Contemporary Art now stands. On the far side of the block next to the Walt Disney Hall is this 453-room, 17-story tower, where today's Downtown literati order martinis and cigars at Noé *(see restaurant listing)*.

The business of Downtown is mostly business, and the Omni efficiently caters to commercial travelers, with spacious, impeccably clean rooms, a business center, dozens of meeting-room configurations, a spa, a fitness center, and outdoor lap pool to work out the kinks from sitting all day.

The Dorothy Chandler Pavilion, home to the Los Angeles Philharmonic and the Los Angeles Symphony, is two blocks away in the same complex as the city's premiere theatrical venue, the Mark Taper Forum and Ahmanson Theater. This is a quiet, safe area at night.

Standard Downtown

550 S. Flower St. (at 6th St.)

Phone: 213-892-8080
Fax: 213-623-4455
Web: www.standardhotel.com
Prices: **$$**

205 Rooms
2 Suites

Tim Street-Porter/The Standard

Back when Elvis was still in high school, the Superior Oil company's owners asked Claud Beelman to design a headquarters building celebrating the technological advancement of the age. They got it. Beelman's Modernist vision, finished in 1956, is an archetype of mid-century Californian architecture. Now part of a hotel, the building's lobby is a designated landmark.

These days, mercantile ambition is a fading ghost here. Downtown LA's revitalization is led less by corporate captains than by those working Beelman's side of the street: designers, artists, media entrepreneurs, writers, filmmakers, and others attracted by the availability of big spaces like those in the Standard.

This is a fun hotel, with large rooms, retro furnishings and décor, a 24-hour restaurant, a fitness center, a DJ live nightly, an AstroTurf sundeck with private cabanas, and a rooftop poolside bar that stays open way past bedtime. When your batteries finally run down, you can fall into feather bedding. Still, 14-foot-long desks, two-line phones and wireless Internet access reveal an underlying truth here: there's a lot of serious work being done Downtown, even if it's not about oil.

Chamberlain

A2

1000 Westmount Dr. (off Holloway Dr.)

Phone: 310-657-7400 or 866-891-0949
Fax: 310-854-6744
Web: www.chamberlainwesthollywood.com
Prices: $$$

104 Rooms
8 Suites

Kor Hotel Group

Part of the Kor Hotel Group portfolio, this West Hollywood hideaway is a boutique hotel whose 112 guestrooms and suites evoke the ambiance of a residential pied-à-terre. The interior design reflects that quality; the décor is personal and intense, far from Minimalist. You'll notice this immediately in the lobby's herringbone-patterned white and green marble floor, mirrored walls, plush seating, jade-green globe lamps, and palette of silver-gray, ice-blue, and aqua-green.

Rooms are spacious, each with a small balcony, gas fireplace, and all the music and video equipment you could want. High-thread-count white linens, down pillows and duvet, and a marble bath stocked with fine towels and toiletries sustain a sense of staying with unstinting friends. If work you must, there's an oversized desk, an Internet connection, and a safe large enough to stow your laptop.

Shady cabanas and wood chaise lounges flank the small rectangular rooftop pool, its five-story-high perch affording a panorama of the Hollywood Hills and LA's vast southerly sprawl. There's efficient room service from the Chamberlain Bistro, which serves Californian fare.

Elan

8435 Beverly Blvd. (at Croft Ave.)

Phone: 323-658-6663 or 888-611-0398
Fax: 323-658-6640
Web: www.elanhotel.com
Prices: $$

52 Rooms

Elan

Housed in a striking concrete-and-glass building near Third Street's better restaurants, galleries, and shops, this boutique hotel is a great value in this area. The lobby and lounge have avocado-colored walls, with furnishings of tangerine, stone gray, and sea-foam green.

Appointments in the 52 guestrooms are colored from a desert palette of sand, cactus, and burnt yellows. The in-room safe accommodates a laptop. Egyptian-cotton linens, down pillows, and a plush robe ensure a high level of comfort, though traffic noise in rooms on the Third Street side of the building can be distracting.

Reasonable garage parking fees, free local phone calls, and free Internet access in the lobby are thoughtful perks. A 25-inch cable television plays videotapes, and the front desk stocks a good film library. Bathrooms are outfitted with plush Irish-cotton towels and high-quality amenities.

You can surf the web while you enjoy a complimentary breakfast of gourmet coffee, fresh fruit, and fresh-baked muffins in the Cyber Lounge. There is no pool, but a fitness room includes free weights and exercise machines. Staff members may be small in number, but they are efficient and friendly.

Le Parc

733 N. West Knoll Dr. (bet. Melrose Ave. & Sherwood Dr.)

Phone: 310-855-8888 or 800-578-4837
Fax: 310-659-7812
Web: www.leparcsuites.com
Prices: $$$

142 Rooms
12 Suites

It's all about comfort at Le Parc. All 154 rooms and suites are classically decorated and range from 650 to 1,000 square feet. Each has a private balcony, a kitchen, a separate sitting area, and a fireplace. The largest have separate bedrooms. All have flat-screen TVs; players for CD's, videotapes, and DVDs; a mini-bar; a safe; and large closets with bureaus so you can completely settle in. You can bring Fido along, too, for a fee.

You could pound the pavement to work out in this residential neighborhood, but if you prefer to stay on the premises, the hotel has a fitness center, a rooftop pool, a tennis court, a Jacuzzi spa, and a sun deck with views of the Hollywood Hills. Feel like eating in? There's a pleasant restaurant and bar, Knoll, serving Mediterranean-influenced fare from early morning to late night (the bar stays open later). That's Le Parc's pitch, appealing to those facing a business trip and wanting to add a bit of pleasure to it.

The hotel offers car service within a three-mile radius. That will get you to Beverly Hills, but it's a mile short of the Hollywood Bowl. Knoll, however, will pack a gourmet picnic meal for your evening at the fabled amphitheater.

The London West Hollywood

1020 N. San Vicente Blvd. (bet. Cynthia St. & Sunset Blvd.)

Phone: 310-854-1111 or 866-282-4560
Fax: 310-358-7791
Web: www.thelondonwesthollywood.com
Prices: **$$$$**

200 Suites

The London West Hollywood

The London made its LA debut in April 2008, making over the former Bel Age hotel into a stylish starlet with a bit of British attitude. More than 200 spacious suites all have an open floor plan, featuring customized designer details such as embossed leather, velvet upholstery, bleached oak, hand-cut mosaic tiles, and Fili D'Oro linens from Italy.

Veranda suites come with terraces equipped with a table and chairs for dining and chaise lounges for sunbathing, while Vista suites on the upper floors afford glittering views of the Hollywood hills. Corner Crown suites provide extra windows and lots of natural light. One-bedroom suites rank as the largest with 1250 square feet. All, of course, include flat-screen TVs, docking outlets for cell phones, iPods, and laptops, in addition to complimentary high-speed wireless Internet access.

When it's time to relax, head for the rooftop pool and sundeck. LA unfolds before you here, amid an English garden-style landscape. For more R&R, a new spa is in the works.

As he does at The London's sister in New York City, Chef Gordon Ramsay lends his name and culinary expertise to the hotel's stellar restaurant (*see restaurant listing*).

Mondrian

8440 W. Sunset Blvd. (bet. La Cienega Blvd. & Olive Dr.)

Phone: 323-650-8999 or 800-697-1791
Fax: 323-650-5215
Web: www.mondrianhotel.com
Prices: $$$$

237 Rooms

Morgans Hotel Group

A hotspot for partying, dining, and occasionally sleeping, the Mondrian enjoys a prime location on the Sunset Strip. Credit Philippe Starck for the minimalist modern design, which begins with the wide glass doors at the entrance and continues throughout the property.

The lobby is a study in neutral tones, with its polished blond wood floor and natural light pouring in from large windows. In signature Starck style, odd pieces of über-contemporary furniture are strategically placed around the space.

This sleek look carries over into the guestrooms, where the furnishings are sparse and the white-on-white color scheme is broken only by accents of robin's-egg blue. On the small side, bathrooms come with toiletries from the in-house Agua Spa. But no matter—it's not about the rooms here; it's about the whole experience. It's about the scene on the elevated teak pool deck, next to the dining patio at chic Asia de Cuba (*see restaurant listing*). It's about the glass-walled pool that affords stunning LA panoramas. And it's about the Skybar, the ultra-exclusive nightspot where a Who's Who of Hollywood hangs out—as a hotel guest, your name will be put on the A-list.

Sofitel

8555 Beverly Blvd. (at La Cienega Blvd.)

Phone: 310-278-5444
Fax: 310-657-2816
Web: www.sofitel.com
Prices: **$$$**

295 Rooms

If Beverly Hills shopping is your goal in LA, book a room at the Sofitel. The hotel's location on Beverly Boulevard, across from Beverly Center mall and near the designer boutiques of Rodeo Drive, Robertson Boulevard, and Melrose Avenue make it the perfect perch for a sojourn spent exercising your credit card.

Opened in 1989, the Sofitel had a complete facelift in 2006, which renewed the rooms and public spaces with a sleek, contemporary look. Black mirrored columns and ultramodern chairs dot the lobby, while the addition of LeSpa, SIMON LA restaurant *(see restaurant listing)* and the STONE ROSE Lounge—styled in sexy red tones by Cindy Crawford's husband, Rande Gerber—make the Sofitel a place to be seen.

Rooms are done in soft earth tones, with flat-screen TVs, Frette robes, luxurious linens, down duvets, and plush beds; many boast views of the Hollywood Hills. In the bathrooms, thoughtful touches include an oversize rain shower as well as Roger & Gallet bath products. Add a spa, fitness facility, pool and sun deck, plus gracious staff members who go out of their way to see to your comfort, and you're set for a *très comfortable* stay.

Sunset Tower

8358 Sunset Blvd. (bet. Olive Dr. & Sweetzer Ave.)

Phone: 323-654-7100 or 800-225-2637
Fax: 323-654-9287
Web: www.sunsettowerhotel.com
Prices: $$$$

34 Rooms
40 Suites

Spa

Sunset Tower Hotel

Architect Leland Bryant's 15-story apartment house was, from its debut in 1929 as the Argyle, hailed as a splendid marriage of Art Deco and Hollywood style. Scrupulously renovated and maintained, it seems unthinkable that rumors of demolition circulated even after it was added to the National Register of Historic Places in 1980. If its walls could talk, they'd gossip about former residents including Howard Hughes, John Wayne, Marilyn Monroe, Errol Flynn, Elizabeth Taylor, Frank Sinatra, and Benjamin Siegel—whom you called "Bugsy" at your peril.

The gangster's 1930s apartment (he was evicted for gambling) is now the lobby and the club-like Tower Bar *(see restaurant listing)*, is decorated with brass-inlaid walnut paneling, suede banquettes, and a fireplace. From electronics to toiletries, rooms are well-appointed. Floor-to-ceiling windows frame unobstructed views, which by night become a glittering brocade of city lights. The top floors have been reconfigured into penthouse suites with wraparound terraces, and town houses with 20-foot ceilings and stairways to sleeping areas.

The spa, fitness center, and pool deck are luxurious; and the service quietly efficient.

The Langham, Huntington Hotel & Spa

1401 S. Oak Knoll Ave. (at Hillcrest Ave)

Phone: 626-568-3900
Fax: 626-585-3700
Web: pasadena.langhamhotels.com
Prices: $$$

366 Rooms
26 Suites

This Mediterranean Revival landmark opened in 1907, setting the Southland standard for grand hotels. A renovation in 1991 raised the bar again, yet the hotel and its 23 acres of lawn and gardens remain anchored in the early-20th-century notion of Southern California as the palmy apotheosis of the American Dream. Debutantes still bow in the ballrooms, and conventioneers still rally over dreams of prosperity like boosters of old.

There's a sense, at this sunny San Marino Valley overlook, of good times past and more to come. Most of the guestrooms are in the eight-story main building. Cottages throughout the grounds account for the rest. All come with featherbeds covered in Egyptian cotton linens, down comforters, pillows, marble baths sumptuously stocked, plush robes, a refreshments cabinet, and a dozen other amenities, including WiFi Internet access. A fully-equipped business center is open 24/7.

The hotel's Dining Room *(see restaurant listing)* serves expertly prepared contemporary fare. For sports fans, a tennis pro presides over three lighted courts, personal trainers staff the fitness center, and two of the four nearby golf courses are championship-rated.

The Ambrose

B2

1255 20th St. (at Arizona Ave.)

Phone: 310-315-1555 or 877-262-7673
Fax: 310-315-1556
Web: www.ambrosehotel.com
Prices: **$$**

77 Rooms

The Ambrose

Santa Monica's handsomest older residences are Craftsman jewels, and this quiet enclave in a residential neighborhood 20 blocks from the beachside bustle blends that style with Asian elements. Earth tones, restrained color accents, and an Asian-inspired garden with a fountain and koi pond reflect the owner's belief in the physical and emotional benefits of applying the Chinese guidelines of feng shui.

That discipline translates into wide, dark-stained wood doors opening into entry areas with wood floors and high ceilings, and the Craftsman signature of dark wood trim. A television hides inside a walnut cabinet; limestone bathrooms use a neutral palette. The effect is an air of tranquility.

Pillows and duvets are down-filled, the linens fine Italian fabric (hypo-allergenic bedding is available on request). Also available are soft bathrobes and plush towels.

Environmentally conscious policies dictate earth-friendly cleaning compounds, comprehensive recycling, wise energy use, and fair-trade organic coffee served in Urth Caffe. Guests are encouraged to self-park in the underground garage. There's a car-rental facility on-site, with, of course, hybrids for hire.

Casa del Mar

1910 Ocean Way (at Pico Blvd.)

Phone: 310-581-5533 or 800-898-6999
Fax: 310-581-5503
Web: www.hotelcasadelmar.com
Prices: **$$$$**

112 Rooms
17 Suites

A $65-million facelift that ended in1999, transformed this seven-story brick and sandstone Renaissance Revival edifice into the grand doyenne of local beach hotels. In the common areas, damask and velvet draperies and fruitwood furnishings honor the hotel's vintage (1926). An arched double stairway rises from the entrance foyer to a lofty, paneled lobby of marble floors, wrought-iron light fixtures, deep-cushioned couches, and armchairs suited for tea or cocktails. Floor-to-ceiling windows along the lobby's back wall afford stunning views of the Pacific, as does Catch *(see restaurant listing)*, the hotel's seafood restaurant.

Guestrooms, spacious and well-appointed, evoke the French Riviera with colorful panache in walls of buttercup yellow framed by white ceilings. Baths of gray Italian marble feature a soaking tub, a separate shower, and an abundance of amenities.

The U-shaped building embraces a pool deck opening onto the beach. Skirting the hotel, a bike and walking trail runs 22 miles from Will Rogers State Park (north of Santa Monica) to Torrance Beach near Palos Verdes. On chilly days, the fitness center offers an indoor alternative.

The Huntley

A2

1111 2nd St. (at California Ave.)

Phone: 310-394-5454
Fax: 310-458-9776
Web: www.thehuntleyhotel.com
Prices: **$$$**

188 Rooms
21 Suites

Jonathan Rouse

An archetype of contemporary design, The Huntley houses 209 rooms and suites on its 18 floors. Each is bright and airy, most rooms located off softly lit, carpeted hallways. Comfy beds are fitted with crisp white Italian linens and down-filled pillows and duvets. There is a 42-inch plasma TV, a desk big enough for paperwork (with a business center for backup), and a choice of Internet hookups.

Beige travertine marble lines the bathrooms, which are equipped with a spacious glass-enclosed shower and quality bath products. A safe, plush robes for lounging about, and closets large enough to stow luggage complete the in-room amenities.

You can order food 24 hours a day, but why eat in your room when you can dine at The Penthouse *(see restaurant listing)* on contemporary American cuisine in a dazzling setting atop the hotel?

Situated two blocks from the Santa Monica bluffs, the hotel boasts views of rooftops and sea in one direction, and palm-lined city streets and distant mountains in the other. Though there is no pool or outdoor garden, there is a fitness center, and nearby Palisades Park has walking paths, a pretty little rose garden, and broad ocean vistas.

Loews Santa Monica Beach

A3

1700 Ocean Ave. (bet. Pico Blvd. & Colorado Ave.)

Phone: 310-458-6700 or 800-235-6397
Fax: 310-576-3143
Web: www.santamonicaloewshotel.com
Prices: **$$$**

329 Rooms
13 Suites

Loews really is on the beach, a short stroll from the San Monica Pier's child-friendly amusements, including a historic refurbished carousel. The all-glass atrium lobby affords great beach views.

Guestrooms on the four floors above open onto balconied hallways overlooking the lobby's potted palms and seating areas. Comfortable and spacious, rooms are done in neutral color schemes with accents of gold, beige, and taupe. Many have sea views; others glimpse the pool area or Ocean Avenue. A pale gray-green day bed with an overhead lamp for reading adds a sophisticated touch. Thoughtfully appointed baths, divided between the grooming and shower areas, are paneled with creamy handmade tiles flecked with crushed seashells; their opalescent glints lend a subtle sparkle.

Ocean temperatures are chilly, so if you want to swim, stick to the large outdoor lap pool. Extra fees gain you access to the spa and fitness center and the Internet. Room service is efficient; but at the hotel's restaurant, Ocean and Vine, you can enjoy expansive beach views, a firepit filled with glass pebbles, and a Californian cuisine mixing various techniques, styles, and influences.

Malibu Beach Inn

B1

22878 Pacific Coast Hwy. (near Sweetwater Canyon Rd.), Malibu

Phone: 310-456-6444 or 800-462-5428
Fax: 310-456-1499
Web: www.malibubeachinn.com
Prices: **$$$$**

41 Rooms
6 Suites

Malibu Beach Inn

A multimillion-dollar renovation in fall 2007 made this 1989 inn worthy of its location on Malibu's "Billionaire's Beach"—so-called for the pricey homes of the rich and famous that line this stretch of sand. With 47 rooms, including 6 suites, one can safely say that they have landed upon the best option for luxurious accommodations in Malibu. Sporting a look that blends beach-house comfort with California chic, the hotel retains an understated aura that appeals to those wishing to get away from it all. Public spaces flow into one another, with plush couches clustering around the lobby fireplace, and contemporary paintings by California artist Glenn Ness ornamenting walls throughout the property.

With Carbon Beach beckoning just outside, you won't want to spend much time in your room. When you are inside, however, count on comfortable ammenities like pillow-top mattress, a gas fireplace, bath amenities, and Trina Turk robes. Bathrooms boast spacious stone countertops—with plenty of room for cosmetics and other sundries—and large showers with shaving mirrors. Glass-walled balconies reveal the crashing waves below.

Seek out seasonal California cuisine and more beach views at the Carbon Beach Club restaurant. For Type-A personalities, even the beach has high-speed Internet access.

The Ritz-Carlton, Marina del Rey

4375 Admiralty Way (bet. Bali Way & Via Marina), Marina del Rey

Phone: 310-823-1700 or 800-241-3333
Fax: 310-823-2403
Web: www.ritzcarlton.com
Prices: **$$$$**

304 Rooms

The Ritz-Carlton, Marina del Rey

If you don't mind trading the nightlife along the Sunset Strip for serene harbor sunsets, this hotel is for you. Just steps away from the largest small-boat harbor on the West Coast, the Ritz-Carlton Marina del Rey offers a respite from the high energy of L.A., a half-hour or so away. A circular driveway leads to the entrance, where the valet staff will park your car. Inside, the deep-green marble-lined lobby is warmed by wood paneling and elegant floral displays. Off this space, Jer-ne restaurant and bar (*see restaurant listing*) dishes up California cuisine and waterfront views.

Recently remodeled accommodations show off a palette of gold and blue, echoing the sunny waterscape outside. Nautical accents—model sailboats, framed maritime prints—continue the theme. Perhaps the best feature of any room here is the private balcony; ask for a room facing the marina if you want a water view.

A new spa pampers guests, and the fitness facility has been refitted with state-of-the-art equipment. Efficient service by a friendly staff, and a hotel shuttle that picks guests up at Los Angeles International Airport (five minutes away) makes this a perfect choice for business travelers.

Shutters on the Beach

A3

1 Pico Blvd. (at Appian Way)

Phone: 310-458-0030 or 800-334-9000
Fax: 310-458-4589
Web: www.shuttersonthebeach.com
Prices: **$$$$**

186 Rooms
12 Suites

Shutters

Bright white, like the building's Victorian trim, the shutters here open onto balconies and, in most cases, views of the sand and water. The lobby's peaked ceiling, wood floors, and potted palms recall Caribbean clubs, with a fireplace for coolers days. The hotel's twin buildings adjoin her sister, Casa del Mar *(see hotel listing)*, and like her sibling, shelters a pool and sun deck framing a view of the Pacific.

Though not always large, rooms are quite comfortable, sporting a casual-chic white beach motif accented by pale blue, sandy beige, and brown. Large wood-framed feather beds are covered with a white duvet and plumped up with feather pillows. Like the rooms' shuttered doors, crown moldings and built-in cabinets for books and electronics are as white as sun-bleached sand. The closet is spacious; the bath boasts a roomy stone shower stall. Fluffy robes and high-quality towels and linens wrap guests in luxury.

Wireless Internet lets you tell friends about your meal at the hotel's restaurant, One Pico *(see restaurant listing)*, and your sightings of celebrity faces gleaming from treatments at One, the hotel's A-list spa.

Viceroy Santa Monica

A-B3

1819 Ocean Ave. (at Pico Blvd.)

Phone: 310-260-7500 or 866-891-0947
Fax: 310-260-7515
Web: www.viceroysantamonica.com
Prices: $$$$

158 Rooms
4 Suites

From the outside, the Viceroy appears to be just a nondescript LA office building, but stroll into the retro-chic lobby and you've clearly entered a stylish cosmopolitan sanctuary. In the lobby, the music is loud, the lights are low, and it's quite a scene at night, populated by young Santa Monica professionals, and the young media and advertising types who tend to stay here.

All ebony and ivory with splashes of emerald green, the room décor takes a modern slant on the English Regency style. Staying in is a worthwhile option when you have a comfy king featherbed covered with Mascioni linens, oversized down pillows, a flat-screen TV, and a well-stocked mini bar. Request a room that doesn't face the pool if you're looking for peace and quiet. While it's too small for serious swimming, the pool often ends up hosting the party that seems to spill over from the bar at Whist (*see restaurant listing*), where refined California cuisine is the order of the day.

Service is warm and welcoming; and while the Viceroy isn't the ne plus ultra of luxury, you can't beat the location—a block from the beach, with easy access to bike paths, the pier, and restaurants and shops galore.

Four Seasons Westlake Village

A1

2 Dole Dr. (at Via Rocas), Westlake Village

Phone: 818-575-3000 or 800-332-3442
Fax: 818-575-3100
Web: www.fourseasons.com
Prices: $$$

243 Rooms
27 Suites

Spa

Peter Vitale/Four Seasons

The proximity of this opulent 270-room hotel to the California WellBeing Institute creates an unusual opportunity to immerse yourself in a regimen of swimming and exercise, yoga and meditation, spa treatments and healthy dining. There are, however, also the posh tables of Hampton's and Onyx *(see restaurant listing for both)*, and the convivial attitude of The Bar, where the crack of pool balls sets the tone. In other words, balance.

An Asian motif adorns the paneled, marble-floored, and flower-decorated lobby, which would put a Swiss banker at ease. A corps of well-trained concierges, receptionists, and valets stands at the ready.

Decorated with English Regency furniture and primary colors of blue and gold, rooms feature Italian-inspired fabrics and include a spacious desk and office chairs, a cushy armchair with footrest, and a plasma TV. Large floor-to-ceiling windows let in ample light. The feather bed is large, and the beige marble bathroom has a big soaking tub and a separate glass-enclosed stone shower stall.

A glass-roofed atrium building shelters an indoor pool. It adjoins the outdoor patio where you can lounge to the soothing rush of a waterfall.

Westlake Village Inn

31943 Agoura Rd. (bet. Lakeview Canyon & Lindero Canyon Rds.), Westlake Village

Phone: 818-889-0230 or 800-535-9978
Fax: 818-879-0812
Web: www.westlakevillageinn.com
Prices: $$

141 Rooms

Located 40 miles from downtown LA, the Westlake Inn maintains 17 acres of manicured gardens, trickling streams, placid lakes, and walkways shaded by flowering-vine-covered trellises. It's a prime setting for weddings and social functions, as well as business meetings. Guest rooms are spread out among several structures, each a short walk from the main building. Despite its sprawling layout, this is an easy property to navigate, thanks to ample parking lots positioned at each building.

Accommodations come in a variety of sizes, from the 300-square-foot courtyard room to deluxe corner suites with 750 square feet of space and golf-course views. All rooms include chenille robes, coffee makers, Bose radios, plasma-screen TVs, complimentary wireless and T-1 Internet connections (available throughout the complex), and a private balcony or terrace. Suites add fireplaces, Jacuzzi tubs, vaulted ceilings, and double sinks.

In addition to the on-site pool and small fitness center, guests here have access to the tennis courts at adjacent Pacific Tennis Club, and to the golf course that borders the property. Rates include a complimentary continental breakfast.

Hyatt Regency Century Plaza

C2 

2025 Avenue of the Stars (bet. Constellation & Olympic Blvds.)

Phone: 310-228-1234 or 800-233-1234
Fax: 310-551-7548
Web: www.centuryplaza.hyatt.com
Prices: **$$$**

680 Rooms
46 Suites

Hyatt Regency Century Plaza

Where cowboys wearing makeup once shot it out on dusty streets, business people now do battle in meeting rooms, most unaware that this recently remodeled 19-story hotel stands on what was once the backlot of the 20th Century Fox studio. The master plan for Century City, unveiled in 1957 as a "second" downtown, included architect Minoru Yamasaki's centerpiece, shaped like a parenthesis and facing a boulevard of fountains.

Recline by its big square pool and your view is of high-rise towers. No wonder business is on the minds of most guests, or that the hotel serves their need for places to meet, entertain, rally the troops, and work off stress. Accordingly, a multilingual staff operates a full-service business center, and the house restaurant, Breeze, serves Californian fare.

Spacious guestrooms follow the hotel's motif of dark browns, beige, and black. Furnishings include a large black-marble-topped desk and slate-gray armchairs. Comfortable down beds are covered with quality cotton linens; bathrooms have wood paneling and marble floors. Enjoy panoramic sunrise or sunset views from your private balcony.

Palomar

B2

10740 Wilshire Blvd. (at Selby Ave.)

Phone: 310-475-8711 or 800-472-8556
Fax: 310-475-5220
Web: www.hotelpalomar-lawestwood.com
Prices: $$$

238 Rooms
30 Suites

David Phelps/Kimpton Hotels

The Kimpton Group does it again—this time bringing the Palomar to the heart of Westwood. A few blocks from the shops of Westwood Village and the campus of UCLA, the hotel is a much-needed newcomer in this area. It is well-located in a high-rise on Wilshire Boulevard—the main drag that runs from downtown L.A. out to the ocean at Santa Monica. Set off wide and softly lit hallways, guestrooms grab you with their bold, contemporary art-in-motion theme. A mix of textures melds a white-linen-clad feather bed with a fake-fur throw and a leather ottoman with faux-snakeskin paneled doors. Turquoise accents add splashes of color to the grey, taupe, and chocolate-brown scheme; while in-room recycling bins, energy-efficient light fixtures, and organic mini-bar options toss in a touch of "green."

Typical of Kimpton hotels, pets are welcome here; when you need to go out, pet-sitters and walkers stand at the ready. There's a well-appointed fitness room on the 6th floor, as well as an outdoor pool, and small sundeck in the back of the hotel. Don't care to leave your room? Check out the yoga and Pilates channel on your TV, or call for an in-room massage. Market-based contemporary fare shines at the Palomar's BLVD 16 (*see restaurant listing*).

W - Westwood

B2

930 Hilgard Ave. (at Le Conte Ave.)

Phone: 310-208-8765
Fax: 310-824-0355
Web: www.whotels.com
Prices: **$$$$**

20 Rooms
238 Suites

The W's 15 ivy-covered concrete stories dominate a residential street near UCLA, but plantation shutters, dense foliage, and a discreet entrance betrayed only by the valet-parking shuffle below camouflage the trendy world within.

One clue is the water running beneath the front steps to glass doors opening into the lobby, where low cushioned benches and tables declare a devotion to modernity. Look left and you'll see the Whiskey Blue bar and the restaurant Nine-Thirty, serving an American menu featuring local produce, artisan cheeses, and boutique wines. Another clue is the names given to the W's one- and two-room accommodations, which range from 400 to 1,400 square feet. The smallest are billed as Wonderful, Spectacular, and Fabulous. Then come the Mega, the Wow, and the Extreme Wow. All have beds with goose-down pillows and comforters, fancy linens, cushy sofas, oversize work desks, and high-speed Internet access (for a fee); plus the full array of video and audio equipment.

With its small pool ringed by lounge chairs and cabana tents, the Backyard is a scene. The palpable ambition of the mostly young, up-and-coming crowd here adds a very L.A. frisson to the air.

Michelin

Western Los Angeles
SANTA MONICA MTNS.
BEVERLY GLEN
BEL-AIR
GETTY CENTER
UCLA
WESTWOOD
BEL AIR CC
MANDEVILLE CANYON
TOPANGA STATE PARK
VETERANS CEMETERY
VA MEDICAL CENTER
WILL ROGERS STATE PARK
BRENTWOOD
PACIFIC PALISADES
RIVIERA COUNTRY CLUB
BRENTWOOD COUNTRY CLUB
WEST LOS ANGELES
WESTSIDE
Page 188
SANTA MONICA
SANTA MONICA MUNICIPAL
SANTA MONICA PIER
SANTA MONICA BAY AREA
Page 142
OCEAN PARK
MAR VISTA
OCEAN FRONT WALK
VENICE BEACH
VENICE
VENICE FISHING PIER
MARINA DEL REY
Stone Canyon Res.
3mi
5km